Prais

Living Simply

"It's so hard to know how to be a good parent these days. Should you pressure your kids to achieve? How do you deal with advertising? What do you do about teen fashions? Marie Sherlock's book is incredibly well written, relevant, and helpful. It's a book you should keep handy to consult whenever you feel overwhelmed or frantic. Better yet, get together with some other parents and talk about it together."

—CECILE ANDREWS, author of
The Circle of Simplicity: Return to the Good Life

"Excellent! Exactly what families with children need to know right now! Sherlock soundly debunks the notion that living simply with children can't be done in today's world. To the contrary, she clearly shows how simple living makes family life richer, instills important values in our kids, and is better for the earth. *Living Simply with Children* is a "must read" for all parents and for anyone wanting to lead a more meaningful and sane life."

—JACQUELINE BLIX AND DAVID HEITMILLER,
authors of *Getting a Life: Strategies for Simple Living
Based on the Revolutionary Program for Financial
Freedom, "Your Money or Your Life"*

"In *Living Simply with Children*, Marie Sherlock writes with wisdom and clarity regarding a crucial subject for all who care about America's children and therefore its future. As an early childhood educator, I believe that the importance of her message to our children's creativity, self-esteem, and well-being cannot be overemphasized. As a parent, I only wish that I had read this book twenty years ago to maximize my own children's chances for joyous, fulfilling lives."

—CAROL HOLST, founder/director, Seeds of Simplicity

Living Simply with Children

A Voluntary Simplicity Guide for
Moms, Dads, and Kids Who Want to
Reclaim the Bliss of Childhood
and the Joy of Parenting

MARIE SHERLOCK

THREE RIVERS PRESS
NEW YORK

Published by Three Rivers Press, New York, New York.
Member of the Crown Publishing Group, a division of
Random House, Inc.
www.randomhouse.com

THREE RIVERS PRESS and the Tugboat design are registered trademarks of Random House, Inc.

Printed in the United States of America

Design by Meryl Sussman Levavi/Digitext

Library of Congress Cataloging-in-Publication Data
Sherlock, Marie.
    Living simply with children : a voluntary simplicity guide for moms, dads, and kids who want to reclaim the bliss of childhood and the joy of parenting / Marie Sherlock.
        1. Parenting—United States. 2. Family—United States. 3. Lifestyles. 4. Simplicity. I. Title.
    HQ755.8 .S5325 2003
    649'.1—dc21   2002009724

ISBN 0-609-80901-6

10 9 8 7 6 5 4 3 2 1

First Edition

To the simple living family I grew up with:
My parents, Gerald and Blanche Sherlock,
and my siblings, Pat, Tim, Dan, and Shelley.

To the simple living family I helped create:
My husband and kids, Marty, Ben, and Scott.

And to all simple living families everywhere.

Acknowledgments

My deepest thanks:

To Marty, Ben, and Scott, for their love, patience, and support.

To David Heitmiller and Jacque Blix, who believed in this project from the start and came to my rescue countless times along the way.

To Beth Vesel, my agent, who found a publisher at mind-bending speed.

To my editor at Three Rivers Press, Becky Cabaza, who, with kindness and wisdom, helped me to make this book much better.

To Carol Holst, Linda Breen Pierce, Cecile Andrews, Janet Luhrs, Vicki Robin, Betsy Taylor, Michael Fogler, Gerald Iversen, and other members of the simplicity movement, who contributed their time, ideas, and encouragement.

To Greta Simonson, my wise and wonderful friend, and all of my other friends and relatives who, with sincere interest, kept asking "How's the book going?" month after month after month.

To Eric Brown and the Center for a New American Dream, for their indispensable assistance in helping me to find parents attempting to raise their kids simply.

And to the dozens of simple living families who shared their stories and insights on living simply with children. I couldn't have written this book without you.

Contents

꩜

Part 2
The "Hows"—How You Can
Live Simply with Children 71

Foreword

It takes a corporation to raise a child.

Say what? Isn't that "It takes a village . . ."?

Well, look at the reality. Advertising jingles have replaced camp songs. Brands have replaced clans as a source of identity. Bonded day care has replaced the stay-at-home mom. Corporations are writing textbooks, funding television programming, setting style trends. In Monty Python's *The Meaning of Life,* an expectant mother, surrounded by a delivery room full of machines, is dismissed from participation in the birthing process by a patronizing doctor. "You're not qualified," he snaps.

Indeed, parents no longer feel qualified to parent. Our hurry-up, competitive, crowded, and commercialized world means you can't just send the kids into the backyard to play or down the street to Grandma or off to public school with the rest of the kids in town. Those days are gone for most of us. Parenting is privatized and professionalized. Parenting skills aren't just knowing when to hug and when to scold. They now consist of a welter of choices involving much insecurity and research. Which diapers? Which preschool? Will they suffer if I don't get them the sneakers? Will they suffer if I do? Do I limit TV? Or throw it out the window? Or just be grateful the kids have some stimulation while I frantically manage the other thousand things on my list? Do I give them an allowance or make them work for it? Do I send them to private school for the academics or to public school for the socialization? Do I give them college or make them work for it?

Back when there were villages that raised us, there was no such thing as a single parent, or even an isolated nuclear family. Parenting came naturally to most because we learned it from all the adults who were parenting all the time. Ample free time and luxurious hours of socializing and ceremony quickly brought collective attention to any individual problem. This way of life persisted for tens of thousands of years. Indeed, ancient languages probably never made the social role—*parent*—into a verb.

The consumer culture, barely a century old, has changed all that. The first empowerment for parents now is just realizing that "the consumer culture" itself is an aberration. This is why it now takes determined, conscious, intentional, heroic simple living parents to raise a healthy child. It takes instructions such as you will find in great measure in Marie Sherlock's wonderful book, which you are lucky to have in your hands. So as you struggle with "parenting," know that you are pushing against a massive surrogate parent—commercialism—that is trying to take your kids and raise them to be consumers.

Andy Lipkis, visionary founder of TreePeople in Southern California, once told me that if there were just a three-day ban on cars in Los Angeles the smog would completely clear. Smog doesn't "happen." People "happen" it each morning when they crank their cars and join the rivers of polluting vehicles on L.A.'s network of freeways.

Would our minds similarly clear if we didn't crank over the 3,000 advertisements a day that keep the pall of consumer culture hanging over our heads? If we were to take the logos off clothing, make everything from panel vans to television to schools (especially schools) commercial-free zones, then how would it be to raise children in America? If we were to quiet the incessant pressure to buy, would we still see ourselves as greedy animals whose basic drive is to have "more"? I think we would so naturally live a simpler life that it would need no instruction or defense.

We would know that who we are is more important than what we own. We'd know that toys "r"n't us. And so would our children. We would have more parks and fewer malls. More libraries and fewer unread books in private collections. More teachers earning more money to guide our most precious resource—our youth—and fewer soldiers to protect our national "possession obsession."

We don't, however, have the social will to constrain the largest uncontrolled psychological experiment on human subjects in the history of the world—the advertising that promotes consumerism, commercialism, and materialism. So we must privatize "simple living." Individuals must choose it for themselves and risk social rejection, loss of status, and even financial insecurity. Because we can't stop polluting our minds, we must cleanse them with refreshing books like *Living Simply with Children.*

Living Simply with Children provides hundreds of ideas for parents. I'd like to single out three threads that speak to me.

First, simple living with children isn't a kind of hands-off program one can institute like day care or summer camp. It really does take a whole family to raise children who don't depend on consumption to make them happy. If parents are shoppers, they will raise shoppers. If parents are snobs about cars and colleges, they will raise brand-conscious kids. As parents go, so go the children—so going down the path to simplicity starts with you choosing simplicity for yourself.

Second, some longings seem almost hardwired in humans. The desire for acceptance and belonging. The desire to stand out in some way. Simple living doesn't change humans, but it provides healthier ways to meet these and other basic psychological and social needs. Television works in part because it hooks into this "hardwiring." Likewise fashion, video games, and all the rest of the allurements of a commercialized childhood. They feed needs—real needs—with small zaps of satisfaction that don't last. Do you feel hopeless as you watch your child succumb, bit by bit, to these electronic seductions and desires bred by ads? This book gives you many ways to reshape your small household cultural environment so that you feed your child's imagination, creativity, and drive to meet developmental needs in simpler, healthier ways.

Third, everything of lasting value takes time—and time is at a premium these days. Parenting—like all arts—requires expanses of empty time for spontaneous, unbidden life to erupt through the humdrum of shuttling between appointments. Time isn't just clock time. It isn't just scheduled "quality time." Time is like a vast, shimmering Shangri-la that is accessed when we leave the manufactured, regimented world behind. It is always there for us, but we need to be there in it or it doesn't show up. Laughter happens in that kind of time. So does love. And meaning. We need time off from clock time. Sabbaths. Rest. Giggling. Lying in the grass. Snoozing with a baby in our arms. Time that is 24/7/365 is totally hostile to the rhythms of love. Simple living means taking time off from clock time, making Sabbath time more important than errands—and e-mails—and even grades and lessons and homework. Marie Sherlock's many suggestions about simple living with children create a bridge from the kind of time that kills love to the kind that fosters it.

So I say "Hallelujah!" for Marie Sherlock's guidance. Even if you don't have children, this guidebook will give you

courage—and a passel of good ideas. Don't let the corporations raise your children. And while you wait (and work) for
the return of the village (real community), be the kind of
simple living parent who can raise a child who will someday
lead us all to wholeness.

VICKI ROBIN
Coauthor, *Your Money or Your Life*
President, New Road Map Foundation
Chair, The Simplicity Forum
Labor Day, 2002

PART 1

The "Whys"—Why Your Family
Should Practice Simplicity

1

Getting Started on
Living Simply with Children

For most American families, "living simply with children" is the *ultimate* oxymoron.

Between Mom and Dad working full-time jobs, the kids being shuttled from day care to lessons to sports—wolfing down fast food along the way—and the never-ending need to buy and spend to "fit in" to America's consumer culture, family life can indeed be incredibly complex.

But in reality, simplicity and childhood are natural counterparts. Left to their own devices, children lead down-to-earth, uncomplicated, *genuine* lives. This truth becomes profoundly clear when you hear an infant squeal with delight over a game of "peekaboo." Or when you see the three-year-old birthday boy playing with the box instead of the battery-operated toy. You realize it when you witness the rapt expression of a kindergartner listening to a bedtime story.

As simple living mom Barbara Thomas notes, "Children are simple creatures. We bring the complexity." Single mom Susan Kelly adds that "consumerism and advertising would have us believe that children need a zillion things to have a good life, but children make the most of simple things."

I heard this theme over and over as I interviewed families for this book: Living simply with children is the most natural and beneficial way to raise kids, parents said. And if families chose to live on deserted islands, far away from all of the forces and pressures of our consumer culture, then living simply with children would be a breeze.

But most of us aren't cut off from the rest of the world. We're trying to live simply within a larger community that leads a much more consumeristic and frenetic existence. Therein lies the complexity.

Living simply with kids in today's American culture presents gigantic obstacles. Among the hurdles are:

- Marketing aimed at kids and parents, indoctrinating them with the belief that happiness can be purchased
- Age-inappropriate and violent media
- The peer pressure of a society that believes more is better
- Overscheduling of children and adults
- Practices that harm the environment and, consequently, children's futures
- The commercialization of schools
- The sheer excess that has become the norm in America

The purpose of this book is to help parents navigate the maze of materialism and the frenzied pace that society sets up for them and their kids. It will show parents how they can shelter their kids from the corporate culture; teach and model important values like compassion, generosity, and respect for the earth; and slow down and enjoy both quality and quantity time with their families. And it will make clear to parents that by doing these things, their kids' childhoods will be focused on the good stuff, which of course isn't stuff at all.

Living Simply—With or Without Children

Focusing on the "good stuff" is what simplicity is all about. Living simply—sometimes referred to as downshifting or downscaling—is both the means and the end to a meaningful life. A downshifter weeds out those aspects of his or her life that are of no lasting value and concentrates instead on those matters that are important. For example, a typical simplifier may consciously conclude that owning expensive cars, designer clothing, and a palatial home are not among her values, but that spending time with her family, working on worthy causes, and showing respect for people and the planet are. Simplicity will help her live with the "good stuff" at the forefront.

Living simply is clearly a financial means to such a life. By living simply—and consuming less—you can work part-time or retire early (or both!), freeing up time to focus on those things that matter most to you. Living simply is also a psychological and spiritual pathway to a more meaningful existence. Without distractions, without financial worries, our minds and hearts are released to pursue our true interests.

Simplicity is also an end in itself. A life focused on the nonmaterial aspects of existence—family, friends, nature, social service, those things that most of us value—is the goal of simplicity. As an end, the adoption of simple lifestyles by Western megaconsumers is truly the only way we're going to save the planet. And living simply is also the method we must employ if we care about global economic and social justice.

A few words on what simplicity is *not*. It's not about being a penny-pinching miser. It *is* about consuming less, which often means saving considerable sums and/or being able to spend that money on other areas, like charitable causes, early retirement, kids, or travel. Simplicity is not about being supremely organized or having some Zen-like interior decorating scheme, although mainstream media might lead you to think so. Decluttering—getting rid of excess—can, however, lead to a natural sort of organization. And simplicity isn't necessarily about an easy life. Even those who manage to retire early by simplifying, by and large devote much time and effort to volunteer work. But while they continue to work, they're engaged in activities that they love—helping others, primarily—without the stress that many Americans feel, so it's easier on their psyches.

Contrary to some reports, simplicity is *not* about deprivation. Those practicing simplicity in North America typically are quite comfortable by global standards. The only thing they've given up is the unnecessary and unsatisfying excess that is common in America. In exchange, they receive the *luxury* of time, peace of mind, and happiness.

Because I believe that this misconception about deprivation keeps many people from simplifying, let me offer another way to look at it. The entire concept of simplicity is relative, both geographically and temporally. If a resident of a third world nation, or even one from one of the "developing nations"—in other words, about 80 percent of the world's population—were to visit my family's modest, by American standards, home, they would be in awe. Our 1,600-square-foot single-family house would stun them. Indoor plumbing! Electricity! Three bedrooms! Telephones! A refrigerator and microwave! CD player! Two computers! A VCR! A mansion of miracles!

The same thoughts would be harbored by my ancestors—even my own parents, who grew up without most of these things.

In other words, my family's "simple ways" don't seem simple at all to most of the world's citizens. They'd consider them opulent. And I do too, to an extent. I consider myself incredibly fortunate to be able to live comfortably—with every *thing* I could possibly need or want. So while some of my contemporaries in this country consider my life a bit austere—

no cell phone, an older car, simple wardrobe, no high-speed Internet connection, DVD, or Palm Pilot—at least four-fifths of the world's people would be happy to trade places with me.

Simplicity, then, is about *not* being a typical American, because in today's society being an average American translates into being a consumer; indeed, a megaconsumer. That lifestyle is best described as materialism—the belief that acquisition and wealth are the highest objectives to be sought, rather than spiritual, intellectual, and humanitarian goals— and it's the opposite of simplicity.

Materialism dictates that you should try to meet your needs through the acquisition of things. It promises, at best, that happiness, acceptance, and love lie just around the corner with a bigger house, newer car, faster computer, trendier clothing.

But materialism never actually delivers on its promises. Each new purchase, latest promotion, bigger and better model, merely sets you up for the next acquisition.

At its worst, materialism ruins the natural environment, creates a situation where billions of people go without adequate resources, while a fraction at the top live in waste. And with its emphasis on things rather than people and nature, materialism robs our souls.

Simplicity is the antidote to all that materialism represents and to all of its soul-sapping, earth-exhausting consequences. Simplicity promises a life that is focused not on the unsatisfying accumulation of stuff, but on those issues, values, people, pursuits, and causes that matter most to you and that make life full and meaningful. And, unlike materialism, simplicity keeps its word.

In the final analysis, simplicity is about living our lives as we know in our hearts they were meant to be lived. This book will help you take that equation a step further and raise your children as you know in your hearts they were meant to be raised.

How to Use This Book

I think it was the Good Witch Glinda of Oz who said, "It's always best to start at the beginning."

Particularly for those of you who are new to simplicity, this is good advice. The values clarification process you'll find in the next chapter is truly essential for beginners. The rest of Part 1—the "whys" or benefits of simplicity—will help you understand why simplicity is such a great lifestyle choice for families.

Those of you who've already embraced simplicity may be inclined to skip the soul-searching exercise, but I hope you'll reconsider. Affirming your values will help you in every aspect of your life. It will reinforce your commitment to simplify and will assist you in living your values on a daily basis.

The balance of Part 1 may not be news to those who've downshifted somewhat. But you may well find that a reiteration of simplicity's benefits will be a source of support and motivation for you.

Whether you're a simplicity novice or a veteran, the second part of the book need not be read in a chronological fashion. If marketing to kids is your pet peeve, then by all means turn to Chapter 8. If the holidays are coming up and you dread the annual ordeal of excess, read Chapter 16 first. Use Part 2 as a resource, for information, ideas, and, hopefully, inspiration.

A Formula for Simplifying

For those of you who may want more of a blueprint for down-shifting, I have included a basic six-step plan that you can start with, adapting it to your family's situation. Here are the steps:

Note: Following this formula is not the only way to sim-plify. If you find that it doesn't fit your family's style, take those steps that *do* work for you.

1. SOUL SEARCHING

Perform the soul searching outlined in Chapter 2 and then read more about the benefits of simplifying in Chapters 3, 4, and 5. Hopefully, this will lead to a commitment to simplify, to live your values, and a foundation for the changes you'll be making.

2. DO YOUR HOMEWORK

Gather information on the "hows" of simplifying. This is essentially what the rest of the book is about. Reading it will be a big step in your research. Other books can and should supplement your search, books like *Your Money or Your Life* and others listed under "Resources" at the end of this and subsequent chapters. Many wonderful organizations, also listed in "Resources," are available for you to tap into. Consider joining the Center for a New American Dream and Seeds of Simplicity. Visit the Simple Living Network website.

Your research will highlight two primary areas: short-term ideas, which you can implement immediately; and long-term possibilities, those actions that will take more time, more effort. Both long-term and short-term ideas should be considered with an eye to honoring your family values (see Chapter 2).

Short-term actions might include starting a Family Night (see below) or other ritual, limiting TV time, doing away with fast food dinners, or paring down the number of outside activities. Long-term simplicity possibilities cover efforts like cutting back work hours or going to a part-time or job share situation. They may also involve selling a larger home and moving to a smaller one, or even moving to a different, less expensive area.

You'll uncover many approaches you'll want to consider with your family. Prepare two written lists from your research.

FAMILY NIGHT

One of the many easy-to-implement simplifying tactics your family may want to consider is establishing a weekly "Family Night."

Setting aside one night each week that is dedicated to family fun is one of the most common rituals that simple living families adopt. Activities on Family Night can run the gamut, but many families take a low key approach to this ritual. Playing board and card games together are common; so are movies or a special meal.

Others plan more focused events. Karen Schneider-Chen, a simple living mom from Seattle, was a contributor to a comprehensive Family Night resource called *Just Family Nights: Activities to Keep Your Family Together in a World Falling Apart* (see "Resources" at the end of this chapter). This book includes details on sixty different "themed" family night concepts. Hundreds of less formal—and nearly effortless—ideas that work well as Family Night activities can be found in *Table Talk* by Steve and Ruth Bennett.

While Family Nights can vary greatly, these homespun gatherings have three important things in common: They should be regular weekly events; they should take precedence over all other activities on those evenings (except emergencies); and they should be fun, something the family looks forward to doing together.

Whether your own Family Night simply involves pizza and a video or a more elaborate affair, it will undoubtedly become a treasured childhood—and parenthood!—ritual.

(See Chapter 12 for more information on family nights and other rituals.)

(You'll be sharing these lists with your family in Step 3, below.) One list will consist of your long-term simplifying ideas and goals. This inventory will have some items that may need multiple actions, and many will be the type that Mom or Dad need to instigate. Your second list will detail short-term goals and actions. Many short-term goals will involve the entire family.

3. THE FIRST FAMILY SIMPLICITY MEETING— BRAINSTORMING

Hold a special family meeting (see "A Primer on Family Meetings" on p. 12) to talk about the long-term and short-term simplifying ideas you're considering. At the beginning of the meeting emphasize that the point of making these changes is to help the family better live its values. Your family will already have been involved in the soul-searching exercise, and this next step will make sense to them. You should also point out that some long-term tactics—for example, Mom and/or Dad cutting back work hours or opting for a job share position—will involve short-term actions on the part of the family, like "brown-bagging" lunches and doing without cable television. The kids can help you make the list of short-term cost-cutting efforts; they'll be happy to do so when they know the goal is more time with Mom and Dad.

At this special family meeting, one parent should first read aloud the list of long-term simplifying ideas you've compiled. Then ask your family to brainstorm further long-term simplifying actions. (See "How to Brainstorm" on page 28.)

Next you'll read aloud the list of short-term simplifying ideas. Again, ask your family to come up with additional short-term strategies.

When you've completed the brainstorming, you'll have two (likely pretty lengthy) lists of ideas covering long-term and short-term actions.

Note: If your kids are still infants—or in the womb!—the two family meetings can be truncated into one discussion between Mom and Dad.

A PRIMER ON FAMILY MEETINGS

Family meetings are optimal times to discuss simplicity changes and to craft a Family Values and Vision statement (see Chapter 2). If you're unfamiliar with the family meeting model, here are some basics to get you started:

1. The primary purposes of family meetings are to promote family bonding and to help the family run smoothly, but they're also educational. Kids—and adults—learn to communicate, negotiate, compromise, troubleshoot, and to respect each other, all invaluable lessons.

2. Your kids should be old enough to participate verbally and tolerate fifteen minutes of discussion—about four or five years of age, depending upon their temperament and activity level. It's a good idea to begin with ten- to fifteen-minute meetings with preschoolers, and once your kids are a bit older—eight or so—to lengthen the meetings to a half hour.

3. Most experts recommend that family meetings take place weekly, although some families meet every other week or even monthly. A regular time—such as after Sunday dinner dishes have been cleared or at the start of Family Night—works well (see "Family Night" on page 10).

4. Each week a blank "Family Meeting Agenda" sheet should be posted for all to see. (Ours is on the fridge.) During the week, family members are invited to jot down concerns, proposed activities, and other issues that could be discussed at the meeting.

5. The meeting should be without interruptions. Unplug the phone or let the answering machine take calls. Keep the meetings short; thirty minutes is usually enough.

6. Use a simple notebook to record "minutes." The notebook is also a good spot to list the "Meeting Rules." One of these should be that all family members will listen and speak respectfully—that is, no "put-downs," eye-rolling, or yelling.

7. At the appointed time, the chairperson opens the meet-

(continues)

(continued)

ing. Many families start by asking each family member to give a compliment to each of the other family members or to comment on something about the family that they're thankful for. This sets a positive tone for the meeting. (Many families rotate the chairperson duties and secretary/recorder role, although younger kids may have difficulty with the writing tasks.)

8. Agenda items are then addressed individually. If the item involves a complaint about a family member's behavior, the involved individuals are expected to present their cases respectfully. Then the entire family can help brainstorm resolutions (see "How to Brainstorm" on page 28). Experts recommend that resolutions be by consensus—that everyone concur in the solution. If a consensus can't be reached, the agenda item can be carried over until the next week.

9. At the end of the meeting, go over family and individual activities for the upcoming week. If you have a family calendar, have it handy and add any activities that the family has agreed upon at the meeting.

10. Consider serving dessert or a special treat after the meeting, as both incentive and reward for a job well done!

4. THE SECOND FAMILY SIMPLICITY MEETING— ADOPTING THE CHANGES

This meeting will be devoted to whittling down the simplifying ideas put forth at the first meeting to those everyone can agree on. Parents should ensure that the perceived drawbacks of particular ideas—for example, not eating out so much—are coupled with fun changes like game and pizza nights every Friday. Read through the two lists and ask for input, "yeas" and "nays." Write the approved ideas on a separate list.

Some worthy ideas may not receive a consensus of approval at first. If you feel that they're important, schedule them for discussion at a future family meeting. Those that aren't as popular may take extra time and effort, or even rethinking entirely.

As a group, decide on three or four actions from the list to implement immediately. Record the simple living actions you decide to take on that week in your family meeting notebook. At your next family meeting, you'll review how those are going and commit to three or four more.

Part of this meeting's function is for each member of the family to figure out their roles in the actions. Parents can help kids determine how they'll be assisting with each strategy. For example, your ten-year-old could set up a recycling center; your kindergartner would be happy to help you bake bread. If your kids are older—say seven or eight or so—you could even assign a specific action for them to monitor that week. Remember that your kids can and should be involved in ways that make sense for them, depending upon their age.

5. THE EXTENDED FAMILY/FRIEND TALK

If some of your changes will impact your extended family or close friends, you'll need to clue them in too. If you've decided to abandon your weekly "night out with the gang," talk with "the gang" about substituting a potluck. If a "TV Turn-Off Week" is on your list, let the relatives know you'd like them to honor that commitment. Chapter 10 includes a section on "Relative Support—or Lack Thereof" that might help you as you attempt to enlighten your extended family.

6. FIND SUPPORT

You can also look to Chapter 10 for details on how to get the support you need to follow through on your simplifying changes. Many of the chapters in the "hows" section will also assist you with details on how to implement your simple living actions.

This blueprint approach may not work for you. Many of us take a zigzag route to simplicity. It's an individual thing! Follow your own path. The important thing is to move in the right direction.

A Few Caveats About This Book

Although I tried to avoid too much repetition, the topics in this book often overlap. This overlap is inevitable. I see it as an outgrowth of the interconnectedness of simplicity. A couple of examples illustrate this: Limiting or doing away with your television will help you deal with marketing aimed at your kids, assist you in protecting them from peer pressure, give you more family time together, and help you teach your kids to manage their money better. Consuming less is perhaps the foremost environmental action, yet it also is the mechanism for working less, for deemphasizing the material world while focusing on people and causes, and for enjoying our communities more.

Something else you may notice about this book is what it *doesn't* cover. I couldn't include every family simplicity–related topic here. My approach was to cover, as comprehensively as I could, those subjects that directly relate to raising kids simply. I especially wanted to address those issues that are "hot buttons" for downshifted parents, subjects like peer pressure, advertising directed at kids, and holiday excess.

I've left several, more general simplicity topics to others. For example, the mechanics of living on less, on economizing, have been covered so thoroughly and so well by others that they're not detailed extensively here (although you'll find some cost-cutting ideas and tactics in Chapters 13, 14, and 15, among others). There are dozens of books out there that deal with living on less financially. Start with *Your Money or Your Life*. If you need more detailed guidance, try *The Com-*

plete Tightwad Gazette. (See "Resources" at the end of this chapter for these and other titles.)

Likewise, I haven't covered organizational and decluttering issues. Again, there are many books available on how to organize your "stuff." (Of course, the primary way to do this is to have less of it!) "Simple" food is also not addressed except in passing in Chapter 14. You'll find much help in books like *The More-with-Less Cookbook,* among others.

If you have a specific simplicity topic you need help with, or find the information in this book inadequate for you, I recommend that you visit the Simple Living Network website—www.simpleliving.net—and go to their Forums. You'll find dozens of subject areas—"Family Matters" is one of them—and hundreds of helpful "virtual" friends to assist you.

Another caveat: Please realize that my family does not hold itself out to be any kind of simple living paragon. We're far from perfect! Through my research on this book, I've become acquainted with many families who practice a much purer form of simplicity than my family does. We're all somewhere on the simple living continuum and we're all trying to live our values as best we can. Some of us will emphasize community more, others the environment, still others rural living. These individual responses to simple living are to be expected. After all, simplicity is about living consciously, mindfully, with integrity—and being true to ourselves.

Finally, before you begin this book, you should know that living simply takes an open mind. If you're not willing to look at the status quo and question it, you'll probably not last long in the simplicity movement. This is particularly true for parents. Kids are the segment of our population most bombarded with commercial messages—and their parents right along with them.

If fitting in is of the utmost importance to you, then saying *"No!"* to the corporate culture's message of "more is better" and "this product will change my life, make me happy, et cetera" will be especially difficult. I hope that if you've made it this far, you've convinced yourself that you don't want to spend your parenting years raising a "good little consumer," that you've questioned the dubious "values" of our consumer culture and concluded you aren't buying them. Keep questioning!

The Wisdom of Many

The materials in this book aren't just my personal thoughts. It contains the collective insights of the more than sixty simple living families I interviewed or surveyed.

I've profiled several families in Chapter 6—my own included—and ideas and quotes from dozens of others are peppered throughout these pages. I occasionally mention a few pertinent facts about these families but often I simply share their anecdotes, words, and feelings. You should know that all of these families are practicing downshifters, at some juncture on the simple living family continuum. They're almost all solidly middle class, they're bright, often well-educated, always caring, always thoughtful. They were certainly an inspiration for me, as I hope they'll be for you.

Over the past year, I've had a number of heartfelt conversations with these families. We've talked about the many roadblocks to raising kids simply in the most commercialized and materialistic country in the world. We've also wondered out loud together why so many others, who seemingly should know better, continue to live the way they do.

As parents longing to bring some sanity into our family's and others' lives, it's easy to feel hopeless today. If millions of other Americans are wedded to the idea that more is better, is there any possibility that we'll make a difference? While we're asking our kids to plan our errand route in order to use the least amount of fuel, our national leaders continue to raise the issue of opening the Alaska wilderness to oil drilling and are reneging on commitments to decrease carbon dioxide emissions. We cringe as our kids' schools struggle financially, turning to corporate "partnerships"—advertising—to make up the difference.

On the other hand, there is also much to be hopeful about. While researching this book, I found that there are many simple living advocates who are getting the word out about this lifestyle. And the sixty-plus parents I interviewed are just a small sampling of those families who've concluded there's a better way.

I have a T-shirt that a dear friend gave me years ago. It's stained, frayed, and misshapen, but I'll never throw it out. In fact, I'm wearing it as I type this. On it is an oft-quoted thought of Margaret Mead's: "Never doubt that a small group of thoughtful, committed citizens can change the world. Indeed, it is the only thing that ever has."

As I interviewed downshifted families for this book, the sentiment on my simple T-shirt has become especially apropos. As we lead downscaled lives, help our kids to embrace simplicity, and spread the word about its many benefits, we can, indeed, change the world. And have the time of our lives in the process!

Resources

Note: Many of the resources mentioned throughout this book are available through Alternatives for Simple Living on the web at www.simpleliving.org; (800) 821–6153 and the Simple Living Network at www.simpleliving.net; (800) 318–5725.

DECLUTTERING

Tara Aronson. *Simplify Your Household* (Pleasantville, New York: Readers Digest Books, 1998).

Jeff Campbell. *Clutter Control: Putting Your Home on a Diet* (New York: Dell Publishing, 1992).

Ronni Eisenberg with Kate Kelly. *Organize Your Family* (New York: Hyperion, 1993).

Ronni Eisenberg with Kate Kelly. *Organize Your Home* (New York: Hyperion, 1994).

FAMILY NIGHTS

Steve and Ruth Bennett. *Table Talk: 365 Ways to Reclaim the Family Dinner Hour* (Holbrook, Massachusetts: Bob Adams, Inc., 1994).

Susan Vogt, editor. *Just Family Nights: Activities to Keep Your Family Together in a World Falling Apart* (Elgin, Illinois: Faith Quest, 1994).

ORGANIZATIONS/WEBSITES

Alternatives for Simple Living: www.simpleliving.org; (712) 274-8875. Numerous resources to help you live simply and justly, challenge consumerism, and celebrate responsibly.

The Center for a New American Dream: www.newdream. org; (877) 68–DREAM. Helps Americans change the way they consume to enhance quality of life and protect the environment.

Frugal/Mindful Living Resources: www.igc.apc.org/frugal. Many great simple living ideas/resources.

Overcoming Overconsumption site: www.verdant.net. Ideas and resources for dealing with materialism.

Positive Futures Network: www.futurenet.org. Promotes sustainability and publishes *Yes! A Journal of Positive Futures*.

Seeds of Simplicity: www.seedsofsimplicity.org; 877–UNSTUFF. Works to help build a strong voice for voluntary simplicity.

The Simple Living Network: www.simpleliving.net. Comprehensive simplicity site, a cornucopia of information and links to other valuable sites.

PERSONAL FINANCE AND COST CUTTING
(SEE ALSO CHAPTERS 13 AND 14)

Jacqueline Blix and David Heitmiller. *Getting a Life: Strategies for Simple Living Based on the Revolutionary Program for Financial Freedom, "Your Money or Your Life."* (New York: Penguin, 1999).

Amy Dacyczyn. *The Complete Tightwad Gazette: Promoting Thrift as a Viable Alternative Lifestyle* (New York: Villard, 1998).

Andy Dappen. *Shattering the Two-Income Myth* (Brier, Washington: Brier Books, 1997).

Joe Dominguez and Vicki Robin. *Your Money or Your Life: Transforming Your Relationship with Money and Achieving Financial Independence* (New York: Penguin Books, 1999).

Jonni McCoy. *Frugal Families* (Elkton, Maryland: Full Quart Press, 1998).

Lisa Reid. *Raising Kids with Just a Little Cash* (Santa Fe, New Mexico: Ferguson-Carol Publishers, 1996).

SIMPLE FOOD

Christine Berman and Jacki Fromer. *Meals Without Squeals* (Palo Alto, California: Bull Publishing, 1997).

Annie Berthold-Bond and Mothers and Others for a Livable Planet. *The Green Kitchen Handbook* (New York: Harper-Collins, 1997).

Doris Janzen Longacre. *More-with-Less Cookbook* (Scottsdale, Pennsylvania: Herald Press, 2000).

Frances McCullough and Barbara Witt, editors. *Great Food Without Fuss: Simple Recipes from the Best Cooks* (New York: Henry Holt, 1992).

Helen Nearing. *Simple Food for the Good Life* (White River Junction, Vermont: Chelsea Green Publishing, 1999).

Eric Schlosser. *Fast Food Nation: The Dark Side of the All-American Meal* (Boston: Houghton Mifflin, 2001).

Carol Simontacchi. *The Crazy Makers: How the Food Industry Is Destroying Our Brains and Harming Our Children* (New York: Tarcher/Putnam, 2000).

VOLUNTARY SIMPLICITY IN GENERAL

Cecile Andrews. *The Circle of Simplicity: Return to the Good Life* (New York: HarperCollins, 1997).

Mark Burch. *Stepping Lightly: Simplicity for People and the Planet* (Philadelphia: New Society Publishers, 2000).

Duane Elgin, rev. ed. *Voluntary Simplicity: Toward a Way of Life That Is Outwardly Simple, Inwardly Rich* (New York: Quill, 1993).

John de Graaf, David Wann, and Thomas H. Naylor. *Af-*

fluenza: The All-Consuming Epidemic (San Francisco: Berrett-Koehler Publishers, 2001).

Doris Janzen Longacre. *Living More with Less* (Scottsdale, Pennsylvania: Herald Press, 1980).

Janet Luhrs. *The Simple Living Guide* (New York: Broadway Books, 1997).

Jerome M. Segal. *Graceful Simplicity: Toward a Philosophy and Politics of Simple Living* (New York: Henry Holt, 1999).

Simple Living Oasis (formerly *Simple Living Journal*); www.simpleliving.com. Quarterly publication that inspires and supports people to live simply; $18 per year; (800)318–5725.

2

♋

First, Some Soul Searching

Like Americans everywhere, I was stunned, saddened, and horrified by the events of September 11, 2001.

Also like many Americans, I immediately began searching for answers. I took to reading, among other sources, the letters to the editor in our local daily newspaper, and saw that people had very divergent views on why this tragedy happened and what we should do about it. But I came across one letter that I think no one could disagree with.

The writer noted that those who made phone calls before their deaths—whether on the planes or in the buildings hit—didn't say things like "I wish I had bought that new car," or "If only I'd gotten that promotion." They said, instead, "I love you."

This is as it should be, said the writer, because in our last moments we realize what truly matters to us. The writer then emphasized that the best way to honor the victims of the attacks is for all of us to figure out what's important to us and then to live each day with those things at the forefront. "This means," the letter writer concluded, "living our lives with no regrets."

"Living our lives with no regrets" is what simplifying allows us to do. As discussed in the introductory chapter, simplicity, by its very definition, involves doing away with the unsatisfying excess in our lives and concentrating on what is really meaningful to us. Simplifying involves distilling our lives down to their essence and then living an existence in concert with our deepest beliefs. As simplicity author Mark Burch notes in his book *Stepping Lightly,* "Simple living begins when people become conscious of their values and live congruently with them, whatever they may be."

A Contradictory Country

That we aren't living our values here in America is pretty obvious. We drive around in gas-guzzling, carbon-dioxide producing SUVs with "Save the Earth" bumper stickers on them. We implore our kindergartners to share with others, yet the U.S. ranks an abysmal twenty-first among industrialized nations in the percentage of our national income earmarked for foreign assistance. We tell our kids that "beauty is only skin deep," that "you can't judge a book by its cover," that it's what's on the *inside* that counts. Yet we buy showcase homes and cars and ensure that our families have the trendiest fashions and hairdos, the latest gadgets and toys.

Our paradoxical nature is a recurring theme. Rabbi Harold Kushner notes, in his best-seller *When All You've Ever Wanted Isn't Enough,* "Ask the average person which is more important to him, making money or being devoted to his family, and virtually everyone will answer *family* without hesitation. But watch how the average person actually lives out his life. See where he really invests his time and energy, and he will give away the fact that he does not really live by what he says he believes."

I feel that the reasons why we're not "living by what we say we believe," why we're not "living our lives with no regrets," are twofold.

One reason is that we haven't actually taken the time to articulate what kind of existence a "no regrets life" entails. We haven't searched our souls and determined what truly matters to us.

The second major stumbling block is that the values of our consumer culture are, in a very real sense, diametrically opposed to our own. Our task of living in concert with our true beliefs becomes an uphill battle in the face of these norms that differ so greatly from our own.

What are those consumer culture values? Here are just a few:

- We should strive to be successful—and "successful" is defined monetarily.
- Happiness can be purchased.
- "Fitting in" is paramount, even if it contradicts our beliefs about the environment, social and economic justice, and other issues.
- All you need is more. (A corollary of this value is that bigger—cars, houses, closets!—is better.)
- All technological innovations are worthy of praise and we should applaud them and buy them, even if we can't afford them and don't need them. (Another corollary here, faster—computers, Internet access, cars [again]—is better.)
- Keeping up with the Joneses—whether they live next door, across town, or only on our TV screens—is essential.
- Outside appearances are more important than what's inside a person, and being "cool" is of greater consequence than authenticity, that is, being yourself.
- Excitement should be sought out, even if it's violent.
- Getting, not giving, is the goal.
- Instant gratification is our right.

If these "values" sound drastic, watch a few hours of commercial television. Browse through magazines, paying particular attention to the ads. Hang out at the mall and observe teenagers, who are, of course, mimicking all of those advertising themes. Watch the Academy Awards! The message the larger culture tells us and our children is *form over substance*. These values are almost the exact opposite of the values we wish to pass on to our kids.

You may say, "C'mon now. Those aren't really American values. Our values are freedom, liberty, independence, good stuff like that." But I didn't say that these are *American* values, I said that they are the values of our consumer culture. And, like it or not, they are the ones we and our kids hear and see most, because the vast majority of the messages we receive from day to day are those of corporations—on TV, in movies, at the mall, in magazines and newspapers, on our "logoed" clothing, even on the backs of toilet stall doors. They're the ones that dictate most of our expenditures, our thinking, our hopes, dreams, and goals—even our interactions with our family, friends, and neighbors. And corporate messages have but one goal: to make you buy more.

If it's difficult for Americans in general to live their values in today's society, it's even more so for parents. Why? The overwhelming pace of our consumer culture leaves mothers and fathers with little energy left for self-reflection. They're on the work-spend-work treadmill along with the rest of the country, *plus* they're trying to raise kids. In addition, parents must deal not only with the influences of culture on their own behaviors, but also with the impact of those forces on their children, who are prime targets for the American marketing machine, as you'll see in Chapter 8.

As one parent I interviewed remarked, "I don't want the values I pass on to my kids to be those of Nike and Reebok." But if you're raising children in North America today and you're not consciously addressing the effects of commercialism on their psyches and beliefs, then you've essentially handed your child's soul over to corporate America. You might as well say, "Here, mold this child into another mindless consumer."

Your active involvement in teaching your child values that truly reflect your own beliefs, values that put people first and "stuff" much further down the list, that promote the preservation of the planet, is essential.

Soul Searching

Discerning your true values—that first hurdle to living a "life with no regrets"—is an indispensable task. You obviously need to know what your values are before you can align your existence with them.

There are two steps to this values clarification process: the first is to brainstorm your values, determining what truly matters to you as a family.

You'll be referring to your brainstorming notes as you tackle the second step of the clarification process: assembling your Family Values and Vision Statement. (You can call it whatever you like, your family beliefs document, values inventory, simplicity statement, or something else; it's up to you.) This document is the end result of distilling your brainstorming ideas down to reveal your highest values, your strongest beliefs, and how you want your family to live those. It's a recitation of what is truly important to you—individually, as a parent, and as a family. You can think of it as a sort of spiritual road map, a document you can refer to time and again to get yourself back on track should you falter or need guidance in making decisions. It's really a blueprint for living a "no regrets" life.

It's important that both spouses/partners participate in this soul-searching exercise, along with your kids, if they're old enough, because participation precedes ownership of the final document—and a much greater likelihood that all members will honor the values expressed. (Your kids are old enough if they can participate in a family meeting. See "A Primer on Family Meetings" on page 12.)

Even if you're convinced of simplicity's merits, you should perform this exercise. The act of contemplating these questions and writing down your answers will bring them to the forefront. Seeing your answers in black and white will help you clarify them, and then internalize them. Unless you're already living an intentional, conscious existence, it is nearly essential to do this.

An aside here: The soul-searching step is of pivotal importance for those couples who aren't "on the same page" regarding simplifying. Through this process, that reluctant spouse will likely realize that his or her values are, in fact, simple values. Soul searching could provide "the big *ah-ha!*" as one simple living parent describes the epiphany that takes place when you finally "get it" about simplicity.

STEP ONE: THE BRAINSTORMING SESSIONS

Use the questions listed below as conversation starters and food for thought. Family meetings are optimal settings for discussing the questions, but you can also use other situations, like mealtimes. You'll need to appoint a secretary—usually Mom or Dad—to draft intermediate and final documents.

The brainstorming questions are getting at two things: what your family's values are, and how those values look in day-to-day life. You'll probably want to break this exercise into at least two brainstorming sessions—one for Values, and one for Vision.

Values Brainstorming Meeting

Some of these questions may speak to you more than others. If so, focus on those. The purpose of asking them is to bring out family members' thoughts and feelings about the values they cherish. Here are the questions:

1. How do *you* define "success"? You might want to rephrase this question, in terms of how you would define a "life with no regrets." What would your life look like without regrets? How would you spend your time?

2. What do you think our purpose is here on earth? Why are we here? As Wendell Berry asks in one of his essays, "What are people for?"

3. What matters to you most? What do you hold sacred? When do you feel most at peace? What brings you the most fulfillment?

4. What characteristics do you value in your friends?

HOW TO BRAINSTORM

Brainstorming is a tried and true method of generating solutions, of unearthing insights, feelings, and even flashes of brilliance. This is how it works:

Introduce the topic or question and then ask for input. You might want to go around the room and ask for each person's opinion. Write down *every* suggested idea or solution. Using a chalkboard or easel with a large piece of paper is a good method, or one family member can simply write down ideas in a notebook.

During a brainstorming session, there are no bad ideas. Everyone is heard and encouraged. The premise of brainstorming is to open your mind to *all* of the possibilities, good, bad, and indifferent. This "no holds barred" approach gets the creative juices flowing. (Ultimately, the suggestions will be narrowed down to those that are truly meaningful.)

If your kids are a little older, you'll likely hear "joke responses." For example, when you ask what family members truly value, kids might say, with mischievous grins, "lots of money," "chocolate," or "a Nintendo game cube." Have a good laugh, then write down their answers and draw them out with, "What is it about video game systems that you value?"—or candy or wealth. You'll get to the underlying value—happiness, security, or fun—and have a good discussion in the process.

---

5. What are families for? What does our family believe in? What's important to us? What do we stand for?

6. What makes you happy? What activities give you the greatest joy? What activities do we like to do together as a family?

Once you've hashed over these questions, the secretary needs to take time to go over the notes and find those values that keep popping up over and over. Some values can be combined—for example, compassion and caring, or generosity and sharing. Keep the inventory of values to a manageable number, no more than about six or seven. These should be listed on a piece of paper, then copies made and given to all family members at the next session—the Vision meeting.

Vision Brainstorming Meeting

At the Vision meeting, family members will review the proposed family values list and agree to it or make suggestions for changes.

Then it's time to brainstorm again. Take each value and ask, "What are some examples of this value in action in everyday life?" Think of daily activities—how time is spent, interactions with others—when asking this question. For instance, the value of kindness might manifest itself in your family becoming a "no put-down zone"; the practice of peace might mean that siblings seek compromises when they disagree.

Next, the family will ask about each value, "What would our family look like if we practiced this value every day?" And, "What would the world look like if everyone practiced this value daily?"

The point to these questions—and the lesson that your children will hopefully learn—is that practicing each of these values begins at home, with our families, but that their impact is much broader. If we all practiced compassion, for example, it would be a very different world indeed. The message is that we *can* make a difference. I believe that this is a very empow-ering and positive lesson for our kids—and us.

STEP TWO: DRAFTING YOUR FAMILY VALUES AND VISION STATEMENT

Your Family Values and Vision Statement can either follow the basic three-step outline I provide below or you can im-provise and draft an original document. The important thing is to include what your values are, examples of those values in daily life, and what difference the practice of those values would make.

The three-step outline looks like this:

1. *Our Family Values. In our family, we value the follow-ing:* List your family's values, with descriptions of each, if desired.

2. *Living Our Values. Our family practices its values in the following ways:* List each value and the differ-ent behaviors and actions that show family members living in concert with that value. For examples, see "A Sample Values and Vision Statement" in the box on pages 31–32. Do this with all of your family's values.

3. *Our Family and World Vision. We believe that practic-ing these values can make a difference:* List each value again and state what would happen if your family—and the rest of the world—practiced that value. Again, do this with all of your family's values.

You might also want to add a declaration of purpose at the beginning of your statement. If you want, you can use the first paragraph of my family's Values and Vision Statement.

When you're finished, take the draft, make copies, and go over it with your family. Add, delete, and improvise as neces-sary.

Once everyone is in agreement on this document, make several copies and post them in appropriate places: on the fridge, in kids' and parents' rooms, in the family room. You

A SAMPLE VALUES AND VISION STATEMENT

This is my own family's effort. It's one example of the format your family can use:

This is our family's Values and Vision Statement. We have listed our most cherished beliefs and many examples of how we can live according to these beliefs. We know that many other situations come up every day that allow us to practice our values. When making a decision, we will try to ask ourselves, "How can I best support my values?" We know that we will be better people, have a better family, and a better world by doing so.

1. Our Family Values. In our family, we value the following:

Caring/Compassion: We care deeply for our family members and friends, our pets too. Love, caring, and kindness are important to us.

Social Justice/Fairness. We believe that all people are entitled to have their basic needs met and to be treated with dignity.

Caring for the Earth: We realize that our natural environment is a miracle and that our planet must be allowed to thrive.

Having Fun (including music, art, self-expression): Laughter and smiling, sharing good times, are part of our family life and are essential components of our humanity.

Learning: We value learning in all its forms—school, reading, research, problem solving, experimenting, and discussion.

Healthy Living: Taking care of our bodies brings well-being, energy, and vitality, all crucial to a good life.

2. Living Our Values. Our family practices its values in the following ways:

Caring/Compassion: Cooperating, helping, being supportive, listening respectfully, and having good manners are all ways that we show that we care.

Social Justice/Fairness: We show our concern for justice when we volunteer to help hungry people and when we donate money to good causes.

(continues)

(continued)

Caring for the Earth: We know that small efforts add up when caring for our planet, things like buying and driving less, turning off lights, and recycling.

Having Fun: Playing cards and board games, having water balloon fights, and telling jokes are some of the many ways we have fun.

Learning: We learn by going to school, reading, talking to others, observing nature—even by making mistakes.

Healthy Living: Eating nutritious food, exercising, getting enough sleep, and relaxing all promote health.

3. Our Family and World Vision. We believe that practicing these values can make a difference:

Caring/Compassion: If our family practices caring, we will all feel loved and cherished. If the world practices caring, no one would be left out or friendless.

Social Justice/Fairness: If our family practices justice, none of us will feel unfairly treated. If the world practices justice, there would be less suffering, less fighting, and perhaps no more wars.

Caring for the Earth: We keep our local environment beautiful and healthy with earth-friendly practices. If everyone did their part, there would be less pollution, more trees, an ozone layer—in short, an abundant planet for us and future generations.

Having Fun: If our family has fun, we'll enjoy each other more and work will be more like play. If people smiled and laughed more, it would be a more relaxed and peaceful world.

Learning: If our family seeks to learn more, we'll discover amazing facts, acquire useful skills, and entertain ourselves. With more learning, there would be less ignorance, bigotry, and prejudice.

Healthy Living: By taking care of ourselves, we're better able to enjoy life, even live longer. If the entire world were healthier, there would be fewer people dying unnecessarily and less suffering.

may want to make a point of reading it at family meetings or on some other regular basis.

Throughout this book—throughout your life—you'll want to consult with this document, asking, for example, "Am I communicating and modeling my values? Is this activity or ritual in sync with our family's beliefs? Does this school— movie, board game, book—teach the standards and principles that I want my children to learn?"

Sometimes you'll forget to ask. And sometimes the answer will be "Not really," but maybe you'll allow the item or activity in question anyway. We're only human! But the mere existence of this document will help keep you on the path. And referring back to it regularly will be a great aid in keeping the values you've expressed at the forefront, leading you to a much greater possibility of "living a life with no regrets."

The Values of Simple Living Families

When I asked dozens of simple living families what their values were, they recited such principles as:

- Compassion
- Love
- Charity
- Family
- Community
- Respect for people and the earth
- Social justice
- Harmony
- Honesty
- Generosity
- Understanding
- Cooperation
- Peace
- Nonmaterialism
- Kindness
- Tolerance
- Diversity
- Responsibility

I will be focusing on these and other similar values in this book, whether the issue is how to communicate them, when and how to protect your kids from sources that oppose them, or how rituals and other practices can enhance them.

Patti Idrobo of Livingston, New Jersey, one of the parents I interviewed, echoed the sentiments of many simple living parents when she spoke of her values: "I am most concerned with contributing toward making a more just world where there is less poverty, fewer human rights abuses, and less suffering. In my own circle of relationships, what matters to me is creating places of kindness and respect." She defines success simply as "doing something important to make a better world."

Nearly every family I interviewed included this concept in some form—contributing to the world, being a positive influence on the planet, giving back to the community, caring about others and the planet—in their values. Perhaps this is the overriding commonality of simple living values: Simple living families don't just want the "good life"—more meaning, less stuff—for themselves; they want it for everyone and for the earth too.

I also asked the simple living families I interviewed what values they hoped to teach their kids. They noted, again almost without exception, that they wished to instill in their children a desire to make the world a better place. Living simply will help them do just that.

Resources

SOUL SEARCHING

Viktor E. Frankl. *Man's Search for Meaning* (New York: Pocket Books, 1963).

Robert Fulghum. *All I Really Need to Know I Learned in Kindergarten* (New York: Ballantine Books, 1988).

Harold Kushner. *When All You've Ever Wanted Isn't Enough* (New York: Simon & Schuster, 1986).

Stephen Levine. *A Year to Live: How to Live This Year As If It Were Your Last* (New York: Bell Tower, 1997).

Bo Lozoff. *It's a Meaningful Life: It Just Takes Practice* (New York: Viking/Arkana, 2000).

3

~~

Quality <u>and</u> Quantity Time

At every stage of my kids' lives, I've wanted to freeze time. To keep them giggling, sweet smelling infants forever. To remain a bit longer as the hub of their toddler and preschooler universes. I hoped, futilely, that my oldest would always tell me stories about his imaginary friend, allowing me a peek into his whimsical four-year-old world. I never wanted my youngest to pronounce his L's properly, wishing he'd keep saying, "Mom, I yuv you a yot!"

My kids are nine and eleven now, but they're still young boys. My eleven-year-old grabs my hand as we walk along, even in public (though not in front of his friends). My nine-year-old still sits on my lap every morning, snuggles, and shares his dreams with me.

But they're growing every day. The time will come soon when my oldest will stop searching for my hand, and then my arm will hang limp at my side. Those spontaneous hugs may even cease along with the little "Love you, Mom" that he adds to the end of every phone conversation. My youngest will stop leaping into my arms and quit delivering on the coupon for "free kisses and hugs for life" that he gave me one year on my birthday. He'll forget to ask me to sit down next to him at night and "have a conversation."

So I keep wishing, as many parents do, that time would stand still. Not for the sake of my aging body. I would gladly accept unlimited gray hair, cellulite, and crow's-feet just to keep these boys young for a few more years. . . .

Childhood is a magical time. It's also fleeting. Those years when you can claim to be at the center stage of your kids' existences pass by all too quickly. And for many of us they coincide with our primary wage earning years. Not long ago I overheard two teachers talking about their upcoming retirements at my sons' school. One teacher said she was looking forward to her leisure time but lamented that it all seemed a bit backward. "Shouldn't we have our free time when our kids are young?" she wondered.

You can—by simplifying.

For those of us with children, more time with our kids is perhaps the greatest benefit that simplifying can offer. To me, simplifying is the closest thing to a magic wand, a sorcerer's spell that appears to make time stand still.

Some individuals outside the simplicity movement are under the impression that the ultimate objective of living simply is to accumulate money. It's not. Rather, freeing up money is one of the tools for achieving the true goals of voluntary simplicity, and chief among these goals for parents is having more time with their families.

Long on Things but Short on Time

That we haven't enough time—for ourselves and for our kids—has been demonstrated over and over again.

We haven't enough time to be with the people we love and to do the things we enjoy because we're putting too many hours into other activities. Chief among these "time burglars" is the ever-increasing portion of our life we dedicate to working. According to the Families and Work Institute, the average American employee now works more than forty-seven hours weekly. That's 3.5 hours more per week than twenty years ago.

Despite our economic slowdown, those numbers are rising. An August 2001 report by the International Labor Organization concluded that Americans added another thirty-six hours to their work year during the 1990s. This means that Americans now work 137 more hours yearly than their closest competitors, the Japanese, 499 more hours each year than German workers. It's rushed and hectic time too, with 60 percent of workers saying they still don't have enough time to finish everything that needs to get done at their jobs.

Commuting times have also increased, according to a recent Department of Transportation study, as well as the time we spend watching television—up almost 40 percent since the 1960s. And then there are those mindless hours we waste "gleaning information" from the Internet. In fact, technology—with all of its "time saving" gadgets—tends to worsen the time deprivation problem. Author Alan Thein Durning notes in his book *How Much Is Enough? The Consumer Society and the Future of the Earth* that "the amount of genuine leisure available in a society is generally in inverse proportion to the amount of labor saving machinery it employs."

If we're spending more time at work—and at the mall, on our cell phones, and figuring out how to work our Palm Pilots—we're obviously spending less time at home. Polls indicate that parents spend 40 percent less time with their children now than they did in 1965. One study found that between 1981 and 1997, "household conversations" all but ceased to exist. We simply aren't hanging out with—or communicating with—our families anymore.

Both adults and kids are feeling this emotional void. In the 1997 Ask the Children survey, 50 percent of parents said

TRACKING YOUR TIME

Where does your time go? To find out, keep a "time journal" for several typical days—a few weekdays and a couple of weekend days. Record the time you spend on the following activities (you can carry a small notebook with you for this purpose or just jot down your estimates at the end of the day):

Sleeping_____

Working_____

Commuting_____

Watching television_____

Web-surfing, e-mailing, other computer/Internet activities (nonwork related)

Shopping and other errands_____

Cleaning_____

Cooking_____

Laundry_____

Lawn care_____

Car maintenance_____

Household repairs/maintenance_____

Exercise_____

Personal care/hygiene_____

Child care (the basics—diaper changing, nursing, discipline— *not* hanging out with your kids, fun stuff)_____

One-on-one time with kids_____

One-on-one time with spouse_____

Fun time with family_____

Hobbies or other personal pursuits_____

Others (name them):

_____

_____

Once you've kept your time journal for at least five days, look at your inventory and ask yourself: "Is this how I want to spend my time? Do I have enough time for my family? For

(continues)

(continued)

myself? Are all of these activities necessary? Are they important to me? Are my activities in sync with my values?"

Now engage in a little fantasy and outline how you would
spend your time if you could choose what to spend it on. What
would your "perfect day" look like? Would you continue working at your current job? Quit? Work part-time? How would you
fill your hours?

Simplifying may not—or it may!—allow you to quit your
job. But as you'll see, it can move you toward your ideal day
and give you more time to spend on those activities that are
meaningful to you.

that they did not have enough time with their kids. A national
poll in 2000 found that "not having time together with
parents" was the top concern of teens, tied with educational
issues.

Our modern dilemma, according to experts, is that kids
actually need their parents more now than they used to because they need that adult contact to sort out an increasingly
complex world—a world that is, in turn, sapping kids and
adults of their time and energy.

A Society in the Fast Lane

We have a bumper sticker on our car that reads, "Slow Down
for Our Kids." It's put out by our city's transportation department as part of a campaign called Reclaiming Our
Streets. It is, of course, meant to remind drivers that kids live
in the area and that driving slowly is a good idea for their
safety.

But I like to think that it has a larger message, that we
need to slow down in every area of our lives—for our kids'
sakes. From our too-fast cruising down neighborhood streets

and our eating fast food on the way to soccer practice to our allowing preschoolers to watch PG-13 movies and giving college entrance examinations to fourteen-year-olds, our society has accelerated.

In fact, our collective solution to our perceived time-shortage problem has been to speed things up. Rather than getting at the root of the issue—that we're spending too much time on those things we dislike and not enough time on those things we value—we've developed a technological solution, in the form of Palm Pilots, day planners, faster computers, high speed Internet connections, and other tools—all, not surprisingly, products to be purchased.

We're also attempting to apply this "faster is better" mantra to ourselves. Our "human" solution is to do two or three things simultaneously. We've even created a new word—multitasking—to describe this approach. The alternative of spending our time consciously, of self-reflection and of making thoughtful choices of the activities we choose to participate in, and then performing them deliberately, is nearly an alien concept.

One outcome of this "faster is better" phenomenon is a generation of "hurried" children. David Elkind's best-selling book, *The Hurried Child: Growing Up Too Fast Too Soon,* makes a strong argument that we're pushing our kids to take on more than they are developmentally capable of handling. And we're doing this due to our own needs rather than their needs as children. "Ours is a hurried and hurrying society," he says. "We hurry our children because we hurry ourselves."

Elkind sees this hurrying in our society's collective pressure for early intellectual attainment; in the trend for both parents to work full-time, thus requiring kids to spend long hours in the care of others; in our inability or unwillingness to monitor our kids' exposure to unsuitable media; in the marketing of inappropriate, "adult" clothing, music, and other products to young children; in our earlier and more frequent testing in schools; in our enrolling kids in numerous sports and activities; and in other practices that rush our children. Corporate marketers even have an acronym for this phenomenon, KGOY: Kids Getting Older Younger. We are, according to Elkind, unnecessarily stressing our kids and, in essence, robbing them of their childhoods.

The problem has only grown worse over the past two decades. Dr. Georgia Witkin surveyed eight hundred children between the ages of nine and twelve about their stress levels and reported her findings in her 1999 book, *KidStress*. She found that kids are indeed under a lot of pressure: Almost one-third of the children surveyed said that they worried "a lot," and another 53 percent said they worried "sometimes."

Anxious kids turn into tense young adults. For fifteen years freshmen at UCLA have been surveyed regarding their stress levels. In 1999, 30.2 percent of them said that they frequently feel overwhelmed. That's nearly double the number who reported feeling this way in 1985.

The Myth of Quality Time

Many guilt-ridden working parents have turned to the concept of quality time to ease their consciences. In the 1990s, "experts" convinced them that it wasn't the amount of time they spent with their children that mattered but rather the quality of that time that mattered. If a parent could devote short yet attentive intervals to their kids, parents were assured that the kids would be just fine.

Books came out with tips for helping readers "be in the moment" more with their kids. Much of the advice in them is worthwhile, but only to an extent. For me—and I'd venture to guess, for many average parents—allowing yourself to "be in the moment" more takes some time itself. Humans don't have an on/off switch that we can flip, transforming us from a frantic pace to a relaxed and responsive condition.

Parents who've simplified agree. Kate Rhoad, a mother of

three from The Woodlands, Texas, finds the entire concept of quality time to be "a false thing. It makes me think of parents who only allot an hour or so for their kids in the evening and they have to be *so* focused because they have such limited time." Kate's family of five has ample unstructured time, which Kate treasures. "If you're living a simpler life, you have more time to just *be*. There's a calmness and a rhythm to your life."

Parents and children need this *quantity* time to find that "calmness and rhythm" Kate Rhoad refers to. Those profound moments when you are really listening to your child and he is really communicating with you—when your child can actually instruct *you* about the meaning of life—don't happen when you've "penciled him in" for a half-hour session. It's only when you've geared down to his speed by having ample time to "just *be*" that those magical times can happen.

Even the experts have come around to this way of thinking. A study by the Families and Work Institute concluded that both quality and quantity time are important, even recommending that we change the terminology to "focused times" and "hang-around times."

Simplifying Gives Families More Time

Downshifted families are aware of the need for time—both quality *and* quantity—and living simply allows them to reclaim it. They've cut back on their expenditures—everything from housing to handkerchiefs—which has allowed many of them to work fewer hours, resulting in more time with their kids.

Many have followed the advice of Vicki Robin and the late Joe Dominguez as explained in their book *Your Money or Your Life*. (See "Your Money or Your Life" on page 76.) Explaining the equation "money = life energy," Robin and Dominguez tell us: "Money is something we choose to trade

SIX WAYS SIMPLIFIED PARENTS MAKE TIME FOR THEIR FAMILIES

1. They work shorter hours. By consuming less (see Chapters 6 and 14), simplified parents are able to cut back on the hours they spend "making a living," and consequently free up time to "make a life" with their families.

2. They turn off their electronic appliances, particularly televisions and computers.

3. They evaluate activities by whether they're in sync with their values and then say _no_ to those that aren't, making their families their first priority.

4. They cultivate interests that the entire family can enjoy, like bicycling, bird-watching, making music, and hiking.

5. They include their kids in more of the everyday activities of their lives—from working around the house to shopping to volunteering together.

6. They establish family rituals, like eating dinner together and observing regular Family Nights (see "Family Night" on page 10 and Chapter 12), that protect family time together.

our life energy for. Our life energy is our allotment of time here on earth, the hours of precious life available to us." For parents, hours spent at work and hours spent buying and maintaining "stuff" equate to hours away from their family.

These families also guard their precious family hours from other "time bandits," like television, shopping, Internet surfing, and other more or less accepted American activities.

Roger Meyer and Dana Murdoch are a good example of how downshifting results in more time for families. They both work only part-time, freeing them to spend unhurried hours with their daughter, Olive. "We both wanted a hand in raising Olive. This way is much more relaxed," says Roger. "I wouldn't do it differently for the world."

Lisa Cunningham is the mother of two daughters and has chosen to be a stay-at-home mom. "I have come to believe that kids need quantity time, not quality time," says Lisa. "You can't schedule those lightbulb moments that happen in the car on the way to the grocery store, while playing in the park, over sandwiches at lunch. It's a cliché, but children grow so fast. The time they are with you and dependent is really a blink. They only go down this road once, and once those moments are gone, they are gone forever. Work, on the other hand, will always be there."

Kate Rhoad says that simplifying sets you up for fewer regrets as far as time spent is concerned. "You don't end up saying, like so many other parents do, 'I wish I had had time for this or that.' You *do* have time for it."

Spending ample time with your kids is, in fact, a win-win proposition. You have, as Kate Rhoad wisely points out, no regrets. Your kids gain access to what they truly want—you.

And, in all probability, your kids will help you recapture the ability to "live in the moment." In fact, they'll likely become your teachers in this regard. They are, after all, the masters of living in the here and now. The world is still a miracle to them—a truth that many of us adults have forgotten—and they view it with awe and reverence.

My nine-year-old son routinely demonstrates this natural capacity. Like when he plays the piano, "just for the sound of it." Or helps me to "star hop" on a clear summer's eve. Or stops me on a walk to point out a cloud that's shaped like a cat. Spending time with him is genuinely therapeutic for me; my pace slows down more or less by osmosis. If I've let the world get to me, I can count on our time together as an antidote.

Living fully—living "in the moment"—is at the core of simplicity. Our kids can help us regain this precious life skill, if we give them the time.

Resources

ON THE NEED FOR MORE TIME

William J. Doherty and Barbara Z. Carlson. *Putting Family First* (New York: Henry Holt, 2002).

Mary Pipher. *The Shelter of Each Other: Rebuilding Our Families* (New York: Grosset/Putnam, 1996).

Stephan Rechtschaffen. *Timeshifting: Creating More Time to Enjoy Your Life* (New York: Doubleday, 1996).

Juliet Schor. *The Overworked American: The Unexpected Decline of Leisure* (New York: Basic Books, 1992).

STRESS IN KIDS

David Elkind. *All Grown Up and Nowhere to Go* (Cambridge, Massachusetts: Perseus, 1998).

David Elkind. *The Hurried Child* (Cambridge, Massachusetts: Perseus Publishing, 2001).

Georgia Witkin. *KidStress: What It Is, How It Feels, How to Help* (New York: Viking, 1999).

OTHERS

Joe Dominguez and Vicki Robin. *Your Money or Your Life: Transforming Your Relationship with Money and Achieving Financial Independence* (New York: Penguin Books, 1999).

Alan Thein Durning. *How Much Is Enough? The Consumer Society and the Future of the Earth* (New York: Norton, 1992).

WEBSITES

www.puttingfamilyfirst.us. Putting Family First is a group of citizens "building a community where family life is an honored and celebrated priority." Includes information on how to start a "Putting Family First" movement in your area.

4

❧

Happier Families,
Stronger Communities—
and a Better World

Happiness. It's such a basic human need that Thomas Jefferson declared its pursuit as one of mankind's "unalienable rights," along with life and liberty. All of us strive for it in life and hope that our children will find it.

Some people joke—or perhaps they're serious—that the Declaration of Independence needs to be reworded to read "life, liberty, and the *purchase* of happiness"; that this revised wording would more accurately reflect the state of our collective relationship with this elusive condition.

But here's a news flash: Money can't buy happiness. No, *really*.

In fact, our pursuit of money and material goods leads not to happiness but to dissatisfaction. It leads to an eternal striving for more and more and more.

Madison Avenue doesn't want anyone to discover the wisdom of this old saying, which is perhaps the key to a satisfied modern life. Those who've simplified, however, want everyone to know it: Doing without the material excess considered normal in America does not decrease one's quality of life or contentment. In fact, simplicity *increases* happiness.

This issue concerns many of those considering downshifting, *particularly* parents. Their fear is that simplifying involves a good deal of self-denial and that their kids will ultimately suffer. David Heitmiller and Jacqueline Blix, the authors of *Getting a Life*, note that as they traveled across the United States promoting their book, they continually heard the same question from parents about adopting a simple lifestyle: "Won't I be depriving my kids if I simplify my life?"

In fact, the opposite is true. Marie McWilliams, a down-shifted mother of four, wisely concludes that "children need love and time more than anything else. Toys break and get boring, even books tear and go the way of all things. Give them yourself. They don't really need a whole lot more than that."

My interviews with dozens of simplified parents confirm this. All of those sixty-plus parents said that their families are happier since they've downshifted. By simplifying, parents contribute to their children's well-being and satisfaction. They promote richer and deeper family ties. They contribute to the health of the greater community; indeed, the entire world.

I want parents hoping to simplify to internalize the wisdom of "money can't buy happiness" because it's essential to really *know* this if you're going to have the courage to say *no* to the insistent din of our consumer culture to buy more and more. So I'm going to give you some facts, some proof.

All You Need Is . . . Enough

Psychologist David G. Myers is one of the leading experts on the relationship between wealth and well-being. In his book

The American Paradox, he cites many surveys that conclude that once life's necessities are within reach, increasing afflu-ence is irrelevant to individual happiness. Myers found this to be true when looking at rich countries versus poorer coun-tries. Well-being rose with wealth but only up to an annual gross national product (GNP) of around $8,000—about the GNP of Ireland at the time of the survey. At that threshold, economic growth became disconnected from subjective well-being. Countries with higher GNPs did not receive a "happi-ness dividend" for all their wealth.

Experts like Myers have also found that this threshold theory holds true when looking at individuals within wealth-ier countries. Once an individual can afford the basic ne-cessities, more money doesn't result in greater happiness. Some evidence even indicates that as income rises, well-being decreases. For example, a study of lottery winners revealed that a majority were *less* content five years after hitting the jackpot.

The disconnect between income and happiness becomes even more pronounced when the studies examined whether, over time, the economic growth of a country improved human morale. Myers points out that in 1957, America's per person income, expressed in today's dollars, was $9,000; today that figure is more than $20,000. He then notes the increase in "creature comforts" that exist today: twice as many cars per person, eight times as many dishwashers, five times as many air conditioners, houses that are twice as big. Added to these are all of those "necessities" that didn't even exist forty years ago: cell phones, high speed Internet access, caller ID, and video game systems. Aren't we happier now?

No, we're not, says Myers. According to the University of Chicago's National Opinion Research Center, since 1957, those reporting that they are "very happy" has *dropped* from 35 to 30 percent, even while our incomes more than doubled, even while we've had increasing access to all of that wonder-ful "stuff."

Another way of gauging the degree of happiness within our consumer society is to look at other factors that have increased (or decreased) while our incomes have grown. Studies show that our free time has dwindled; that the rates of child abuse, drug addiction, and teen suicides have all risen; that the number of children with emotional problems has grown; and that global warming has increased. Our quality of life clearly is not improving with the quantity of items we purchase.

How to Be Happy

If it's true that material acquisitions and increased income beyond a certain level of sustenance do not impact one's happiness, then what *does* affect happiness?

There is hard evidence that an emphasis on nonmaterialistic values and virtues *does* increase contentment. Research shows that those individuals who value helping their communities, being close to people, growing as a person, and making the world a better place experience more well-being and a higher quality of life than those who don't value these things. "Those people who internalize the belief that it's important to be wealthy—those who have materialistic values—are less happy than those who have nonmaterialistic goals," says Tim Kasser, an assistant professor of psychology at Knox College specializing in happiness research. He adds that those nonmaterialistic strivings, not coincidentally, mesh almost perfectly with the pursuits of those who seek simplicity.

"There is empirical research to support what voluntary simplicity is saying," Kasser concludes—that happiness comes from close relationships with family, strong ties with your community, and a feeling of making a difference.

I think the story of my mother's childhood illustrates this concept pretty well. My mom was born in 1918. Her family was poor, even by the standards of the early 1900s. By the time she was six, her father had abandoned her mother with five kids, ages nine and younger. The house they lived in was twenty miles from town and had no running water or indoor plumbing of any sort, no phone, radio, or central heating, not even electricity.

"At first," my mom recalls, "there were times when we didn't have enough to eat. I remember a stretch when all we had to eat was potatoes and not even any oil to fry them in. My mother cooked them on the woodstove as best she could. And it was cold. We wore our coats and hats to bed to keep warm."

The family soon moved into town and found a place where they were allowed to live rent-free. Her mother took in wash—which, of course, she did by hand—and the kids delivered it in a small wagon. They somehow made ends meet in the most simple fashion. Mom can't remember any toys— except a ball (made of yarn), a baseball bat (in reality, a stick), and a jump rope (a length of twine)—but she does vividly recall the neighbors who came over in the evenings to play cards and tell stories. "Our neighbors were wonderful. They'd bring food over when someone was sick. They were there when we needed them. We all helped each other," Mom recalls.

"I don't remember feeling deprived," she says. "Not at all. You were happier with what you had then. You weren't always wanting something else."

Of course, I'm not advocating a return to such harsh times. I'm also not saying that every household in this country has reached the level where increased income brings diminishing returns. There are certainly millions here in America who still need to be lifted out of poverty and a hand-to-mouth existence.

But a return to what made those earlier times memorable for folks like my mother, the very things that we know to be essential for authentic happiness—family time together, an emphasis on community and on relationships—is long overdue.

Without a revolution in the meaning of our lives, without a cultural epiphany regarding those things in life that are worthy of our ambition, our kids are destined to keep searching for happiness in all the wrong places. Indeed, more and more American kids are growing up with those "yuppie values." UCLA and the American Council on Education gather statistics from nearly a quarter million college freshmen each year.

HOW HAPPY ARE YOU?

Through studies and research, psychologists have determined what beliefs and practices lead to happiness. To discover whether you're on the "happiness track," ask yourself the following questions based on the findings of David G. Myers and Tim Kasser:

1. Do you have *non*materialistic goals—like growing as a person, devoting time to family—rather than goals of achieving great wealth? Are you satisfied with basic financial security rather than riches?

2. Do you volunteer on a regular basis?

3. Do you smile and laugh frequently?

4. Do you have several close, intimate friendships?

5. Do you have strong ties to your community? Do you know your neighbors and interact with them often?

6. Do you have employment or hobbies that you feel are challenging yet not unduly stressful? Do you look forward to each new day?

7. Do you enjoy good health? Do you get enough sleep and exercise regularly?

8. Do you pause to reflect on all of the good things in life often?

9. Are you a religious or spiritual person?

10. Do you give priority to those things in your life— people, causes, activities—that are most important to you?

The more yes answers you have, the greater are your chances for being a contented, happy individual.

Between 1971 and 1998, the share of Americans entering college who believed it essential or very important to be "very well off financially" rose from 39 to 74 percent. Sadly, as Professor Kasser's research concludes, this increase in materialistic values means that more and more of these young people will not find happiness or satisfaction.

Simple Families Are Happy Families

Simplified families know that there is no point in pursuing "material happiness." The responses I received when I asked downshifted families if simplifying had made them happier were emphatic: *"Yes!"* "Absolutely." "Definitely." "Immeasurably happier." "It makes life much more enjoyable."

They also unanimously said that their kids were happier too. The Merck survey corroborates this overwhelming satisfaction: 87 percent of the downshifters surveyed reported that they were happy with the change. Betsy Taylor of the Center for a New American Dream confirms this contentment among simplifiers: "They don't want to go back once they've started down this path. They're pretty darned happy!"

The equation is amazingly straightforward: Cut back on consumption, on the need to acquire more and "better" stuff, on the illogical race to "one up" the Joneses. Refocus your time and energy on those things that matter to you. And—voilà! Happiness.

How does this look in real life?

Diana Wright and Steve Hoffman of Vermont are a good example. They both began working part-time when their first daughter was born in 1994. "It felt so good," says Diana, "we were so happy when we quit working full-time." Why this contentment? "We've made a conscious effort to be happy with what we've got," Diana says. "We're not going to spend our life searching for the perfect house, the perfect car . . . "

Roger Meyer and Dana Murdoch are parents in another

downshifted household who've chosen to work part-time, for their happiness and sanity. "If it's stuff you're after, you'll never have enough," says Roger. Besides, he feels that he's creating the kind of childhood for his daughter, Olive, that will be memorable and magical.

Linda Farris notes that she and husband Paul Wilson could easily have gotten caught up in the work-spend-work tread-mill. But Linda, who was working as a physician at the time, recalls: "I looked around at my colleagues and saw them work-ing more, spending more—and they still weren't satisfied." Instead of joining them, Farris and Wilson downshifted—and were able to retire in their forties.

Contented Communities

To rephrase a term used by a former President, happiness has a "trickle up" quality to it. If we're happier as individuals with less stuff and more time, then we feel better, we're less stressed, and our families reap the benefits of more time to-gether focused on each other. Hence, happier families. We also have more time and energy—and we actually feel the *need*—for more community. We feel more civic commitment; we get to know the folks who live down the street. Our neigh-borhoods are, consequently, enhanced, safer, healthier, and happier.

A 1992 survey found that 72 percent of Americans didn't know their neighbors. This is astounding—and depressing. I think of my mother growing up in the 1920s and how much more difficult her life would have been without the neighbors who shared their meager possessions, their stories, and their lives with each other.

Simple living families have the time and energy to focus on their communities, but it's really a reciprocal phenomenon. Tara Strand-Brown says that her family depends on friends and neighbors in their rural area more since simplifying: "We share tools so we don't each have to own them. We have a community garden and chickens. This sharing breeds intimacy."

Roger Meyer has seen firsthand the difference that simplifying can have on the community. "I'm able to keep in touch with my neighbors, deepen roots in the neighborhood," he explains. He even started a weekly play group for other parents and toddlers with both moms and dads attending. "I really feel like I'm part of the community."

Another way that many downshifted families feel more like "part of the community" is by volunteering together to help those less fortunate. By volunteering together, these families impart meaningful values, create treasured family rituals, "do the right thing"—and have a good time in the process. See "Communicating and Modeling Compassion and Social Justice" on page 90 and Chapter 12 for more information on volunteering with kids.

A Better World

Mahatma Gandhi, who personified social justice, nonviolence, and simplicity, gave us the profound words "Live simply that others may simply live." That phrase captures the simplicity movement's deepest convictions about the relationship between those of us who have much and those who have little.

Almost all of us in the United States are among the world's "haves." According to the 1992 United Nations Human Development Report, the top fifth of the world's people—that's you and me and most Americans—holds 83 percent of the world's wealth, while the bottom fifth claims only 1.4 percent.

Lisa Cunningham, who spent two years in the late eighties in Gambia with the Peace Corps, describes daily life in that poor, third world country, which ranks among the bottom fifth (Lisa refers to her Gambian friends and neighbors here as brothers and sisters):

> In my village, where the annual per capita income at the time was roughly $250, children were often malnourished. Water-borne diseases flourished. Sanitation was rudimentary. Mosquito nets were a luxury in an area rife with malaria. My brothers walked miles to gather increasingly scarce wood for cooking fuel. My sisters performed a backbreaking array of chores for the family. So precious were school supplies that the students would memorize the tiny serial numbers on their Bic pens so that they could identify them should they be lost or stolen.
>
> It is mere accidents of birth that have placed them in incredibly harsh climates and environments, places that would challenge the most educated, technically savvy Westerner. They deserve basic food, shelter, sanitation, health and education every bit as much as we do on our not-really-so-far-away side of the planet.

But it gets worse. The Gambians whom Lisa describes are among the *lucky* members of that bottom 20 percent. According to the World Food Programme, 50 million in that group are not just malnourished, but suffering from what they term "acute hunger," due to a combination of drought, war, crop failures, politics, and simple bad luck. In this group, more than 15,000 children die *each day* from hunger-related diseases. Daily life for these millions is, alas, much harsher.

Dr. John Schultz, president of the Christian Children's Fund, visited a remote section of Ethiopia in the spring of 2000 and reported that "the village was hushed, like a hospital ward. Many of the people were in the last stages of starvation. . . . In one home, a widow whose daughter had died the week before was cradling another daughter in her arms. Her son was lying on the floor wrapped in what would likely

HUNGER AND POVERTY IN AMERICA

Almost a billion people worldwide are considered undernourished. Over 30 million of those hungry people live right here in the "land of plenty." Here are more sad statistics on hunger and poverty in America:

- Nearly one in five American children lives in a "food insecure" household—meaning they may not know where their next meal is coming from.
- Twelve million American kids live below the poverty line.
- Child poverty is more widespread in the U.S. than in any other industrialized country.
- A person working full-time at the federal minimum wage makes less than $11,000 a year. The average annual compensation of the thirty highest paid executives in the U.S. is $112.9 million.
- The gap between rich and poor in America has been widening for three decades.
- The ratio of the average CEO's pay to the average U.S. blue-collar worker's is 531 to 1, which means we have the greatest wage inequality of any developed nation.
- Three-fifths of American workers earn less than what the Economic Policy Institute concludes is needed for a minimum "living wage."
- Almost 40 million Americans have no health insurance.

become his burial shroud. They had had nothing to eat for days and were on the brink of death."

If you're an average, middle-class American, you are, as you read this, sitting in a 2,000-square-foot home, amply furnished with thousands of dollars' worth of sofas, armchairs, china cabinets, and down comforters. You own two cars, at least one computer, several televisions, and various other electronic "toys." You probably eat a good deal of red meat—that is to say, you're on the top of the food chain—and, except when dieting, have never gone hungry in your life.

Your kids are relatively carefree, likely receiving more than the Gambian per capita income of $250 for allowance each year, spending it on the latest kid-targeted fads.

Patti Idrobo is a simple living mom from New Jersey who feels strongly that the contrast between our American lives and those of destitute third world citizens is the strongest argument for us to live simply. "When I look around and see all the waste and excessive consumerism in middle-class United States, I am truly appalled and saddened," she says. "How can we live this way when others in other countries and also in this country are living in conditions of extreme poverty and poor health?"

At the very least, living simply allows us to send some of our excess to relief organizations, or to groups like Bread for the World, working at eradicating the causes of poverty and hunger around the world. "By 'living simply,' " observes Kathleen Murphy of Ottawa, Canada, "I have more income available to give away to various charities." This is the simplest expression of sharing—writing a check in the comfort of our "lavish" North American homes.

But "live simply that others may simply live" signifies more than the moral imperative that we share our excess with those less fortunate. By living simply and consciously, we can ensure that others around the world do not endure sweatshop conditions, labor in pesticide-ridden fields, or are forced to clear-cut their rain forests so that we can have access to inexpensive food and other products. These are the people who sew the clothes that we browse on racks at Nordstrom; they work long hours for pennies, harvesting our produce and coffee. The majority of Americans don't see this connection; it's missing from the tags on our capri pants and our Folger's labels.

Simple living parents understand the relationship between our consumption and the lifestyles of billions around the globe. Kathleen Murphy emphasizes that "in North America, *not* 'living simply' ultimately means that someone else is being forced to live in poverty to support the North

RAISING YOUR CHILD TO BE A GLOBAL CITIZEN

Most of us can't just pick up our families and travel around the world or sign up for a stint with an overseas relief agency. But we can take steps to ensure that our kids are aware of and connected with others in the global community. Here are a few possibilities:

- Read to your kids about other countries. Books such as *Children Just Like Me* and *Children from Australia to Zimbabwe* (see "Resources" at the end of Chapter 7) help your kids to identify with and understand foreign cultures.
- Model global citizenry. Discuss world affairs, not just what's happening down the block or at city hall. Write to your members of Congress regarding international issues. Donate to overseas relief groups. Let your kids see you doing these things. Explain your actions in terms they can understand.
- Post a world map in a prominent location. Ours is in our living room and we use it frequently, locating countries that are in the news, where ancestors lived or where friends and relatives are currently visiting.
- Embrace other cultures' traditions. Attend cultural events, listen to the music of other lands, read about the practices and rituals of faraway places.
- Join organizations that support efforts to create just and humane conditions for all people around the globe like Bread for the World, Amnesty International, and Co-op America. Tell your kids about the important work these groups do.
- Encourage your kids to donate to overseas relief groups. A simple effort is the "Trick or Treat for UNICEF" program. You might want to include a charitable donation as part of your allowance scheme (see Chapter 13).
- Shop with a global perspective—and tell your children

(continues)

(continued)

why you do so. Remember the impacts that your purchases may have on the rest of the world, from promoting sweatshop conditions to destroying rain forests.

- If you're able to and want to travel, look into a "volunteer vacation." These short-term commitments give participants a taste of life abroad while making real contributions to poor communities. See "Resources" at the end of Chapter 10 for more information.

- Become world travelers from the comfort of your own home, as my family has, with a monthly Globe Trotter Sunday tradition. On Globe Trotter Sunday one country or region of the world is featured and the purpose is to learn a bit more about that country. We always have at least a sampling of ethnic cuisine, read a few short paragraphs about the region from a children's atlas (we use *Scholastic Atlas of the World*), and point out the country on our world map, mentioning any current events that involve the country. If we have more time and energy, we might watch a feature film or documentary on the country. Your own family could go further by enjoying ethnic music or learning a few phrases from the country's language.

American lifestyle. By 'living simply' I am reducing the demand for cheap goods made by overseas wage slaves."

To Lisa Cunningham, "living simply that others may simply live" means "that the consumption choices that I make have a direct impact on the lives of people around the world—what crops are grown, what resources are mined, what pollution is generated, what lifestyles people aspire to."

Patti Idrobo points to another reason why simplifying can help others around the world: "The middle-class lifestyle not only hurts [us] as we chase after illusory sources of happiness, but also keeps us focused on ourselves so we are blind or ignorant of the problems of the rest of the world." It also separates us from the many struggling citizens of our own country. (See "Hunger and Poverty in America" on page 56.)

In addition, living simply shows solidarity with the majority of the world, those who really have no choice, who are living in *involuntary* simplicity. Living simply then is both symbolic *and* functional in allowing others to live.

Peace on Earth

"If you want peace, work for justice" is another of the simplicity movement's mottoes. But it also is more than a bumper sticker platitude. When we make efforts that contribute to the eradication of hunger, poverty, and human rights abuses, we are working for a more just world—and we're helping to promote peace too.

This is really the ultimate "trickle up" benefit of simplicity: a peaceful world to pass on to our children.

Resources

A BETTER WORLD

Alan Thein Durning. *How Much Is Enough? The Consumer Society and the Future of the Earth* (New York: Norton, 1992).

Alan Thein Durning and John Ryan. *Stuff: The Secret Lives of Everyday Things* (Seattle: Northwest Environment Watch, 1997).

Scholastic Atlas of the World (New York: Scholastic, Inc., 2001).

Ronald Sider. *Rich Christians in an Age of Hunger* (Downers Grove, Illinois: Intervarsity Press, 1977).

HAPPINESS IN GENERAL

Robert Frank. *Luxury Fever* (New York: The Free Press, 1999).

David G. Myers. *The American Paradox: Spiritual Hunger in an Age of Plenty* (New Haven: Yale University Press, 2000).

David G. Myers. *The Pursuit of Happiness: Discovering the Pathway to Fulfillment, Well-Being, and Enduring Personal Joy* (New York: Avon, 1992).

Juliet Schor. *The Overspent American: Upscaling, Downshifting, and the New Consumer* (New York: Basic Books, 1998).

FAMILY HAPPINESS

William J. Doherty. *The Intentional Family: How to Build Family Ties in Our Modern World* (Reading, Massachusetts: Addison-Wesley Publishing, 1997).

William J. Doherty and Barbara Z. Carlson. *Putting Family First* (New York: Henry Holt, 2002).

Mary Pipher. *The Shelter of Each Other: Rebuilding Our Families* (New York: Grosset/Putnam, 1996).

ORGANIZATIONS/WEBSITES

Amnesty International (www.amnesty.org) and Amnesty International USA (www.aiusa.org); (212) 807–8400.

Bread for the World: www.bread.org; (800) 82–BREAD. Antihunger citizens' lobby.

Co-op America: www.coopamerica.org; (800) 58–GREEN. A nonprofit organization with a goal of promoting the values of social justice and environmental sustainability within the marketplace by educating consumers and companies.

Food First: www.foodfirst.org; (520) 654–4400. Frances Moore Lappe and Joseph Collins's organization to eradicate world hunger.

www.networkforgood.org. Information about many charities.

OTHERS

Barbara Ehrenreich. *Nickel and Dimed: On (Not) Getting By in America* (New York: Metropolitan Books, 2001).

David Heitmiller and Jacqueline Blix. *Getting a Life: Strategies for Simple Living Based on the Revolutionary Program for Financial Freedom, "Your Money or Your Life."* (New York: Penguin, 1999).

5

〰

Caring for the Earth

In Portland, Oregon, where my family lives, curbside recycling has been provided by the city for almost a decade. For no extra charge, residents can set out their recyclables for pickup by their garbage hauler. The program has been enormously successful. Portland now recycles more than 54 percent of its waste, making it the number one recycling city in the country, according to an industry publication.

Yes, folks here in Portland consider themselves to be pretty environmentally correct; they feel that they're doing their part. But the other day as I took my daily run, I started thinking maybe this environmental smugness isn't such a good thing.

My running route takes me through an upscale neighborhood in a very politically correct part of town. Friday is this neighborhood's garbage/recycling day, and the city-issued yellow recycling bins sit neatly outside every home, glass, tin, paper, milk jugs, and newspapers painstakingly separated. With its meticulously landscaped yards, impeccable streets, and magazine-cover-quality homes, this neighborhood could be the poster child for Portland's reputation as an environmentally progressive city.

But looking closer, it becomes obvious that something is amiss. Homes here run a half million dollars and up, with easily 3,000 to 4,000 square feet and lot sizes that are far above the average. Those lush green lawns eat up a lot of water and chemicals. Parked in the driveways of most of these residences are usually one—sometimes two—decidedly *un*earth-friendly vehicles. Expeditions, Suburbans, and Navigators are popular, as are luxury SUVs (another oxymoron) made by Lexus, Mercedes, and Cadillac. It takes a lot of stuff to fill a 4,000-square-foot house, and, of course, secondhand couches and mismatched end tables just won't cut it.

What many Portlanders have conveniently forgotten is that the environmental motto *begins* with "Reduce" and *ends* with "Recycle." Our first obligation to the environment is clearly to consume less, *not* to recycle more. Our unquenchable thirst for stuff—everything from mammoth homes and cars to the latest technological gadget—is the true environmental culprit, and all the recycling in the world isn't going to justify our excess.

It isn't just Portlanders who are missing the point. This attitude of "I recycle, don't ask me to reduce" is a nationwide phenomenon. A Gallup poll conducted in the spring of 2001 found that 57 percent of Americans *say* they support environmental protections even if they might hamper the economy. The same percentage felt that the quality of the environment in the U.S. is declining. A poll by Opinion Research Corporation International in the summer of 2001 revealed that 96 percent of Americans believe that individuals should take personal action to conserve energy and protect the environment.

And yet America, with about 4 percent of the world's population, consumes a third of the planet's resources. According to Northwest Environment Watch, Americans deplete 120 pounds—nearly their average body weight—*every day* in natural resources extracted from farms, forests, range-lands, and mines. This is far, far more than the consumption rates of less wealthy countries.

Americans are willing to recycle—but heaven forbid any-one ask them to quit consuming. During the 1992 Earth Sum-mit, the first President Bush said, "The American way of life is not up for negotiation," meaning we're not willing to con-serve if it impacts our consumer lifestyle.

The apple didn't fall far from the tree. President George W. Bush's press secretary said recently, explaining the President's stance on the growing energy crisis, "The President believes that [the amount of energy Americans consume is] an Ameri-can way of life, and that it should be the goal of policy-makers to protect the American way of life. The American way of life is a blessed one."

Blessed? Certainly not in Mother Earth's estimation. Our complicity in the global warming problem is one example. Early in 2001 the United Nations–sponsored Intergovern-mental Panel on Climate Change issued their long-awaited report on global warming. The news was not good. The sixty international scientists participating in the report said that the earth's average temperature could rise as much as 10.4 de-grees by 2100. The scientists reported that there was "new and stronger evidence" that most of the warming of the planet was due to human activities, such as the burning of oil, gasoline, and coal. The 4 percent of the world's population living in the United States currently produces 25 percent of the world's carbon dioxide, making us the chief contributors to global warming.

The Bush administration abandoned the Kyoto Protocol—the 1997 treaty aimed at cutting emissions of the green-house gases linked to global warming—saying that America was being asked to do more than its share to avert the problem. Besides, the needed actions could impair our faltering economy.

America's out-of-control consumption, though clearly detrimental by environmental and social welfare standards, is

WHAT IS YOUR FAMILY'S "ECOLOGICAL FOOTPRINT"?

Environmental advocates often use the metaphor of a footprint to describe the extent of damage an individual or nation causes to the environment. An individual's "ecological footprint" represents the amount of land and water it takes to provide the resources that one person consumes and to accommodate the waste he makes from birth until death.

The earth has about five acres available for each of the 6.1 billion people on the planet to use. Unfortunately, the "ecological footprint" of the average American is about thirty-one acres. We're obviously using resources at an unsustainable—and unfair—rate.

If you're interested in discovering whether you're a typical Big Foot American, visit these websites:

- www.earthday.net/goals/footprint.stm
- www.rprogress.org/programs/sustainability/ef/quiz
- www.bestfootforward.com/footprintlife.htm
- You can also calculate your "carbon footprint," that is, how much carbon dioxide is added to the atmosphere due to your family's practices, at www.safeclimate.net.

Take the time to complete one of these short questionnaires, determining your own family's footprint. Then refer to Chapter 14 for more information on how to lessen your impact on the earth.

unfortunately seen as the saving grace of our economy. If Americans consume heavily, we're said to be experiencing an economic boom. The "R" word—recession—gets mentioned when buying goes down. It's almost unpatriotic to spend less. In the end, we are an entire country that gauges its success on its accumulation of "stuff."

Lisa Cunningham, the downshifted mother of two from Maryland, believes that "consumption is the elephant in the room that no one wants to talk about."

"Consuming," she reasons, "really is the American way of life, the ability to waste resources profligately."

And this is the message we're teaching our kids too. While schools now have plenty of environmentally friendly messages intertwined in the curriculum, they're typically focused on the need to recycle or on esoteric discussions about endangered species. The connection between our own consumption and the decline of biodiversity is not clearly made.

Even if it were, how can we expect kids to absorb the message when they see excess all around them? Obviously, our own example is ensuring that our kids will continue to focus on less effective environmental actions. A child who watches Mom and Dad buy a $40,000 vehicle that gets only ten or twelve miles to the gallon is learning a clear lesson on priorities.

In 1999 the Center for a New American Dream conducted a poll of four hundred parents on the topic of "kids and consumption." Two-thirds of the parents said that their kids care about the environment, yet only 20 percent of the parents said their kids think that buying too much stuff is harmful to the earth. We're teaching our children well—and they're turning out much like their parents.

We aren't, of course, the only country that makes a habit of consuming far more than it needs. The 1992 United Nations Conference on the Environment—the Earth Summit—concluded that "the major cause of the continued deterioration of the global environment is the unsustainable pattern of consumption and production, particularly in the industrialized countries." That conference called on those countries to "take the lead in achieving sustainable consumption."

But we stand out even among our conspicuously consumptive peers. The average American uses twice as much fossil fuel as a British citizen and consumes 2.5 times as much meat as the average Japanese citizen. The typical American discards nearly a ton of trash per person per year, two to three times as much as the typical Western European throws away. Americans consume approximately twice as much energy per capita as the British, French, Swedes, Norwegians, or Japanese.

As with so many other things, we are setting the pace for the rest of the world with our consumption patterns and our indifference regarding their impact on the planet.

Living Lighter on the Earth—with Kids

Simple living advocates with children should be especially concerned about the environment. Why? Because those of us with children have even greater stakes in preserving the planet.

For one thing, it is our children and grandchildren who'll be inheriting the earth—and we want to ensure that the world we leave them will be vital and sustainable.

Also, by becoming parents, many of us acknowledge that we're exacerbating the degradation of the environment. We've brought more people into this already overtaxed world, and what's more noteworthy, we've brought them in as *Americans*.

And that's bad news for Planet Earth. According to experts, a baby born in the United States creates thirty-five times as much environmental damage over the course of its lifetime as a baby born in India. An average American consumes about fifty-three times more goods and services than the average resident of China. The amount of energy used by one American is equivalent to that used by 531 Ethiopians.

So, in effect, my family of four causes as much environmental damage as 140 residents of India, consumes as many goods and services as 212 Chinese citizens, and uses as much energy as 2,124 Ethiopians. This view of American parenting emphasizes our responsibility to limit the damage our families cause. Unless we intercede, our children will likely turn into typical American megaconsumers. For this reason alone, all parents should be committed conservationists.

Downshifting parents are, for the most part, strong environmentalists, and hope to raise their kids to care about the earth too. John Davis of Greensboro, North Carolina, is a

SHOW YOU CARE: START AN ECOTEAM

One constructive and fun way to cast a vote for the planet is to start or join an EcoTeam. EcoTeams are neighborhood-based groups of families learning together how to live lighter on the earth. The EcoTeam effort is a program of Global Action Plan (GAP), a nonprofit group based in Woodstock, New York. Since the program was started in 1990, more than 150,000 people worldwide have participated.

An EcoTeam is created when five or six households within a neighborhood commit to going through the program together. Over the next four months, the group works through the EcoTeam handbook, learning about environmentally friendly changes they can make within their households, and then commits to take action. The handbook covers five different areas—garbage, water and energy use, transportation, and consumption.

EcoTeam participants keep track of the changes they make and forward that information to GAP. Households report sending up to 51 percent less garbage to landfills, using one-third less water, 17 percent less energy, 20 percent less fuel, and saving almost $400 yearly on average by adopting EcoTeam strategies.

Three options are available for those interested in forming EcoTeams:

1. If you live in one of the seven local communities that sponsor EcoTeam programs—Columbus, Ohio; Kansas City, Missouri; Portland and Bend, Oregon; Madison, Wisconsin; Philadelphia, Pennsylvania; and Rockland County, New York— call your local EcoTeam or Sustainable Lifestyle Campaign office. (A materials fee of $35 will be charged.)

2. You can start an "at large" group by contacting GAP (see "Resources" at the end of this chapter). The materials fee for each household in at-large groups is $38.95.

3. You can lobby for your city or county to sponsor the EcoTeam program. Contact GAP and they'll guide you through the process.

good example. He teaches his son, by example and discussion, the importance of keeping our planet healthy. John feels so strongly that he says he hopes to pass on a respect for the earth to his son "or my life will have been wasted."

If we do our jobs right—as John is doing—we can make an impact on many generations to come, and our actions might well mean the survival of the planet.

A New American Dream

The survival of the planet is what simplicity is all about. Living simply—and teaching our children to do the same—is the best, possibly the *only*, way to have a sustainable future. If we are to do this, we'll have to adopt some habits that on the surface may seem almost un-American.

Perhaps, then, a revised definition of the American Dream is in order. Simple living families have an organization to help them with this goal—the Center for a New American Dream—whose mission is to assist "individuals and institutions to change the way they consume, to enhance quality of life and protect the natural environment."

Part of that American Dream is also to find the true meaning of happiness, which all of us hope to pass on to our kids. Fortunately, those activities that lead to happiness are almost always low consumption, earth-friendly practices, things like volunteering, appreciating nature, connecting with family and friends, and enjoying music and art.

The Future of the Planet

When my oldest son was just beginning to talk, my mother-in-law gave me a blank book in which to record those wacky, witty, and wise things he would say. As a mother she knew they would come. All kids, after all, are profound.

When he was four or so, I wrote down this proclamation of his: "Mom, I think people were sent here to save the earth."

After recording that little insight, I editorialized with my own comment: "If so, we're sure doing a lousy job of it."

I should have added, " ... so far." If enough parents practice simplicity, and pass on this way of life to their children, there is hope.

Resources

Alan Thein Durning. *How Much Is Enough? The Consumer Society and the Future of the Earth* (New York: Norton, 1992).

Alan Thein Durning and John Ryan. *Stuff: The Secret Lives of Everyday Things* (Seattle: Northwest Environment Watch, 1997).

Mark Hertsgaard. *Earth Odyssey: Around the World in Search of Our Environmental Future* (New York: Broadway, 1998).

Paul Wachtel. *The Poverty of Affluence* (Philadelphia: New Society Publishers, 1989).

Edward O. Wilson. *The Future of Life* (New York: Alfred A. Knopf, 2002).

ECOLOGICAL FOOTPRINT WEBSITES/BOOKS

Donald W. Lotter. *Earthscore: Your Personal Environmental Audit and Guide* (LaFayette, California: Morning Sun Press, 1993).

www.bestfootforward.com/footprintlife.htm
www.earthday.net/goals/footprint.stm
www.rprogress.org/programs/sustainability/ef/quiz
www.safeclimate.net

ECOTEAM INFORMATION

Global Action Plan: P.O. Box 428, Woodstock, NY 12498; (845) 679–4830; www.globalactionplan.org.

PART 2

The "Hows"—How You Can

Live Simply with Children

6

≪≫

What Does a "Simple Living Family" Look Like?

As I researched this book, the thoughts I'd had about simplified families were confirmed: No two downshifting families are alike. There are as many variations on "simple family life" as there are families who adopt this way of living.

As Vicki Robin, coauthor of *Your Money or Your Life,* has noted, "People come to simplicity through different doors." Many are attracted by the personal finance sanity of simplicity, and many long for more time and less stress for their families. A large number feel the pull of environmental concerns, while still others are motivated by economic and social justice matters and by the prospect of stronger community ties. Most of the parents I spoke with ultimately felt strongly about all of these issues, even if their initial reasons for simplifying involved only one or two factors.

Along with our varied incentives for simplifying, Robin emphasizes that we all come to simplicity from diverse backgrounds. In short, we're all unique and our interpretations of simplicity will all be a bit different.

So, simplicity is a continuum. The simplest existence might

be the cabin in the woods, living off the grid, eating home-grown, organic, and vegetarian foods, and home-schooling the kids. There probably are families who fit this description somewhere out there, although I didn't uncover any in my search.

There are, on the other end of the simplicity spectrum, those who have cut back in an effort to allow one spouse to work part-time or stay home until the kids are in school. In the middle are the vast majority of simplicity seekers, and their methods are diverse as well.

The variety of approaches taken actually makes complete sense. If simplicity is about living authentically—living consciously and mindfully—and if we're all individuals, then we'll have different takes on this lifestyle.

Six Ways to Simplify

Just what a simple family looks like can vary greatly. The following examples represent just a few of the many approaches families are taking to simplifying, with an emphasis on the big financial "how tos:"

1. PART-TIME PARTNERS

Roger Meyer describes it as "the best of both worlds." He's talking about how he and wife Dana Murdoch both work part-time, at jobs they enjoy, and spend the rest of their week home with daughter Olive, age two. Roger and Dana have arranged their days at home so that Olive is in the care of others for only four hours weekly—and even then, the caregivers are Roger's parents.

The family makes ends meet and is still able to save by utilizing a number of downshifting strategies—from owning only one car and purchasing used clothing to entertaining at home and simply buying less. "The material stuff that people work two jobs to get just wasn't worth that much to us," says Roger.

Roger and Dana are expecting another child in a few months. Except for the six-month maternity leave Dana plans to take, they will continue their part-time partner setup. "We wouldn't do it differently for the world," says Roger, "we're lucky to have this situation." They're also, I might add, wise and farsighted enough to take advantage of it.

But, yes, they're lucky too. Before Olive was born, Roger and Dana approached their employers about working part-time—and both employers were amenable to their proposals. Dana, who works as an architect, found that a three-fifths-time option was already in place where she works. Roger was allowed to switch from full- to half-time in his job as coordinator of a social service agency, and he now consults half-time, typically as an interim director for nonprofits.

Good part-time positions aren't always so easy to find, as many simple living parents have discovered. For example, Laural Ringler and Tom Caldwell of Bellingham, Washington, have two young children and work in education. Over the past five years, they've switched back and forth, with one parent working full-time and one at home, and they even had a year of each working half-time. They preferred the "part-time partners" situation but they're back to one parent working full-time because their employers weren't able to accommodate them. They'll keep trying to secure half-time positions.

2. UN-JOBBING

Because finding good part-time jobs can be a difficult proposition, some downshifting parents try to find home-based work, often as freelancers or consultants and sometimes by teaching or tutoring on an occasional basis or as small—very small—business owners.

Michael Fogler calls this "un-jobbing." Michael and wife

Suzanne McIntosh live in Lexington, Kentucky, where they "un-jobbed" over a decade ago. Michael's written a concise yet extremely helpful book about this approach to simple living called *Un-Jobbing: The Adult Liberation Handbook.*

Michael believes that the "institution of 'making a living' has gotten way out of hand." Americans, he says, are plagued by "terminal professionalism," taking their jobs way too seriously, so much so that "our way of life is dominated by jobs

YOUR MONEY OR YOUR LIFE

Perhaps a majority of downshifting parents have used *Your Money or Your Life* to help them make financial changes. This book, written by Vicki Robin and the late Joe Dominguez, is often called the bible of the simplicity movement due to its comprehensive handling of personal finance issues.

The book guides readers through a nine-step program which, if the plan is faithfully followed, results in *financial intelligence* (knowledge about the true nature of money), *financial integrity* (aligning financial decisions with values), and, ultimately, *financial independence* (the point at which income from savings covers expenses).

The nine steps range from creating an inventory of all of your assets and recording every cent that you receive and spend, to utilizing cost-cutting techniques and reaching the "crossover point" where earnings from your investments equal your expenditures. The core of the program, according to the authors, is Step 4, which asks readers to determine "How much is enough?" for them. This step guides readers to "develop an internal yardstick for fulfillment" and to gauge whether their financial life is in sync with their values. It's the crux of the simplicity experience.

Those interested in receiving help in tackling the nine steps can visit www.newroadmap.org or www.fiassociates.org, where support and on-line study groups are available.

and not by meaningful, fulfilling work." Much of the problem is our acquisitiveness, he says; we spend as much or more than we make.

Michael came to these conclusions from personal experience. For over a decade, Michael, who has a Master of Music degree in guitar performance, continually sought to be, as he puts it, "a career success story." Instead he was invariably frustrated. Full-time college faculty positions in his specialty are extremely rare (the year he received his master's there were only five such positions in the entire country).

But Michael kept trying. In the meantime, he found part-time teaching jobs and performance "gigs" to make ends meet along with the occasional half-time salaried position. He also completed the *Your Money or Your Life* cassette tape course—available before the book came out in 1992—and he and Suzanne made a number of downshifting changes, such as reducing to one car and selling their house and buying another in a less expensive neighborhood.

By 1990 he came to the realization that he really didn't need that coveted full-time job's money or status, that he enjoyed his home-based freelance lifestyle. "I decided to embrace the notion of part-time work instead of being furious with the world," Michael recalls.

Michael and Suzanne quit their jobs in 1990—hers as a tenured music professor, his, at that time, as a half-time college counselor. They concluded that they could live simply yet comfortably on the income from their combined part-time freelance work.

And they are. Michael likes theologian Matthew Fox's definition of work as "the joyful return of one's gift(s) to the community." He feels he's now doing that as a freelance musician and part-time peace activist. Suzanne, likewise, is a freelance musician and finds other unrelated work. Their son, Benjamin, thirteen, is "unschooled"—more about this home schooling option in Chapter 15—another decision in keeping with their simple lifestyles.

THE HIGH COST OF HEALTH CARE

Affordable health insurance is a major stumbling block for many parents attempting to cut back on their work hours. If they choose to work part-time, freelance, or "un-job," they may find that health insurance premiums are prohibitive or, worse, that they simply can't qualify for coverage. And, unlike our neighbors to the north, America has no national health insurance program. Medicare, which isn't comprehensive in any event, doesn't kick in until you're sixty-five (or disabled).

Consequently, decent health insurance keeps many downshifting parents from quitting those full-time, "with benefits," positions. One downshifter I interviewed a few years back indicated that inflation wasn't a big simplifying concern, "not when you do your shopping at garage sales." But we can't get secondhand health insurance. We can be savvy consumers, however, and most simple living people are. We can and should shop around, get quotes, do research.

Some families opt for lower cost, high deductible, "major medical" policies that aren't really triggered until you've incurred significant medical costs. For healthy families—and, of course, another benefit of the simple life is good health—these can result in significant savings. But even if all of the members of the family are healthy, more traditional insurance plans, like HMO (health maintenance organization) coverage, can be costly. And if anyone in the family has a health issue, both types of coverage can be denied them.

This is my family's situation. We currently pay $795 monthly for an HMO plan, over $9,500 annually, and considerable annual increases are to be expected. With preexisting conditions for one family member, and without employment that provides access to group health coverage, our only current option is the Portability Plan, the medical insurance option available after COBRA coverage runs out. (COBRA stands for Comprehensive Omnibus Budget Reconciliation Act, a federal law that requires

(continues)

(continued)

companies with more than twenty employees to offer group health coverage to former employees for eighteen months after they leave their jobs if the employees pay the premiums themselves.)

We've explored other group policy possibilities, through a couple of professional organizations, but have yet to find a suitable alternative. Many national organizations only offer coverage in more populous states, but Oregon, where we live, is a small state. (Alumni groups sometimes offer group insurance too. Call your college alumni office.) Our state does offer a "high risk" insurance option for people in our situation, but the premiums would be higher than our Portability Plan. These insurance pools and other health insurance options vary from state to state. Contact your state's insurance commissioner for more information.

Some simplicity movement members are looking into ways to help those in similar situations find affordable group coverage. If they're successful, information will likely be posted on the Simple Living Network website, www.simpleliving.net. Until then, all parents contemplating quitting their jobs must seriously consider the health insurance issue.

Michael's life—his part-time work and his "light on the earth" practices—feel right to him. "They're in alignment with my values," he says, "and that's a good feeling."

3. MOM'S AT HOME . . .

Lisa Cunningham has one of those classic setups that we hear are fast becoming a thing of the past: She's a stay-at-home mom to daughters Natalie, seven, and Stephanie, four. Husband Mike works full-time.

But Lisa is hardly June Cleaver. She and Mike joined the Peace Corps after college and spent more than five years in

Africa, in Gambia and Botswana. In fact, daughter Natalie was born in Botswana. Lisa's experiences overseas have had a huge impact on her decision to live simply.

"There was nothing like living in a poor village in a developing country to drive home how materially 'rich' we were and yet how 'rich' our local [overseas] community was in many ways," says Lisa thoughtfully.

Mike now works for the EPA, and both Lisa and he are attracted to simplicity not only because it can make a difference to the world's poor, but also because it's an environmentally friendly lifestyle. They own only one car, try to eat organic, and are raising their two daughters TV-free.

Lisa wishes that everyone could visit a third world country, and in particular hopes that her daughters have a chance to live overseas. "It opens your eyes, forces you to evaluate yourself and your perspective," she says. If all Americans were to engage in this "experiential soul searching," perhaps simple living would become the status quo.

4. . . . DAD'S AT HOME

I read once, in a major women's magazine, one writer's opinion that simplicity was yet another movement with the ultimate goal of sending women back to the kitchen.

Lest anyone come away with that impression, I'd like to point out that based upon my research, this is hardly the case. The simple living parents I interviewed were very much equal partners. When it makes sense, Dad stays home.

I mentioned Tom Caldwell and Laural Ringler in the "part-time partners" section. They've switched back and forth, between one staying home and one working full-time, and currently Tom's the stay-at-home parent. Paul and Kathleen Murphy of Ottawa, Canada, are another example—he's home with daughter Alison, while Kathleen works. Paul was able to take early retirement—he's in his fifties—so, Kathleen notes, "it made sense for him to become a stay-at-home dad."

Diana Wright and Steve Hoffman of Vermont had both worked part-time for many years, but now Steve's home and Diana's back full-time because an opportunity came up that she felt strongly about, to be the director of the Sustainability Institute, a nonprofit group helping individuals and institutions to adopt environmentally sustainable practices.

Simple living parents take a mindful approach to the "who stays home" question, much as they do about other matters. Decisions are not made on gender differences but rather on the basis of whose job pays more, which one has better benefits, who feels more strongly about continuing to work, and other issues. It just depends on what works for the family in question.

5. SIMPLE, SINGLE PARENTHOOD

Let me first say that I think single parents are amazing. Their jobs aren't easy—and they deserve all of the help they can get.

But if I'm amazed by single parents generally, I'm positively in awe of Linda McDonough. Linda is a single mom by choice. At age thirty-nine she concluded that if she was ever going to become a mother, she was going to have to do it alone. So she did. Molly was born in November 1994. Then, in January 1999, Linda brought infant Brianna into their family as a foster child, and two years later adopted her. In what surely must be the ultimate testimonial to the benefits of simplicity for families, Linda says she couldn't have done it—that she couldn't have had a family at all—without living simply.

Linda emphasizes that simplicity is a *choice,* and says sincerely, "I had a choice between using disposable diapers and having a child," referring to the costs involved in raising kids. "I chose the child," says Linda. She adds that she also chooses to not eat out, to drive a smaller, older car, and to wear second-hand clothing, all of which allow her to afford the *luxury* of children.

Linda works thirty hours a week as the Christian Education Coordinator for an Episcopalian church in upscale Chapel Hill, North Carolina. Daughter Molly attends public school, and Brianna goes to day care while Linda works. Linda budgets religiously and is even able to give her kids a few extras, like sports and dance classes.

Linda is still able to save—although admittedly not a lot—despite being the sole breadwinner for her family. Tougher than the financial side for her, however, is the psychological effort it takes to go against the grain, particularly with her decision to be a simple living single parent. "A lot of folks admire me, I think, but they think I'm a little weird!" Linda jokes. She finds support from friends, family members, and her church.

6. SEMIRETIRING EARLY

You've probably read in the press about how living simply has allowed some individuals to retire in their thirties and forties. An early retirement is indeed one of the many perks of downshifting. But while many simple living practitioners without children are able to retire several decades before their Golden Years, few of those with children still at home are financially able to do so. This isn't to say that simple living parents can't retire earlier than the norm. But as Diana Wright explains, "the biggest benefit of simplifying for us is more time all along rather than a firm retirement date."

If I could prescribe a "simple living formula" for both parents being able to retire while their kids are still young, it would be this: Both partners work full-time once they finish school. They live simply, save substantial sums, and pay off their mortgage early. They postpone having kids until their early or mid-thirties. By then they've accumulated enough savings that they can quit work altogether.

That's it. Oh, except for that *huge* dose of luck. Luck

in the sense that both partners simplify early in life, that they have kids later, that they're fortunate enough to get well-paying jobs, a good deal on a house, that they remain healthy—all of these factors.

Not surprisingly, simplifiers don't follow this formula very often. I guess my husband and I have sort of followed it, after a fashion and without any real plan to do so. We had simplified and saved considerably before we had kids—but not to the extent that we didn't still need an income.

Then, when *Your Money or Your Life* came out in 1992, we read it with great interest. The authors' description of reaching the "crossover point"—that point in time when the earnings from your savings cover your expenses—was the motivation we needed to work toward my husband Marty's goal of quitting his job. We hadn't really contemplated such a concept—early retirement, with kids?!—until we read this book. Marty was able to quit work in 1999, when the kids were nine and seven. I continued to write part-time from home.

To be sure, luck played a role in our semiretirement—for example, buying a home and a rental house before prices sky-rocketed in our area. But we also saved religiously—and, in our minds, pretty painlessly. We simply quit buying stuff we didn't need—or even want, for that matter. We drove older cars, wore preowned clothes, invited friends over for dinner instead of meeting at restaurants. My husband and I were both thrilled to realize that our environmental concerns meshed pretty well with downshifting.

I think we're living proof that you can downshift with kids, in truth *because* of them, and still semiretire early. I've been saying "semiretire" rather than "retire" for a good reason: After more than two years home with the family, my husband has returned to part-time work, largely due to the cost of our family's health insurance. (See "The High Cost of Health Care" on page 78.)

For now, my husband and I are back in the "part-time partners" category—and feel lucky to be there. Like part-timers Dana Murdoch and Roger Meyer, we think it's the best of both worlds.

Resources

Joe Dominguez and Vicki Robin. *Your Money or Your Life* (New York: Viking, 1999).

Michael Fogler. *Un-Jobbing: The Adult Liberation Handbook* (Lexington, Kentucky: Free Choice Press, 1999).

The New Road Map Foundation; nonprofit group started by Vicki Robin and Joe Dominguez, authors of *Your Money or Your Life* (YMOYL); www.newroadmap.org and www.fiassociates.org. Information on the foundation and on YMOYL on-line study groups and contacts in your area.

The Simple Living Network; www.simpleliving.net

7

*

Communicating Your Convictions
and Practicing What You Preach

Sometimes I wonder if all that I've said and done to instill simple values in my kids has worked. Then, out of the blue, one of them will say or do something that demonstrates that they really *were* listening, that they really *did* absorb a bit of our simple ways.

Like a while back, on allowance day, when it came time to put aside money for charity. (The kids are required to "earmark" 10 percent of their allowance in this way. More information on simple allowances can be found in Chapter 13.) My youngest said, "I want to give an extra twenty dollars to charity." This was coming from his savings; he doesn't receive that much monthly. "Are you sure, Scott?" I asked. "Yes," he said. "I'm sure."

My older son had a class assignment last year to produce a magazine. He chose to devote one to cars, his current obsession. In it he included a feature story on hybrid vehicles and several spoof advertisements, one on a new monster SUV called the *Extravaganza,* with fuel "efficiency" of two gpm—

gallons per mile. "Impress Your Friends! The biggest SUV ever made! You can stuff a bedroom in the backseat!" the ad read.

On the other hand, there've been times when I've suspected that babies were switched at the hospital. . . .

I *do* know this: Even if kids don't totally absorb your simple lifestyle, they're taking in everything you say—and do. Simplicity advocate Cecile Andrews, author of *The Circle of Simplicity,* says that "when parents feel strongly about simplicity, sooner or later kids catch on to those values."

Your commitment to simplicity will surface in two primary ways: your communications and your behavior.

Communication: Talking to— and with—Your Kids

The importance of talking with kids about simplicity—and about your simple living values—was brought home recently when I was reading postings on an Internet simplicity discussion board. A woman wrote in about how her parents had always lived simply even though they'd had good, professional jobs. But the parents didn't talk to the kids about their reasons for low consumption choices. The woman, now an adult, said she always felt "out of it" because she didn't have as many clothes and toys or the big house or new cars that her friends and classmates had. She wished, in hindsight, that her parents had talked with her about their decision to be frugal. She felt that had her parents discussed their reasons for living simply, those underlying values, she may have understood more and had a stronger foundation to sustain her when she felt "different."

In the new millennium we can be even more up front about our choice to live frugally, because the many reasons for doing so are more widely accepted. For example, back in the sixties and seventies, few families had caught on to the environmental rationale for living simply. Now, our kids can point to the environment, social justice, and other reasons for their families' simple lifestyles.

VALUES-BASED COMMUNICATION

Explaining the "whys" of your actions—why you may not drive a new car, why you limit TV, why you haven't yet

---

COMMUNICATING YOUR VALUES

Along with taking advantage of those spontaneous "teachable moments" to reinforce your family's values, you'll want to make an effort to purposefully and *deliberately* bring up values discussions with your family. Here are a few ways to do this:

1. Perform the soul-searching exercise in Chapter 2. The process of brainstorming and composing your Values and Vision Statement is, of course, a major method of instilling those beliefs in your kids.

2. Post your Family Values and Vision Statement where all can see it—and be reminded of it. Next to the family meeting agenda is ideal. My family has also placed copies of the first section of the statement—the listing of values and short descriptors—in each kid's bedroom.

3. Discuss values at family meetings. Another way to highlight the family's beliefs is to pick one value from your Values and Vision Statement to reflect on at each family meeting. (See "A Primer on Family Meetings" on page 12.) One agenda item could read "Values discussion," and then indicate that week's value. For generosity, for example, family members could point out examples of generosity in action witnessed within the family that week—and perhaps brainstorm on other behaviors that would demonstrate generosity. Rotate through the values—and then start over again. You might also consider using the book *The Family Virtues Guide* (see "Resources" at the end of Chapter 10) as a handbook for these values discussions.

---

bought a DVD player, why you buy organic—is both important in teaching simplicity and it's respectful of the child. You'll discover that most of the "whys" of these types of behaviors connect neatly to your values. You'll find yourself saying things like, "We don't watch television because we value our family time together," or, "We buy organic because we care about the health of the earth and our own health."

Seize every "teachable moment" to enlighten your kids with values-based explanations. You'll find that there are dozens of daily situations and activities that allow for— sometimes *beg* for—explanations related to simple living and simple values. Here are just a few examples of those recurring opportunities: trips to the grocery store—or the farmer's market; paying your bills; visiting grandparents; meal preparation; running errands in the car; packing lunches; volunteering together; garbage/recycling day; buying/making birthday gifts. Keep your radar on for these opportunities— and use them.

EARTH-FRIENDLY EXPLANATIONS

The environmental explanation is a frequent one for simple living parents, because it's a common value among these families. When Patti Idrobo's older daughter clamored to have juice boxes like the other kids, Patti recalls, "I kept refusing, but then realized I had never explained to her my reasons. As soon as I explained that juice boxes have too much packaging and that makes too much garbage for the earth, she never asked me again."

Pointing to environmental impacts has also been a major tactic for Lisa Cunningham and husband, Mike. "We both talk about environmental issues in our daily lives. Why we only have one car and Daddy rides the Metro. Why we use Tupperware instead of juice boxes and plastic bags. Why we should only use a few squares of toilet paper, not yards. Why we shouldn't waste X or needlessly drive to Y when we could combine trips."

Ann Halstead of Liberty, Canada, often uses explanations related to the earth when discussing lifestyle choices with her children. For example, she tells her kids that one of the reasons the family is vegetarian is that meat and dairy production wastes a lot of water, and that buying disposable items means natural resources are depleted and more and bigger landfills are needed. "Every choice we make that affects the environment is explained," Ann notes.

These environmental discussions resonate with kids. I loved Tara Strand-Brown's description of how her four-year-old son, Tevon, has absorbed her earth-friendly rationales. She said he's "definitely a strong environmentalist. He often tells people that if George Bush wants to cut down the redwood trees on our land, he's going to defend them by climbing into them. He has also offended a few other shoppers as he asks me, 'Mommy, why is that man buying poisoned food?' Ahhh, well."

The environmental explanations have worked well in our family too. I've discussed my "transport pod" theory with my kids many times   that is, that cars are not toys, status symbols, or reflections of our egos, nor are they fortresses-on-wheels, protecting their occupants from the other Hummer look-alikes on the roads; they are environmentally devastating transportation devices, meant to move people and goods from point A to point B—and we should use them sparingly. They've absorbed these lessons well; our Car Free Sunday ritual was the inspiration of my younger son, readily accepted by the rest of the family.

PEOPLE-FRIENDLY EXPLANATIONS

Simplified parents frequently use explanations related to compassion and social justice (see "Communicating and Modeling

Compassion and Social Justice" below). Several parents commented that kids inherently care about those less fortunate. Tapping into these natural compassions and linking them to simplicity help them internalize the simple life.

COMMUNICATING AND MODELING COMPASSION AND SOCIAL JUSTICE

Compassion and social justice are on nearly every simple family's values' list. Instilling these beliefs in our kids takes repeated discussion and modeling. Here are some strategies to use based upon your child's age:

Toddlers. Look for your youngsters in acts of compassion—and praise them. For example: "Sharing your candy was a very kind thing to do. You must really care about your brother." Each incident in which a child hurts a sibling or friend also presents an opportunity to teach compassion. Name the behavior and the resulting consequence. "When you hit your sister, she feels bad. In our family, we care about each other and we talk about our angry feelings."

Preschoolers. Begin discussions with your preschool-age kids about hunger and poverty. This is a good age to tell your kids that there are people who haven't enough to eat in your own community. Tell them what you think, for example: "I feel sad when I know others go hungry." Then take them with you to bring food to your local emergency assistance agency or food bank. You could also bring them along as you deliver food to shut-ins with an organization like Meals on Wheels.

Picture books with themes of helping are also good at preschool age, for example, *Uncle Willie and the Soup Kitchen* (see "Resources" at the end of this chapter).

Elementary school–age kids. Continue talking about hunger and poverty and begin discussions on the more abstract elements of these issues. Teach your kids the meaning of the term social justice, that all human beings deserve fundamental free-

(continues)

(continued)

doms and have the right to basic necessities like food, shelter, and medical care; that human suffering is wrong, and that we can and should do something about it. The book *For Every Child: The UN Convention on the Rights of the Child in Words and Pictures* is an excellent tool for introducing this concept, as is *If the World Were a Village* (see "Resources" at the end of this chapter).

Other books about families in need will pull at your kids' heartstrings—and bring out their innate empathy. Consider *The Hundred Dresses* and *The Family Under the Bridge*. (See "Resources" at the end of this chapter for more ideas.)

At a family meeting, present your kids with information on hunger and homelessness in their community. (Your local food bank should have this information. Also, see "Hunger and Poverty in America" on page 50.) Ask your kids what they think they could do to help hungry and homeless people. Listen to their answers and help them implement their ideas, or suggest similar actions that the family could take on. Examples include helping out at your local food bank or a nearby soup kitchen. Your church—or any church in your neighborhood—may have a hunger outreach or homeless family program.

Middle and high school–age kids. Keep talking about social justice and modeling charity to and with your kids. Point out newspaper and magazine articles about homelessness and hunger to your teens.

Continue or begin volunteering together as a family. Many middle schools require "community service hours" of their students. This is an ideal way to introduce your teens to the joys of volunteering. (See also the discussion in Chapter 12 on volunteering.)

Kathleen Murphy, like many simple living parents, tries to ensure that the products she purchases haven't been made in sweatshops by mistreated workers. She's found that even her young daughter can grasp the idea of socially responsible shopping—and empathize with the victims—if the concept is explained in simple terms. "I've told her, at a level a six-year-old can understand, about how companies keep the price of products down by not paying their employees enough." Recently Kathleen used this explanation for rejecting Alison's request for a specific pair of shoes. Kathleen believes that Alison felt "genuine sympathy for the poor employees, which allowed her to accept the fact that she would not get those particular shoes."

Some parents find that other deeply held sentiments can work in explanations too. Victoria Mead tells her three young children that "the empty space you sometimes feel can't be filled with 'stuff.' Love, internal peace, and compassion are the only ways to fill that up." Wise words for all of us.

FAMILY, FUN, AND FINANCE-FRIENDLY EXPLANATIONS

Explaining the economic trade-offs of cutting back on consumption—for example, if we don't buy all of these things, Mom and Dad can spend more time at home with you—is another significant method of conveying your beliefs about simplicity to your children. You are, of course, simultaneously communicating that you value time with family over more stuff.

I like to use the terms that Vicki Robin and Joe Dominguez used in *Your Money or Your Life*. We talk with our kids about trading our "life energy"—our time, especially our time spent doing fun stuff with them—for money. And we're pretty straightforward about saying we *choose* not to spend our money—our life energy—on new/fancy/trendy stuff. We emphasize that it really is a choice, and that buying things just doesn't appeal to us as much as having time to spend with our family and friends.

Downshifted parents I spoke with were pretty adamant

that the "whys" shouldn't include the phrase "because we can't afford it," unless that's literally true. Linda McDonough is a single mom supporting herself and two young daughters on a thirty-hour/weekly job. She does a lot of explaining. "Every time we shop or make other decisions about our lives, I explain why we do this. I try never to say 'We can't afford this,' even if that is true, if the *real* reason is that it goes against our values." She'll give these values-based explanations, for example, when the kids ask for highly packaged, nutrient-poor foods, pointing out that they're bad for the environment and for their health, not that "we can't afford it."

Linda often talks about *choices*—for example, "We *choose* not to buy these things because we want to save money for a vacation." I heard the word *choice* over and over when I interviewed downshifted parents. Laural Ringler was typical: "The fact that [simplicity is] a choice makes a huge difference. We *choose* to live simply. It's more fun!" Jan Anderson of Clearview, Washington, has five children and emphasizes the choice concept too. "It's really important for your kids to understand that simple living is a choice," says Jan, "that it's not about deprivation."

Since our two sons were very young, we've been explaining the reasons for our purchases—or *lack* of purchases—to them. And I can't remember ever saying "because we can't afford it." The truth is, for those things we wanted the kids to have—say piano and swimming lessons, museum visits, travel—we've had the money.

My husband and I have also been able to say, truthfully: "If we bought all of this stuff, Mom and/or Dad would have to go back to work full-time and we think you kind of like having us around, right?" They do. Michael Fogler's son Ben feels the same way. Michael notes, "When there is some [discussion] about material things, I remind my son about my time with him and the trade-off of earning more money and being away from home more. My son gladly trades more time and connection with me for more money/stuff in the house."

This "less spending, more time, more fun" formula should be repeated often. Kids really *do* want to spend time with their parents and they *do* understand trade-offs. This message will sink in.

YOUNG CHILDREN

If you're fortunate enough to have simplified early in your kids' lives, you'll find them eager receptacles for your simple view of the world.

Lisa Cunningham knows that young children are like sponges, and she's used that to her advantage with her daughters, ages seven and four. "I flat out say what I think, for starters. My kids are at an age where they still actually listen to me. I've spent these early years filling their little heads with my view of the world."

Propaganda? Well, all parents do this; perhaps Lisa is just more honest about it. Shelby Pawlina, a mother from Boulder, Colorado, calls this technique "frontloading." "Giving [daughter Shae] as many of the tools as possible in as many arenas as we can manage seems like a good start," she explains, in helping Shae build a foundation of simple living values.

Your explanations should be age-appropriate. For younger children, clear, uncomplicated connections are best. "I try to explain using simple language," says Patti Idrobo, "and talk about one thing at a time as opposed to trying to explain everything at once."

Another communication method that many simple living parents use with young children is to read simplicity-related books with them. On an Internet discussion board thread on this subject, one participant said that to fix a case of the "poor me's" or the "gimmes" she brings out her copy of *Material World,* a book that features photos of average families from around the globe along with all of their worldly possessions. She and her kids then discuss the unequal distribution of wealth on the planet—and how very lucky they are. The

"Resources" section at the end of this chapter contains a number of books that other simple living parents recommend.

TALKING WITH OLDER KIDS

Some parents I've spoken with have bemoaned the fact that they came to simplicity later in their—and their kids'—lives. It's true that beginning your simplified life when the kids are young is preferable, but if you didn't, you didn't. And it's never too late to start!

Most of the same strategies that work for younger kids work for older kids too. Communication is critical. Especially if your kids are older when you begin simplifying, explaining your family decisions in terms of impact on the environment or solidarity with the less fortunate will help them "hear" what you're saying.

At the outset of your downshifting, a family meeting to discuss what may be some very different family realities is in order. The values clarifications meetings will also be a great help (see Chapters 1 and 2). Listen to your kids' concerns; respond with the truth. A conversation, versus a monologue, makes much more sense as kids grow up. If they feel that they're truly heard, they're much more likely to go along with the changes. They may well have some good ideas of their own!

As Lynne Cantwell knows, lectures directed at teens often fall on deaf ears. Lynne is a single mom with two daughters, ages fourteen and twelve. "They're sick of me pestering them about bringing home their Ziploc bags! Seriously, I do try to communicate to them that I am doing this specific thing, such as recycling, because it's good for the environment. I try not to lecture, because lecturing doesn't work real well at this age." (See also "The Teen Years" on page 165.)

If discourses on simplicity topics delivered by Mom or Dad aren't the answer, what might appeal to older kids? For some, presenting information from a neutral third party can be the answer. My older son was clamoring for soda on a regular basis a while back. Then the local newspaper ran a feature on those exclusive soda contracts that schools are entering into, which highlighted the negatives of all of that highly sugared, carbonated, caffeinated liquid for kids. I handed the article to my son, he read it, and now he only rarely asks for soda. Kids might not want to read an entire book on a subject but they'll often read an article or listen to a documentary, and the facts and logic presented will stick with them.

LISTENING TO YOUR KIDS

Lynne's observation that lecturing can be futile with teens brings up the flip side of talking, which is, of course, listening. To me, listening is all about respect, and we need to respect our kids *as individuals*. Some kids will absorb simplicity easily, others won't. Sometimes this means taking different approaches with different kids—and *always* this means being mindful of their uniqueness.

Also, as our kids grow older, they are exposed to many forces beyond their simple living parents, to ideas and viewpoints that we need to understand, if not agree with. (See "The Teen Years" on page 165.)

So, while we're talking, we also need to listen. We can try to figure out *why* a kid is insistent about getting a scooter, or a Harry Potter watch, or whatever the latest gadget is. To jump-start a conversation with your kids, ask open-ended queries—essay-type versus true-false inquiries. Begin your questions with "Why" or "How." This helps kids to open up.

A specific example in the listening arena involves the concept of "cool." Ask your kids why people want to be cool, what it means to be cool, and whether or not it's important to be cool. Listen as they figure out *on their own* what cool is all about. My kids and I have had the "cool discussion" many times, and I think that they now have a good grasp on Madison Avenue's use of "cool" to get folks to buy things. I also feel that they've internalized that the most important facet of an individual's personality is that they are kind and follow the Golden Rule, not whether they're cool by some always changing materialistic standard.

Everyone wants to be heard, to have their feelings—and often their *fears*—respected. Sometimes listening is all that's required.

Behavior: Walking Your Talk

Instead of lecturing her teens, Lynne Cantwell puts faith in the old axiom "Actions speak louder than words." She says: "I try to be a role model, and hope that they pay attention."

Practicing, to be sure, drives home your message quicker than preaching. This is true whether your kids are still in preschool or about to enter college. If you aren't committed to living simply—both in theory and in practice—they'll call your bluff.

Most of the simple living parents I interviewed said that the chief way they communicate the value of simple living to their kids is by example. Asking yourself, "Is this activity in concert with my values?" and then putting your answer into action will model and communicate those values to your children better than any lecture ever could.

Janice Arnold has taken her "walk" a bit further. Recently a new Wal-Mart was proposed near her home. Janice learned that its construction would require a considerable amount of clear-cutting. She took her two young daughters, ages five and three, to the city council meeting to protest the rezoning that would allow the Wal-Mart to be built.

As you could probably predict, Wal-Mart won. But Janice values the experience nonetheless. After the hearing, she and her daughters drove by the area where the Wal-Mart will be constructed. They saw the trees that would be sacrificed for the department store and, Janice recalls, "we all vowed never to shop in Wal-Mart again."

"I'm really glad we went to the meeting," she adds. "The kids still talk about the place where they are going to cut down the trees and how we aren't going to go there when the shop is there."

Modeling this kind of political action for your kids is important. First of all, they'll hear your message loud and clear if you're willing to march down to city hall with it. They'll also be more likely to emulate you.

It will also give them hope and help make them more optimistic, even well-adjusted, individuals. A study a few years back found that kids whose parents were taking some sort of political action regarding nuclear war—letter writing, petitions, et cetera—were much less likely to be fearful of a nuclear holocaust. When we take action that says we believe individuals can make a difference, our kids absorb that message and are empowered by it.

Shelby Pawlina makes this to-the-point conclusion: "Modeling is the easiest way to get our children on the same page. Just make it a way of life."

Making it a way of life is key. Embrace nonmaterialism in all that you do. There are dozens of great books out there to help you with the mechanics of simplicity. Study them. If you read no other book, read *Your Money or Your Life,* which combines philosophy and practicality as well as any simplicity guide.

SHOW YOUR KIDS HOW MUCH FUN SIMPLICITY IS

It's not just your acts of practicing simplicity that your kids need to see, it's *how* you practice it. It goes without saying that you shouldn't whine about not having a new car or more stylish clothing. But you need to be more than *neutral* about the benefits of simplicity; you must be clearly upbeat about your chosen lifestyle. A positive attitude goes hand in hand with living simply, and loving it.

Simplicity advocate Cecile Andrews feels that Mom and Dad need to demonstrate that they delight in living simply, that it's the lifestyle that brings more joy. "Parents have to show their commitment and how much fun [simplicity] is. It should never seem like self-deprivation. It's meant to allow you to have more fun in life, not less."

Showing kids the fun side of simplicity is pivotal. The alternative of working long hours to buy more stuff, then working more, even going in debt, isn't my idea of a good time. At our house, we try to keep fun at the forefront, and it's much easier to do without tight schedules and shopping trips. Because both my husband and I work part-time, we are rarely in a rush. It's relaxed around our house—and relaxation and laughter are natural counterparts.

Show and Tell

The combination of both talking *and* walking your values is particularly potent.

My parents—and my large extended family—were as much "showers" as "tellers." I was raised in a solidly blue-collar environment. Most of my uncles worked at the local sawmill. My father was a meat cutter who opened a small grocery store in the 1950s but he was always a devoted union man. He talked about the labor movement, but he also acted on his beliefs. Although it meant that he sometimes paid his workers more than he made himself, he insisted on being a union shop.

My point? I'm now a strong union supporter. My father's example—and actual sacrifice to practice what he preached—stuck with me.

By both telling and showing our kids the reasons and benefits of simple living, they'll understand why, as parents, we live simply, and they'll be much more likely to embrace simplicity themselves.

Resources

BOOKS FOR KIDS

Maya Ajmera and Anna Rhesa Versola. *Children from Australia to Zimbabwe: A Photographic Journey Around the World* (Watertown, Massachusetts: Charlesbridge Publishing, 1997).

Jim Aylesworth. *The Full Belly Bowl* (New York: Atheneum Books for Young Readers, 1998).

D. C. Beard. *The American Boy's Handy Book* (Jaffrey, New Hampshire: David Godine, Publisher, 1983).

Jeff Brumbeau. *The Quiltmaker's Gift* (Duluth, Minnesota: Pfeifer-Hamilton Publishers, 2000).

Natalie Savage Carlson. *The Family Under the Bridge* (New York: HarperCollins, 1958).

DyAnne DiSalvo-Ryan. *Uncle Willie and the Soup Kitchen* (New York: Morrow Junior Books, 1991).

Adam Eisenson. *The Peanut Butter and Jelly Game* (Elizaville, New York: Good Advice Press, 1996).

Nigel Gray and Philippe Dupasquier. *A Country Far Away* (New York: Orchard Books, 1998).

Eleanor Estes. *The Hundred Dresses* (New York: Harcourt, Brace, and World, 1971).

For Every Child: The UN Convention on the Rights of the Child in Words and Pictures, text adapted by Caroline Castle (New York: Phyliss Fogelman Books, 2001).

Mem Fox. *Feathers and Fools* (New York: Harcourt Brace, 1989).

Anne Frank. *The Diary of a Young Girl* (Garden City, New York: Doubleday, 1967).

Barnabas and Anabel Kindersley. *Children Just Like Me* (London, New York: Dorling Kindersley Publishing, 1995).

Peter Menzel. *Material World: A Global Family Portrait* (San Francisco: Sierra Club Books, 1994).

Scott O'Dell. *The Island of the Blue Dolphins* (Boston: Houghton Mifflin, 1960).

Dr. Seuss books, most of them, but particularly *The Lorax, The Butter Battle Book, The Sneetches, Horton Hears a Who,* and *Horton Hatches an Egg.*

David J. Smith. *If the World Were a Village* (Toronto: Kids Can Press, 2002).

Alternatives for Simple Living. Visit www.simpleliving.org or call (800) 821–6153 for their catalogue of simplicity-related children's titles.

Chinaberry Book Service; www.chinaberry.com; (800) 776–2242; another great resource for children's books.

BOOKS FOR OLDER KIDS

Phillip Hoose. *It's Our World, Too! Stories of Young People Who Are Making a Difference* (Boston: Little, Brown and Company, 1993).

Elizabeth Rusch. *Generation Fix: Young Ideas for a Better World* (Hillsboro, Oregon: Beyond Words Publishing, 2002).

COMMUNICATION IN GENERAL

Adele Faber and Elaine Mazlish. *How to Talk So Kids Will Listen and Listen So Kids Will Talk* (New York: Avon, 1999).

Carl B. Smith with Susan Moke and Marjorie Simic. *Connect! How to Get Your Kids to Talk to You* (Bloomington, Indiana: Family Literacy Center, 1994).

OTHERS

Cecile Andrews. *The Circle of Simplicity: A Return to the Good Life* (New York: HarperCollins, 1997).

Joe Dominguez and Vicki Robin. *Your Money or Your Life: Transforming Your Relationship with Money and Achieving Financial Independence* (New York: Penguin Books, 1999).

Deborah Spaide. *Teaching Your Kids to Care: How to Discover and Develop the Spirit of Charity in Your Children* (New York: Citadel Press, 1995).

8

Reclaiming Your Kids from the Corporate Culture, Part I: Marketing Mania

"Question Authority."

Most baby boomers remember this slogan—and omnipresent bumper sticker—from the sixties and seventies. Those two words encapsulated an entire generation's attitude about being told what to do by those in power. For many of us, this sentiment coincided neatly with our teenage years, when we, of course, knew better than anybody else—particularly our parents—what was best for us.

Three decades have elapsed and some simple living advocates have amended the slogan to reflect the current trend of corporate marketing experts to target every facet of our lives—from the clothes and shoes we wear to the vehicles we drive and the coffee we drink. It's not our parents or our government that is telling us what to do now; it's Coke, Nintendo, and General Motors. Now some of us boomers are saying "Question *Corporate* Authority"—and we're hoping to teach our children how to do so too.

Why? Following corporate messages in lockstep has devastating effects for the environment, for our pocketbooks—

and for our souls. And the ramifications for children, the most vulnerable and impressionable segment of our society, are even greater, as this chapter will illustrate.

Parents have never been able to completely control their children's environments. There have always been outside influences, from peers and schools to fads and music. Everyone had to buy a Hula-Hoop in the fifties; even back in the twenties the Charleston was all the rage.

But the extent to which the corporate culture has usurped parental authority—indeed, all other influences—in recent years is mind blowing. The sheer number of advertisements that all of us, parents and kids alike, are exposed to has skyrocketed. One source estimates that each of us, on average, sees 3,000 advertisements each day, from television commercials to stickers on our banana peels.

The tactics used have become more and more invasive and psychologically damaging to all of us, especially our children. In the introduction to *Children First: A Parent's Guide to Fighting Corporate Predators,* by Linda Coco, consumer advocate Ralph Nader warns us that parents "are losing control over their own children to the omnipenetrating hucksterism of companies."

If Nader's warning sounds like overkill, consider these statistics:

- Marketing aimed at kids has skyrocketed. Corporations now spend more than $2 billion annually on advertising directly targeting children, a more than twentyfold increase in the last decade.
- It isn't just the amount that's spent on advertising that's changed, but also the *type* of marketing used. In recent years, the advertising industry has added "cross marketing" to its arsenal. Cross-marketing occurs when, for example, a fast food restaurant gives away plastic toy figures from a just-released children's movie, or entire TV cartoon shows are based, essentially, on prod-

ucts, resulting in half-hour commercials. It amounts to a double whammy for our kids, designed to induce the "gimmes."

- Ad agencies are spending an increasing amount on psychological research regarding children. One outgrowth is that ads now target our kids virtually from birth. Experts say that at six months of age babies can form images of corporate logos and mascots; at twelve months they're capable of "brand association." Most American children begin requesting products by brand name by age three.

- Judging by the corporate bottom line, all of that advertising money is well spent. Purchases by children have soared in the past two decades. In 1984 kids from four to twelve years old spent $4.2 billion of their own money; by 1994 that figure had reached $17.1 billion, and only three years later, $23.4 billion.

- Purchases by parents that are influenced by their kids have also skyrocketed. In 1984 children from four to twelve influenced about $50 billion in adult expenditures; by 1997 that figure had more than tripled to $188 billion. Some experts estimate that the amount of spending "indirectly influenced" by kids is now more than $500 billion annually.

The result of all of this is that most of the messages our kids take in on a daily basis now come from corporations rather than from their families, friends, and teachers. Marketing aimed at kids is, in fact, the chief concern of many downshifting parents. Debbie Newman is adamant—but very typical among simple living parents—in her feelings: "We want our chidren to buy from actual need and desire, not artificially created desire. We don't want them to fall into the 'Collect all four!' trap. We resent the blatant, targeted marketing toward children, particularly in the school environment."

Lisa Cunningham is another of these "had it with the marketing mania" parents. "While one can argue that adults can make informed decisions," she explains, "young children cannot, yet they are being singled out not only in their leisure time, but even in school, where they are more or less 'captive.' "

"This Spelling Lesson Is Brought to You By . . . "

Indeed, advertising can't get much more kid-targeted than when it's incorporated into our schools. The commercialization of educational institutions is a true "hot button" for downshifted parents. And these are *public* schools we're talking about. This is probably the most depressing development in corporate marketing in recent years.

For example, more than 234 corporations offer "instructional material" to schools, such as films, textbooks, and computer software. This material is corporate-inspired yet it's designed to look like classroom lesson plans and activities. An example is the free lesson plan that Campbell distributes to 12,000 schools. In it, schoolkids are urged to compare the thickness of Campbell's product, Prego, versus a competitor, Ragú. The conclusion to be reached is that—surprise!—Prego is thicker. Another example is a Chips Ahoy–sponsored counting game in which kids are asked to determine the number of chocolate chips in their cookies.

Not surprisingly, a Consumers Union study found that these "academic" materials had little or no educational value and that 80 percent of them had biased or incomplete information.

In addition to these supposedly benign "free" corporate educational materials, many schools simply sell advertising space. A company called YouthStream has installed promotional message boards in 7,200 high school locker rooms around the country. Other schools sell advertising space on buses and in school hallways.

A huge culprit in the school commercialization phenomenon is Channel One, which broadcasts a daily eight-minute "soft news" program, accompanied by two minutes of advertisements, to more than 8 million children in 12,000 schools around the country. In exchange for allowing children to view the programs, the schools receive the loan of the televisions and video equipment. The president of Channel One has been quoted as saying, "The advertiser gets a group of kids who cannot go to the bathroom, who cannot change the station, who cannot listen to their mother yell in the background, who cannot be playing Nintendo, who cannot have their headsets on." A study by the University of Wisconsin Center for Analysis of Commercials in Education found that taxpayers actually pay $1.8 billion annually for class time lost due to the airing of Channel One. There is broad-based opposition to Channel One—from Ralph Nader to Phyllis Schlafly!—yet it continues to flourish.

Exclusive soft drink contracts are another example of corporate intrusion into the schools. Brita Butler-Wall is a mother of two daughters and lives in Seattle, where the school district has an exclusive contract with Coke. She points out that the soft drink companies actually lose money on many of these contracts, but "it's worth it to them because they can 'brand' kids at a young age." Commercial Alert (see "Resources" at the end of this chapter) reports that hundreds of school districts around the country are considering such contracts.

The Negatives of Marketing to Kids

The corporate invasion of schools is one marketing trend of concern; the increasing sophistication of advertisers is another. Corporations now use psychologists and psychiatrists to perform research on children's developmental process to better perfect their kid-targeted marketing. The results are advertising campaigns designed to promote parental pestering by kids until they get what they want, and other campaigns that attempt to undermine the authority of parents.

The goal, says author Linda Coco, is "to get past the parent, the 'gatekeeper.' To do this, the marketers try to separate the parent from the child by nagging or making [the parents] look stupid."

Did you catch that last sentence? "To do this, the marketers try to separate the parent from the child by nagging or making [the parents] look stupid." We really are working at cross purposes with these groups. As if parenting in the twenty-first century weren't difficult enough!

The marketers have gone so far that in 1999 a group of psychologists joined together to send a letter to the American Psychological Association protesting the trend among some members of the association to perform psychological research that allows corporations to "bypass parents and influence the behavior and desires of children," resulting in the "commercial exploitation and manipulation of children." (The APA has appointed a task force to study the issue.)

Other countries have laws protecting children from such abuse. Commercial Alert reports that Sweden and Norway both prohibit television advertising directly targeting children below twelve years of age. Greece bans television advertising of toys to children between 7:00 A.M. and 10:00 P.M. Belgium, Denmark, and the Canadian province of Quebec prohibit all advertising to children on television and radio.

So one enormous negative is that these marketing efforts actually pit parents against their kids. Not an outcome any family wants, and certainly not what a nation that professes "family values" should allow.

But there are several other pernicious side effects of marketing to kids. For instance, many of the techniques used by advertisers are also damaging to kids' fragile egos. One marketing consultant, Nancy Shalek of the Shalek Agency, remarked that "advertising at its best is making people feel that without their product, you're a loser. Kids are very sensitive to that. If you tell them to buy something, they are resistant. But if you tell them that they'll be a dork if they don't, you've got their attention. You open up emotional vulnerabilities, and it's very easy to do with kids because they're the most emotionally vulnerable."

She's talking about our kids here!

Other experts point out that advertising directed at kids—and, indeed, at adults—is not just selling one product but, in essence, peddling a complete value system that preaches that purchasing material items will make you happy. As discussed in other chapters, this is the facet of corporate marketing that most troubles many downshifting parents. Whose values, they wonder, will their children adopt? Tommy Hilfiger's, Disney's, or their own families'?

The sad truth is that this marketing works: Our children are "learning" that purchasing the right stuff will make them happier, better liked, more accepted. In a recent poll by the Center for a New American Dream, 87 percent of parents of children of ages two to seventeen indicated that advertising and marketing aimed at children makes kids too materialistic. Two-thirds of the parents said that their children define their self-worth by what they own.

Allowing our kids to absorb the commercial message is, in essence, teaching them that they can fulfill their deepest, nonmaterial human needs—like acceptance, love, true joy, self-confidence—with purchases.

How to Fight Back

There's also the strong possibility that marketing—and media exposure generally—is actually destroying childhood. According to Neil Postman, author of *The Disappearance of*

EDUCATING OTHER PARENTS ABOUT COMMERCIALISM

It's very difficult to combat commercialism if other parents around you don't see the harm in it. As simple living mom Lisa Cunningham notes, "I can make all the 'right' choices in the world for my kids, but unfortunately other people's choices affect them."

You can take the lead in educating others by offering to facilitate a class or to lead a group on simplicity or media literacy and inviting parents from your child's school and your community. Here are some resources:

1. The Northwest Earth Institute (NWEI) offers Voluntary Simplicity discussion courses (among other topics) for a nominal charge. Contact NWEI—(503) 227–2807—or one of its "sister earth institutes," located in over a dozen cities across the country. Log on to www.nwei.org to find out if there is an earth institute in your area. If not, NWEI will assist you in becoming a local organizer.

2. Participating in a simplicity study group or "simplicity circle" helps educate the members *and* is a great source of support for lifestyle changes. You'll find information on how to start one of these groups in Chapter 10.

3. Several media literacy groups can also help, with courses on that topic. For example, the Center for Media Literacy—www.medialit.org; (800) 228–4630—produces a number of Media Literacy Workshop kits on topics ranging from "Sexism and Media" to "Parenting in a TV Age." The kits contain lesson plans, a leader's guide, and handouts, and are reasonably priced from $15.95 to $19.95. The New Mexico Media Literacy Project—www.nmmlp.org; (505) 828–3129—offers a Just Do Media Literacy video and discussion guide (cost $29) for parents and teachers. The National Institute on Media and the Family—www.mediafamily.org; (888) 672–5437—has a Media-Wise Parent Education Program that includes a leader's guide, video, and materials for twenty-five participants for $24.95.

(continues)

(continued)

4. Another way to educate parents in your area is to per-form a "commercial walk-through" of your child's school, not-ing all commercial presences—from corporate-sponsored textbooks to soda machines. Your findings are then presented to your school board. The Center for Commercial-Free Public Education—www.commercialfree.org—has more information on how to conduct the walk-through.

5. Contact the Center for a New American Dream—www.newdream.org—and request copies of their brochure "Tips for Parenting in a Commercial Culture." Make them avail-able to parents in your community.

Childhood, the blame can be attributed in large part to the media.

Postman urges parents to conceive "of parenting as an act of rebellion against American culture." His recommenda-tions are similar to those that simplicity endorses: help kids stay connected with elders and insist that children learn the discipline of delayed gratification. "But most rebellious of all," says Postman, "is the attempt to control the media's ac-cess to one's children."

What's a concerned parent to do? I, for one, think that Postman's advice is sound: Let's rebel! Reclaim your youthful skepticism and say "NO!!!" to corporations. This "rebellion" approach has the big plus of potentially being of great inter-est to teenagers too!

There are a number of specific actions parents can take to help their kids handle this marketing onslaught. It's not easy, but it's essential if we are to equip our kids with the ability to deal with our society and its emphasis on "stuff."

Most simple living parents take one of two general ap-proaches in dealing with the consumer society's impact on their kids. One group of downshifters attempts to provide a sanctuary for their kids from an increasingly materialistic world by raising them in a noncommercial environment as much as possible. These parents have no televisions, may home-school their kids, and perhaps ban media-themed items from their homes.

Other simple living families take a "we have met the enemy and subdued him" approach, permitting their children to sample more of the culture's marketing temptations while balancing that exposure with limitations and plenty of time explaining and modeling simple lifestyle choices for them.

What you decide to do will depend upon your view of our society and how best to prepare your kids for dealing with it, and even your own child's temperament and learning style. The following ideas can help you form your approach.

1. TERMINATE YOUR TV

Most experts and simple living parents agree that doing away with or strictly limiting your kids' television viewing is the biggest factor in protecting your children from corporate marketing. It's such a huge issue that I've devoted Chapter 9 to it. The following actions are in addition to what you do to tame—or terminate!—your television.

2. ENSURE THAT YOUR KIDS ARE "MEDIA LITERATE"

As a society, we've become deluged with "information" from an ever-expanding number of sources. Rick Seifert, cofounder of the Northwest Media Literacy Center, believes that media literacy is pivotal for kids in today's world because they're being inundated with those media messages earlier and earlier. Media literacy, he says, is all about being able to critically assess all of that information.

Seifert encourages parents to help their kids become media literate. Talk to them about all types of media—from television and movies to magazines and newspapers. Point out that all media is based on economics, on profits, on money. Seifert puts it this way: "You aren't really being sold products but rather *you* are the product being sold to advertisers by TV stations and magazines."

Lisa Cunningham, mom to two girls, says, "We talk about it directly. Even four-year-old Stephanie knows that the reason they put a picture of Arthur on Juicy Juice is so that kids will nag parents to buy it. We talk about how advertisers use bright colors and packaging to hook kids. We talk about advertising and the media and how things are made to make you want to spend your money foolishly."

Lynne Cantwell, also a mother of two daughters, adds, "I have always tried to point out to my kids that stuff never looks as good as it does on TV, the toy never works like that, Barbie doesn't walk by herself, et cetera. As a result, I think, my kids are actually significantly less hooked on name brands than others their age."

More media literacy strategies as they pertain to television viewing are detailed in "Help Your Kids to Become 'Media Literate' " on page 139. Take those steps further and apply the techniques to all types of media—newspapers, websites, junk mail, and the backs of cereal boxes. Additional information is also available from the media literacy resources listed at the end of Chapter 9.

3. BE INVOLVED IN YOUR KIDS' LIVES— AND BE WILLING TO TAKE CONTROL

One way to help your kids handle corporate marketing is to be there when they're faced with it. This is where simple living parents have a distinct advantage over other families. With more time to devote to their kids, the children of downshifted families are 1) less likely to be exposed to marketing pressures because their parents have restricted access to them; and 2) when problems arise—inappropriate movies, clothing, video games, et cetera—the parents of these kids will be aware of the situation, can talk to their kids about it, and prohibit the activity or product in question, if necessary.

To accomplish this, you'll have to monitor what your kids are doing, watching, playing, wearing. You need to determine if this is an activity—card game, TV show, computer program, movie, et cetera—that you want your child to participate in and that is in sync with your family's values. And then you have to be willing to take the heat by saying, "No." Using the strategies in Chapter 7—that is, explaining your reasons in terms of family values—will help your child understand and respect your decision.

4. LIMIT OR BAN "LOGOED" ITEMS AND OTHER COMMERCIALLY THEMED PRODUCTS FROM YOUR HOME

Parents and kids can now purchase nearly every item imaginable—from pajamas, underwear, and bedsheets to tennis shoes, baseball caps, and backpacks—with a media- or corporate-themed identity. Marketers do this not just to sell the product by association—for example, getting kids to clamor for the "Bugs Bunny" toothbrush—but also to "brand" the child (infant!) as early on as possible.

A complete ban on these products is difficult, especially if you're a garage sale/hand-me-down kind of consumer. But limiting their presence is essential because the cumulative effect of dozens, perhaps hundreds, of corporate-themed possessions is both a proclivity to keep buying them and a tendency for kids to identify themselves and others by what they wear and own. Discuss the issue with your older kids, for example, "Why does Nike put the swoosh on all of their products?" "Are kids who wear Tommy Hilfiger cooler, more popular?" "Aren't you a walking billboard with that on? Shouldn't you be paid by Old Navy to wear it?" And tell relatives and friends who want to shower your kids with these items that you'd prefer products that don't sport a corporate logo or advertise the latest movie or hit television show.

5. TALK WITH YOUR KIDS ABOUT THE NEGATIVES OF COMMERCIALISM

Simple living parents overwhelmingly use this approach. Discussing the downsides of materialism generally, particularly its environmental impacts, can be very persuasive with kids. For example, when Brenda Scearcy's daughter asks her for a new product, Brenda describes all of the resources and energy needed to produce the article in question—raw materials needed, manufacturing, waste, transportation, marketing. This usually works to stop the "gimmes."

It's gratifying to see how talking with your kids about marketing and advertising—over and over, for years and years—actually works. My youngest often volunteers comments like, "That's not good for the environment," and, "We really don't *need* that." Music to my ears.

6. WALK YOUR TALK

Once again, you need to back up your words with the right behavior. If you can model that it's easy—and fun!—to resist commercialism, your kids will absorb the message much faster and deeper.

If you tend to buy all the latest electronic toys or fashions, your kids will wonder what's wrong with their requests for similar items. Parents who are slaves to fashion or need to have their houses "just so" also shouldn't be surprised if their kids follow suit.

In addition to being an example of nonmaterialism for your kids, remember also to model the "wheres" and "whats" of consumption. Try to avoid chain stores and, instead, support local businesses. Opt for the most environmentally friendly and worker-friendly alternative, whenever possible. And explain your choices to your kids. Organizations like Co-op America (see "Resources" at the end of this chapter) can help with support and information.

7. LISTEN TO YOUR CHILD

If your child has descended into "nagging mode," it's important to listen to him or her. Whether your children have fallen victim to the seduction of TV commercials or the excess of other kids, their "gimmes" may be laden with emotional needs—the need to be accepted, liked, to feel part of the group. Treat your child gently and remember that living in this culture of consumption can be very conflicting for kids— adults too. Talk with them about why they're asking for an item, ask them if they really need it. If they persist, let them pay for it with their own money (assuming the item isn't objectionable for other reasons).

SELECT TOYS FOR YOUR CHILDREN WITH CARE

Corporate marketers try their darnedest to get you—and your kids—to buy stuff. High on the shopping list for American parents and children is toys.

Instead of purchasing endless plastic crap—the kind that kids may nag you to buy—parents should stick with a few good quality, "timeless" toys. I asked simple living parents which toys they considered to be the most worthwhile for kids. Over and over they said that the following playthings were the best-liked and most-played-with by kids, and—perhaps not coincidentally—the most acceptable to parents: Legos, wooden blocks, K'nex and other quality building toys; arts and crafts supplies; books; bikes; dollhouses; Brio; make-believe/ dress-up clothes and props; Frisbees; and puppets. Some

(continues)

(continued)

suggestions weren't even toys—like cardboard appliance boxes, pots and pans, chairs and blankets for forts—*really* simple stuff!

The best toys, according to the experts, are those that lend themselves to creativity and to imaginative play. Low tech play-things allow the child to devise the theme of play and foster originality and inventiveness. High tech toys—invariably the ones that need batteries—stifle the child's fantasy world. Simple living parents, hands down, endorse the low tech vari-ety. Kathleen Murphy says it well. After listing the best toys her daughter has, she notes that they are "all toys that require more from the kids than from the toy."

What's the verdict on Barbie? Many parents are wary of allowing Barbie, with her inhumanly proportioned body and airhead image. But a few point out that Barbie—"and friends"!—have actually been part of their kids' creative play. Lynne Cantwell discovered that her kids "would play these in-tricate invented Barbie games for hours on end—Barbies go into outer space and meet Luke Skywalker and his dad, all kinds of wacky stuff."

It's not just the quality and type of toys that parents need to be wary of—it's also the sheer quantity of playthings that can accumulate. A childless friend of mine once said, "What can be wrong with toys? Their purpose is fun. How can a kid have too many?"

What's wrong with endless toys? For one thing, a surfeit of these possessions is bad in the same way that leaving too many possessions is bad for adults. They need to be picked up, maintained, organized, cleaned, and stored. They cost a lot. And, too, all of that nonrecyclable plastic takes a huge toll on the earth.

Mary Kalifan is the director of the Parent Child Resource Service at Cedars-Sinai Medical Center. In a paper called "Cur-

(continues)

(continued)

ing the 'Gimmes,' " published by Seeds of Simplicity, she adds these reasons for not giving our kids so many toys:

1. Constant indulgence breeds a feeling of entitlement.

2. Excess breeds boredom.

3. We deprive them of the joy of anticipation.

4. Too much choice is confusing to kids.

5. Kids appreciate something more when they have come by it through the sweat of their brow.

6. They may learn to equate love with material objects.

All are good reasons to limit the number of toys your kids have—while ensuring their quality.

8. TEACH YOUR CHILDREN THAT THEY ARE NOT THEIR POSSESSIONS

The message of our consumer culture is that you are what you wear, eat, drive, watch—in short, what you buy and own. That message is exactly the opposite of what most Americans actually believe. Most of us, if we're honest, would say that individuals should be judged not by their possessions, but by their creations, their activities, their character. Make sure that you teach and model this for your kids. Make it one of your family values. (Chapter 10 explores the issues of self-acceptance and acceptance of others.)

9. ADVOCATE FOR YOUR KIDS— AND AGAINST KID-TARGETED MARKETING

We live, ostensibly, in a democracy. As voters and taxpayers, we should demand that marketing to kids be curtailed. Groups like Commercial Alert (see "Resources" at the end of this chapter) are lobbying for restrictions on corporate tactics. Support these groups generously! Join them and, when asked, contact your senators and representatives to be heard on these issues.

Parents who are particularly outraged over corporate intrusion into public schools are taking action. Brita Butler-Wall and other parents in Seattle formed a group called Citizens' Campaign for Commercial-Free Schools. The school board proposed selling advertising space in the schools as a fund-raising technique but withdrew the plan when parents—organized by the Citizens' Campaign—turned out in force to oppose it. The group was also instrumental in the school board's adoption of a commercialism policy.

These Seattle parents are good role models for the rest of us. What started as a handful of outraged moms and dads has evolved into a powerful voice for protecting kids, now numbering over a thousand members.

You can start in your own community by gathering a few like-minded parents and asking your school board—or your school's parent/teacher organization—to hold hearings on the presence of commercialism in schools. Of course, if your school district is considering one of these corporate presences, you'll need to act *now.* If they're already in your schools, lobby to get them out. Gary Ruskin of Commercial Alert and Jim Metrock of the Alabama-based group Obligation Inc. have drafted a model school board policy and a model state law called the Public Education Protection Act. See "Resources" at the end of this chapter for more information.

Clearly another lesson here is that our public schools need to be adequately funded so that these corporate "giveaways" aren't so enticing to school administrators. Support efforts to amply finance our public schools. And support those organizations like Commercial Alert that are leading the fight to decommercialize our schools.

10. EDUCATE YOUR CHILD—
AND OTHER CHILDREN

Lynne Cantwell, a single mother of two from Alexandria, Virginia, wrote a study guide for middle schoolers based on *Your Money or Your Life.* It's available as an on-line download at the simpleliving.net website. Lynne says that the increase in commercialism aimed at kids was the main impetus for her writing the guide: "I wanted to give my kids—and everybody else's kids too—a way to evaluate the hype that they're constantly exposed to."

Lynne's study guide is well-written, funny, and accessible for the eleven- to fourteen-year-olds it was intended to reach. The guide can be used individually with your own kids and in organized settings; for example, with church youth groups.

Another way to educate all kids about marketing is to include media literacy in school curricula. Organizations like the Center for Media Literacy, the Northwest Media Literacy Center, and the New Mexico Media Project hope to accomplish this. Contact them and assist them with this goal.

All of these strategies will help you safeguard your kids from marketing efforts that have none of their best interests at heart, and in fact have a goal of teaching them values contrary to those you hope they'll learn.

They'll help you protect yourself too.

Resources

KIDS AND MARKETING

Linda Coco. *Children First: A Parent's Guide to Fighting Corporate Predators* (Washington, D.C.: Corporate Accountability Research Group, 1996).

James Garbarino and Claire Bedard. *Parents Under Siege: Why You Are the Solution, Not the Problem, in Your Child's Life* (New York: The Free Press, 2001).

Sylvia Ann Hewlett. *The War Against Parents* (Boston: Houghton Mifflin, 1998).

Michael F. Jacobson and Laurie Ann Mazur. *Marketing Madness: A Survival Guide for a Consumer Society* (Boulder, Colorado: Westview Press, 1995).

Jean Kilbourne. *Can't Buy My Love: How Advertising Changes the Way We Think and Feel* (New York: Touchstone, 1999).

Neil Postman. *The Disappearance of Childhood* (New York: Vintage Books, 1994).

David Walsh. *Selling Out America's Children: How America Puts Profits Before Values and What Parents Can Do* (Minneapolis: Deaconess Press, 1994).

KIDS AND MARKETING AND ANTICOMMERCIALISM
ORGANIZATIONS/WEBSITES

Adbusters: www.adbusters.org. A great general resource for anticonsumerism; also publishes *Adbusters* magazine.

Center for Science in the Public Interest: www.cspinet.org; (202) 332–9110. Information on a variety of health-related and marketing topics.

Citizens Campaign for Commercial-Free Schools (Seattle): www.scn.org/cccs

Commercialism in Education Research Unit: www.school commercialism.org; (480) 965–1886; researches commercialism in the schools.

Consumer Reports' Center for Kids Online: www.zillions. org. Helps kids eight and up "evaluate products, see through ad hype, be money smart, and think for themselves."

Co-op America: www.coopamerica.org; (202) 872–5307. Informs consumers on companies' track records regarding environmental issues, sweatshop conditions, et cetera.

The Lion and Lamb Project: www.lionlamb.org; (301) 654–3091. Organization with a goal of stopping the marketing of violence to children.

For a free copy of "Tips for Parenting in a Commercial Culture" call (toll-free) 877–68–DREAM or visit www.new dream.org

Parents interested in lobbying against the commercialization of schools can contact these groups:

The Center for Commercial-Free Public Education: www.commericalfree.org; (510) 268–1100

Commercial Alert: www.commercialalert.org; (503) 235–8012

Obligation, Inc. helps parents remove Channel One from schools; (215) 822–0080; www.obligation.org

MEDIA LITERACY

Gloria DeGaetano. *Screen Smarts: A Family Guide to Media Literacy* (Boston: Houghton Mifflin, 1996).

Media Literacy Organizations/Websites: See "Resources" at the end of Chapter 9.

TOYS FOR KIDS

Nancy Carlsson-Paige and Diane Levin. *Who's Calling the Shots? How to Respond Effectively to Children's Fascination with War Play and War Toys* (Philadelphia: New Society Publishers, 1990).

☙

9

Reclaiming Your Kids
from the Corporate Culture,
Part II: TV or Not TV?

Directly outside my second story office window there is a good-size maple tree. There's also a bird feeder, and I'm frequently entertained by robins, finches, and sparrows.

And the occasional cat. The other day I looked up to see a large orange tabby staring back at me and in that moment of feline confrontation, it finally dawned on me why I've never seen a nest in this tree.

Birds are smart—or at least instinctively savvy—and there's no way they're going to risk their young by building a nest this close to the ground, in cat territory.

It's a dangerous world for birds—and for our kids. While predators aren't exactly imagining our babes as their next meal, they're still out there, and their motives aren't benign.

A large part of our job as parents is to protect our kids. And yet many of us have invited one particularly voracious predator into our homes, set up an altar to it, and gathered around to allow this interloper to eat up our time, sap our energy, even shape our values.

Of course, I'm talking about television. It's been called "a

vast wasteland." It's been implicated as the cause of a number
of problems, as I'll detail later. It provides an eternal struggle
between parents and children in many households. I've yet to
hear any parenting expert, teacher, marriage counselor, or
cleric urge parents or kids to spend more time, zombielike, in
front of this little box.

Sometimes I wish there were no televisions anywhere—
that the darned thing had never been invented. I wish that
families and whole communities could come together as they
used to, pre–boob tube.

When my mother was growing up in the 1920s and
1930s, there were no televisions and Mom's family couldn't
afford a radio. But my mom doesn't remember feeling deprived. Instead she says, "I really think we were happier back
then.

"Neighbors would come over in the evenings," she recalls. "They'd sit around and tell stories—some they made up
and some true. Many were handed down from parents and
grandparents." Mom says that they often played cards with
the neighbors and did a lot of reading—out loud and
on their own—but it's the stories she really remembers. "The
storytelling was special; it was important. We don't take time
for that now," Mom laments. "The TV has taken over."

Much later, in the fifties when televisions were first
readily available to the public, my parents had saved enough
money that they had the option of either buying a clothes
dryer or a television. Mom, at home with four kids age five
and younger, living a few miles out of town, and desperate for
a little adult "conversation" and entertainment, chose the TV.
Who could blame her?

But TV was a different animal fifty years ago. Television
has changed dramatically, from the lone channel that my
mom was able to get on her old Philco to the virtually unlimited network and cable options now available. Programming
has shifted, along with the type and number of commercials.
Even news programs aren't really news anymore, with their

"Entertainment Tonight" format and their lack of depth and analysis.

With ever more sophisticated methods of drawing in viewers, television has evolved into a major—predominant, even—influence in most Americans' lives. It's estimated that the average child spends 60 percent more time watching TV each year than he or she spends in school. It's the top after-school activity chosen by children ages six to seventeen. Often kids needn't even get out of bed to be impacted, influenced, and impaired by television: According to a study by the Kaiser Family Foundation, two-thirds of kids ages eight through eighteen have TVs in their bedrooms, and one-third of those seven and under do also.

While television was always a means of advertising to the masses, the number of commercials that the average child views each year has increased from perhaps a few hundred in the fifties to 20,000 annually in the 1970s to about 40,000 commercials per year today. Additionally, via television, the average American child has witnessed 200,000 dramatized acts of violence and 40,000 dramatized murders by the time he or she reaches eighteen. (Another sad estimate: By age eighteen, kids have seen 100,000 ads for alcohol.)

Yet we watch. Why? Ostensibly, because it's just so darned entertaining. Oh, and then there's the whole *zeitgeist* thing. Alan Reder, Phil Catalfo, and Stephanie Renfrow Hamilton, authors of *The Whole Parenting Guide,* say that television provides "the zeitgeist, or the spirit of the times . . . [Your] children will experience limitations in almost any social arena . . . if they don't watch some television because TV puts them on a cultural wavelength with their peers, obnoxious as that culture may be."

The Negatives of TV Viewing

Even if I felt those two flimsy reasons had any substance, the negatives associated with television viewing far outweigh the benefits, if any. What are those negatives?

1. TV TRANSFORMS OUR KIDS—AND US— INTO "CONSUMER UNITS"

If there was ever any question about the relationship between TV viewing and kids wanting more "stuff," a study reported in the June 2001 issue of *Journal of Developmental and Behavioral Pediatrics* concludes that, yes, indeed, kids who watch more TV bug their parents to buy more toys. The study involved a school-based effort to reduce television. By the end of the school year, those students who'd watched less TV were 70 percent less likely to have requested a toy during the previous week.

TV advertising works on adults too. A survey by economist Juliet Schor concluded that respondents spent an extra $208 annually for each hour of television they watched weekly. Betsy Taylor, Executive Director of the Center for a New American Dream, aptly calls the television a "direct I.V. of manufactured want."

2. TV GIVES US INFERIORITY COMPLEXES

The premise of most TV advertising is to make the viewers feel *less*—less cool, less attractive, less popular—if we don't buy whatever they're selling. The message is that, by buying these items, we'll be complete, we'll be part of the "in crowd."

And the "in crowd" has changed too. Television shows and movies aren't portraying the Cleaver family anymore but a very upscale Jones family. We essentially need to keep up with ever more affluent reference groups. Consequently, we need to spend more and more to keep from feeling "out of it."

3. TV PROMOTES VIOLENCE AND OTHER NEGATIVE VALUES

Remember the statistic quoted above about the 200,000 dramatized acts of violence and 40,000 dramatized murders that our children, on average, witness on television before they turn eighteen? According to a variety of sources, there is overwhelming evidence that violence on television—and at the movies and in video and computer games—is one of the causes of violent tendencies among young people.

Any doubt about the cause and effect of violent programming was put to rest by a joint statement in July 2000 by the American Academy of Pediatrics, the American Medical Association, the American Psychological Association, and the American Academy of Child and Adolescent Psychiatry. They said: "The conclusion of the public health community, based on over 30 years of research, is that viewing entertainment violence can lead to increases in aggressive attitudes, values, and behavior, particularly in children. Its effects are measurable and long-lasting. Moreover, prolonged viewing of media violence can lead to emotional desensitization toward violence in real life."

It isn't just the violence on TV that is harming our kids. Other negative "values" are reinforced on television, among them disrespect, greed, the notion that looking good and being cool is of paramount importance, and an attitude of entitlement and selfishness.

4. TV INDUCES AN ADDICTIVE, TRANCELIKE STATE

Another reason to be TV-free involves the psychological effects of televison viewing. A number of studies conclude that the simple act of watching TV is harmful to children, whether it's "Sesame Street" or "NYPD Blue." Among the many negative effects that television viewing has on children is the trancelike state it produces, the sensory overkill, and its addictive qualities. The pernicious effects of viewing are amplified by the quantity of TV the average American kid watches. A twenty-year longitudinal study conducted at Yale University concluded that children who watch excessive amounts of television tend to be less imaginative, more restless, more aggressive, and have poorer concentration.

Television's hypnotic, addictive effect is only getting worse. In his book *Culture Jam: The Uncooling of America,* Kalle Lasn explains that television content contains "jolts" that he describes as "any 'technical event' that interrupts the flow of sound or thought or imagery—shift in camera, angle, gunshot, cut to commercial." In 1978, television shows contained about ten jolts per minute; by 1998, the number of jolts had doubled. Some channels and programs deliver many more of these "technical events," like MTV with sixty events per minute. Lasn and others contend that jolts release hormones that trigger the fight-or-flight response, and that the viewer's attention is riveted by upping the incidence of jolts, inducing essentially an addiction to that release of hormones.

The real world does not work this way, notes downshifted mom Debbie Newman. She believes that this aspect of television programming may even be the cause of the "epidemic" of kids with ADD and ADHD. "If we were going to take, say, an alien from outer space and train him to have a short attention span, what would we do?" she asks. "Probably we would sit him in front of a screen and flash pictures in front of him that change every fraction of a second." Just park him in front of the tube—instant attention deficit.

5. TV CREATES COUCH POTATOES

Excessive TV viewing contributes to weight problems in children. According to the Third National Health and Nutrition Examination Survey, the more children viewed TV, the heavier they were. Children who watched four or more hours of television a day were, on average, 17 percent heavier than those who watched less than two hours per day. A recent study at Tufts University revealed that kids who watch a lot of television end up eating more of the types of foods advertised—that is, fast foods, convenience foods, candy, and soda—than children who don't watch as much television.

6. TV INHIBITS LEARNING

Too much television also leads to poor academic performance. A number of studies conclude that the less TV a child watches, the better that child will score on achievement tests. Similarly, as TV viewing increases, reading ability decreases.

The negative effects of television on young children are so pronounced that, in 1999, the American Academy of Pediatrics issued a statement recommending that pediatricians "urge parents to avoid television viewing for children under the age of 2 years."

7. TV IS A TIME VAMPIRE

So far the negatives I've listed have, more or less, been related to the programming, advertising, or psychological impacts of viewing television. But there's another, more straightforward and potentially much more negative impact of television viewing: the simple amount of time it takes away from other activities. A 2000 study by the Annenberg Public Policy Center found that kids ages two through seventeen spend an average of 4½ hours *each day* in front of screens—TV, computer, and video game systems.

That it takes away from time spent on physical activity and reading is implied in the last two negatives discussed. But there are many other activities that are lessened and sometimes obliterated because we're zoned out in front of the tube.

Family time together is a huge one! A 2001 study by Professor Barbara Brock of Eastern Washington University revealed that TV-free families spent an average of 385 minutes each week in meaningful conversation with kids, ten times the national average. Families without televisions spend much more time playing, creating, and just "hanging out" together than their TV-immersed peers. TV-free families also have more time to spend getting to know neighbors, helping younger siblings, working around the house, learning to play an instrument, volunteering—in short, virtually any of those activities listed later in this chapter and in Chapter 12. This failure to spend time on pleasurable, relaxing activities could explain why, as a 1999 Kaiser Family Foundation study revealed, youngsters who watched more TV tended to be less content than their TV-free peers.

. . . And Yet We Watch

Marie Winn has written extensively on the effects of television on us and our kids. In 1974 she instigated what may have been the first "TV free" experiment in Denver, Colorado. Fifteen families turned their televisions off for a full month and kept diaries on the results. The improvements in family dynamics and happiness seen during that month were impressive. The families reported better communication between children and adults, a more peaceful atmosphere in the home, greater feelings of closeness as a family, more help around the house by the children, more leisurely meals with more interesting mealtime conversations, more reading by both parents and children, and more real play among children. The negatives, says Winn, were minor. Some family members missed their favorite TV programs, some kids mentioned experiencing a "weird" feeling (could it have been withdrawal?), and parents reported a few discipline problems without TV deprivation to use as a threat!

The positives of doing without television are noted over and over again by experts. Family therapist and author Mary Pipher notes that her standard suggestion for families in crisis is that they turn off the TV for at least a couple of nights a week and, instead, watch the sun set or take a walk.

But here's the rub: Having experienced all of these benefits—and with knowledge of the many negatives of TV viewing—all fifteen families in Winn's Denver experiment returned to watching TV to some extent after the experience!

With virtually no positives to recommend it and numerous negatives, television continues to hold the country in its viselike grip.

It doesn't have to. Simple living families almost universally have taken one of two actions with regard to television viewing: Either they have no TV in their home or they strictly limit TV viewing. Here's a look at each of these alternatives.

Alternative One: Become TV-Free

Clearly, the easiest route to becoming a TV-free household with children is to never have had one. Evicting your television can be a colossal battle if the kids, and that nutty sports-loving spouse, put their collective foot down.

Many simple living parents have just continued their TV-free lives once they had kids. Diana Wright and her husband, Steve Hoffman, are in this group, having been without television since the seventies. Now, with daughters Claire, six, and Eliza, two, they're too busy doing other fun things to give a second thought to television. "We can't imagine having a TV," Diana says. "We wouldn't have the time to watch it." Diana prefers their TV-free existence. "It's not there creating desires," she says.

Laural Ringler, Tom Caldwell, and their five- and three-year-old sons in Bellingham, Washington, are also TV-free. "We don't have time for it!" says Laural. "We are busy being active, creating music, dancing, being outside, playing, adventuring. . . ."

Kate Rhoad and family are another TV-free household. (Note: The Rhoads own a TV/VCR but use it solely for occasional family movies.) Kate asked her three kids how they felt about being TV-less. Her nine- and eight-year-olds mentioned that it might be nice to see cartoons occasionally, but had no real problems about not watching TV. Her thirteen-year-old said he could tell that his "thinking about 'things' " was different from his peers'. He pointed out that his friends often have struggles with their parents over stuff that they want that they see on TV. "He just doesn't have that problem and he's glad," says Kate. "The difference between our three kids when it comes to materialism and wants is so pronounced that I can't imagine ever making the decision to introduce a TV," she concludes.

Tara Strand-Brown of Occidental, California, eloquently explains her family's decision to be TV-free. They did it, she says, "because of all the negative effects of television. It's like smoking—we know it's bad for us, still we do it. We feel it's simpler not to face the question. No TV in the house means no struggle with kids or anyone else as to whether it's on or not. I believe TV breeds violence, makes people dissatisfied with what's in front of them (since real life is never as high-speed and dramatic as TV), and decreases our brain capacity. We want nothing to do with it. Oddly, though we have friends with similar values, we don't know any other families without a TV. *Why?*"

Good question!

So here's great advice if you're just starting married life or your kids are still in diapers: Get rid of the TV. It will never be easier to do than prekids, with just two rational—one assumes!—adults to contend with.

GOING COLD TURKEY

If, however, your kids have already been exposed to that vast wasteland, other tactics may be in order. If your goal is to do away with your television completely, your best bet, according to experts, is to go "cold turkey"—that is, rather than wean yourself from TV viewing, just bite the bullet and pull the plug (to throw two clichés together). As with any other addiction, the toughest part will be the first few weeks—but it *will* get better.

A great way to terminate your television is to participate in "TV Turn-Off Week," the last full week of April. Alternatively, you can do it yourself, with help from the TV Free America websites, www.tvfa.org, or www.tvturnoff.org, and other resources, like Marie Winn's books. The advantage of participating in TV Turn-Off Week is that you'll have lots of company, hopefully, among your kids' friends' families. After the official week, your family would just continue to enjoy the pleasures of TV-free living.

Whether you're attempting to turn the tube off for seven days or permanently unplug it, your first step will be to sell the idea to your family. Rather than dropping this on your family by declaring an edict, a less suicidal approach is to call a family meeting (see "A Primer on Family Meetings" on page 12) and present the TV turnoff as an adventure and as an opportunity to do more cool family stuff together (which, merely by coincidence, involves eliminating television). Ask family members to brainstorm about fun things to do and write the ideas down. (For more ideas, see "Alternatives to TV Viewing" on page 134.) You might even want to have a small budget for outings, crafts items, et cetera. Focus on the positives—the fun to be had!—of doing without television. For more cerebral kids, a listing of the *proven* negatives of television might work too. You could simply show them the first part of this chapter.

THE RELUCTANT SPOUSE

Spouse? Let's face it, we're probably talking about your "dear husband" here, and the likely programming in question is "Monday Night Football." Hopefully, your spouse will be persuaded to relinquish the remote control by reading this chapter or one of the books suggested below. If your spouse remains unconvinced, perhaps he (or she!) will at least agree to tape shows and watch them when the kids are not around. Then you and your kids can begin your adventure—and he'll probably eat crow later and beg to be included in your fun evenings.

A reward system is a good idea for bringing around any fence-sitting kids. A special sleepover, family party, or new books are all possibilities. If your kids are dead set against any such plan, experts recommend that parents go ahead and conduct their own TV turnoff, which *not* coincidentally involves doing a lot of fun stuff with the family. They'll likely come along, much like the reluctant spouse.

THE BATTLE PLAN

In *Unplugging the Plug-In Drug*, Marie Winn recommends that all family members sign contracts, stating their resolve to do without the one-eyed monster for X length of time. She also urges families to write up a "Battle Plan." I think at a minimum the brainstormed list of alternate activity ideas should be posted and reviewed regularly. A trip to the library at the start of your turnoff is a near must (for most simple living families this is a regular family outing anyway). I also feel that the television should be relegated to a closet or the basement, with the long-term hope of it staying there. At the very least, put a large towel/cover over the TV for the duration.

The first night might be a good time to go *out*—that is, away from the TV—for a family activity. A bike ride, bowling, or a concert all make sense. Just make it FUN.

At the end of your week—or at the end of each week, if you're attempting a longer TV-free period—hold another family meeting and discuss how the week went. Ask: Were there enough fun TV alternatives available? What did family members like—and *not* like—about being TV-free? What are the benefits to the family of being TV-free? If your turnoff is for a week, a celebration party at the end of the week makes sense too.

One note for those who are tempted to give the TV-free life up after a week or so: While I believe you'll see the benefits immediately, you'll also likely notice withdrawal pains. Remember that it will get better.

ALTERNATIVES TO TV VIEWING

Many families resist killing their televisions for fear they simply won't know what to do without them. Those who've given up the tube or at least curtailed their addictions emphasize that the "I'm bored" syndrome, if it occurs at all, will give way in short order to an amazement that you ever had time to watch television.

If, however, you're having difficulty initially in coming up with fun things you can do when you're not watching television, consider the following easily expandable list. (See also Chapter 12, "Simple Pleasures and Family Rituals.")

- Play board games and cards.
- Read—and visit the library frequently!
- Call friends up for a "pickup" game of soccer or baseball.
- Swim at your local public pool.
- Make dinner together.
- Play charades.
- Write letters.

(continues)

(continued)

- Visit grandparents and other relatives.
- Volunteer together.
- Cuddle with the cat.
- Play with the dog.
- Go for a walk or bike ride.
- Visit a museum.
- Listen to music.
- Have the kids put on skits and recitals.
- Make music together. If you don't have a piano or guitar, you can sing!
- Listen to selected radio programs. (My kids love "Car Talk" and "Prairie Home Companion.")
- Learn a foreign language.
- Work in the garden.
- Share your hobbies—knitting, woodworking, et cetera—with your kids.
- Fill up a photograph album or leaf through an old family one, perhaps borrowed from grandparents (looking through one *with* grandparents is even better).
- Make a scrapbook about a favorite trip or activity.
- Find a tape recorder and record the kids asking grandparents questions about their pasts.
- Put on an oldies station and do housework together.
- Declutter closets and donate items to a nonprofit.
- Work on a home improvement project—a satisfying, do-it-yourself, low cost one, like painting or stripping furniture.
- Mix up some barbecue sauce, strawberry jam, or just a batch of cookies to share with neighbors.
- Tell stories.
- Attend a local high school play or concert.
- Listen to books on tape.
- Have friends or family over.

(continues)

(continued)

- Bake bread.
- Sit on the front porch and blow bubbles.
- Go on hikes or "nature walks" around the neighborhood.
- Play outdoors.
- Attend a town meeting and get involved.
- Go bowling.
- Do your homework.
- Teach your kids how to balance a checkbook.

I've taken a number of these "alternatives to boredom" and posted them on our refrigerator. And, yes, the kids have actually consulted the list on numerous occasions; they've added to it too.

All of these things take time, and some take a bit of effort. You'll find the time by not watching television. The effort or energy may seem to be lacking occasionally. Some of these activities are less physically demanding than others; you can choose those that fit your energy level at the time. If you've simplified financially and have thus been able to quit work or work part-time, you'll have more time and energy to put into these projects with your family.

The possibilities for TV-less fun are endless. And remember: TV-less fun brings you closer together as a family—and likely to your community too.

Alternative Two: Limit Your Child's Exposure to TV and Other Media

Some parents feel, for whatever reason, that the option of doing without television entirely isn't the route they wish to take. If the TV-free lifestyle isn't your cup of tea—or you simply can't pry the remote from hubby's hand—then limiting the amount of TV your child views is imperative.

All of the negatives of television viewing become more serious as those viewing hours increase, and the hours can really pile up. According to the Nielsen people, the average twelve-year-old spends more than four hours each day watching television, totaling over 1,500 hours yearly. Nevertheless, half of all parents have no rules regarding what or how much TV their kids watch, according to a study by the Kaiser Family Foundation.

The American Association of Pediatricians recommends a one-hour-per-day limit to children's exposure to all screen media combined—television, computer, Nintendo, GameBoy, et cetera. The American Academy of Pediatrics has further warned that kids age two and under should watch no television whatsoever.

CLEAR, CONSISTENT RULES

The above recommendations are a good place to start, although I hope you will want to take them further. For example, many parents have a "no TV on school days" rule; others prohibit the tube before school and before homework is completed. Many also ban certain types of programming; you'll likely need to watch programs with your kids to make those determinations. Ratings provided at the www.mediafamily.org site can help. Others limit the one-hour daily ration of television to noncommercial TV and/or acceptable videos, particularly for younger children. A few require the kids to keep TV diaries, writing down every program viewed.

One rule that should be obvious is "no TV during meals." Chapter 12 lists the many benefits of family mealtimes. If the one-eyed monster is drowning out all conversation, those benefits are lost.

If your decision is to limit rather than to do away with the television altogether, you'll likely need very clear rules for television usage. And you'll need to stick to them. It takes more energy and time to enforce TV rules than it does to give in and say, "Whatever." Your rules should also extend to Internet, computer, and video game system usage. (I say that you'll *likely* need clear, consistent rules because I did discover a few simple living families who really had no television usage rules, yet had no problems with their kids overdoing it. It will depend upon your family, your children, and your style.)

An excellent way to get started on the path of less TV is to participate in a TV Turn-Off Week program or have your own family turnoff week, as discussed above.

Another very good tactic is to physically relegate the television to a nonprominent spot in the house. Reclaim your living and/or family room as a TV-free zone. It will lend itself to numerous other more family-friendly activities. Besides, research proves that we watch less television if the boob tube altar is not the focal point of our living rooms. Our television is in the basement; it's out of sight—and, for the most part, out of mind. Other families actually put the TV in a closet/wardrobe and take it out only on special occasions.

MONITORING TV VIEWING

The Newmans of Austin, Texas, use a coupon system, a popular TV regulation method. Their kids, ages seven and six, are allowed four hours of screen time—computer, TV, movies—weekly. Each Saturday both kids receive eight "TV tickets," good for thirty minutes of screen time each. "This has taken the pressure off us as parents from always being the bad guy saying no," says Debbie Newman. "It's taught the kids about economics and time management, and more important, has kept them from watching so much television."

The Newmans also prohibit television viewing on weekdays during the school year. "We still use the tickets," says Debbie, "but we find that they are so accustomed to occupying themselves during the week that they hardly ask for the TV much on the weekends. Mostly they have many tickets left over."

You can borrow the Newmans' coupon approach or devise another that suits your family. Some parents add a little incentive for their kids by allowing them to "cash in" their coupons for special outings or family activities. Alternatively, you can simply state your limits and expect cooperation. Again, it's whatever works for your family.

Help Your Kids to Become "Media Literate"

Whether you opt for a TV-less existence or not, you will want to assist your children in learning to process and understand media. After all, even kids from TV-free households come into contact with one at some point in their lives. They'll be better prepared to deal with television and other media if you've taught them a few things about their function, their reliance on advertising, and other factors.

You can do this by watching TV with your kids and talking with them about what they're seeing. Critique the programs and the advertising. This process is educational, as well as fun. (For households without television, borrow a TV or ask a relative or friend if your family could watch a few programs for this purpose at their house.) Here are a few media literacy questions and activities you can use with your kids:

1. Have your kids count the advertisements in a thirty-minute program; have them time them too. Ask them how much commercial time there is in a half-hour show and how much is actual programming.

2. Then discuss the function of advertising. Tell your kids that the purpose of commercials is to get you to buy things—period!—and that the advertisers pay the television people a lot of money to put their ads on the air; indeed, that advertising money pays for the television shows themselves. Especially with younger children, point out that the people in the ads are actors, hired to look excited and say positive things about the items advertised. Emphasize that sports figures and superstars get paid *big* bucks to endorse products. (An example: When Michael Jordan retired from basketball the first

time, in 1993, he was raking in about $30 million annually—
just in endorsements!)

3. Help your kids "deconstruct" those ads. See if they can
tell you why the advertisers use different techniques. Ask
open-ended questions of your kids, like, "Why do you think
they have kids skateboarding when they're trying to sell
candy?" and "Why do they have a rock star singing in this
soda commercial? Can drinking a certain kind of soda make
you 'cool'?" Even the occasional hilarious commercial can
make your case: Ask your kids, "What does humor have to
do with buying this product?" Point out the use of music and
special effects to mesmerize viewers too.

Ask your kids if they think the product advertised will
really live up to its claims. "Will those action figures really
move like that? Can a car actually make it to the top of a
mountain?" Look at what the ad is selling *beyond* the product. "Does this advertisement imply that you'll be more popular, happier, prettier if you use their product? Do you think
that's true?" Invite your kids to name the *emotion* the ads are
exploiting. Love, insecurity, loneliness, and the yearning to
belong are all possibilities. Ask them how a product can sat-
isfy these needs.

Question out loud whether products are even necessary.
Point out that most advertisements are trying to get you to
think you need something when you don't. Ask your kids if
the products advertised are good for the environment. (The
answer to that one is almost always no!)

Throughout your deconstructing efforts, tell your kids
how you feel, and listen to their feelings.

4. Critique programs as well. Ask: "Does this program
have a moral or message? What is it? Do you agree with it?
What kinds of lifestyles do the characters lead? Do you think
this show represents what 'real life' is like?"

The most important factor in all of this is for your kids to
hear and see you *talking back to your television,* especially
commercials.

I think that this is a wonderful way to empower kids to have the self-confidence to question things, whether it's the necessity for a new CD player or the wisdom of doing drugs because "everybody else is doing it." It also plays a big part in helping your kids "question corporate authority," as discussed in Chapter 8.

I've engaged in this dissing dialogue with my television and my kids since they were young (also about advertising on radio, billboards, magazines, et cetera). I've been completely candid about how I have little respect for commercial television—or advertising generally. We've talked to our kids extensively about the commercials they see and how they're trying to get them to buy stuff, stuff they don't need and that often isn't good for them. They've become pretty savvy consumers at tender ages. I believe they are much less gullible than even most adults I know.

Media literacy should be included in school curricula. It's already included in countries like Canada, Australia, England, and Scotland. Rick Seifert of the Northwest Media Literacy Center says that "we need media literacy in schools because the single most pervasive influence on kids is mass media." The result? We have the most "electronically entertained" and the most acquisitive children on the planet. "We need to help kids be able to critically assess all of those messages," says Seifert.

Some Final Recommendations

Consider these additional strategies for taming your TV:

Physician, Heal Thyself

No surprise here: Studies show that children whose parents are heavy television watchers are themselves excessive viewers. So, step away from the remote! And keep moving . . .

Don't Use TV as a Babysitter

As tempting as it may be—particularly when your children are young and physically demanding—resist using TV as a babysitter. Television is not a benign nanny, not even public television. In *Endangered Minds,* Jane M. Healy warns against allowing children to spend significant time with Barney and the Teletubbies, even devoting an entire chapter to "Sesame Street and the Death of Reading." Some experts add that, while you may buy yourself a few hours of peace by employing the electronic sitter, you'll end up with kids who are less able to entertain themselves.

Whatever You Do, DON'T Allow Televisions in Kids' Bedrooms

You may conclude that television restrictions don't fit your family's style. If that's the case, I can make only one last plea: Keep televisions *out* of your kids' rooms. Then, at the very least, they'll have to come out of their caves to pay homage to the little box. And you might be able to talk them into a game of chess or Scrabble instead.

Resources

ON THE NEGATIVES OF TELEVISION

Roy F. Fox. *Harvesting Minds: How TV Commercials Control Kids* (Westport, Connecticut: Praeger Publishers, 1996).

Dave Grossman and Gloria DeGaetano. *Stop Teaching Our Kids to Kill* (New York: Crown Publishers, 1999).

Jane M. Healy. *Endangered Minds: Why Our Children Don't Think* (New York: Simon & Schuster, 1990).

Kalle Lasn. *Culture Jam: The Uncooling of America* (New York: Eagle Brook/William Morrow, 1999).

Jerry Mander. *Four Arguments for the Elimination of Television* (New York: Morrow, 1978).

Joyce Nelson. *The Perfect Machine: TV in the Nuclear Age* (Toronto: Between-the-Lines, 1987).

David Walsh. *Dr. Dave's Cyberhood: Making Media Choices That Create a Healthy Electronic Environment for Your Kids* (New York: Simon & Schuster, 2001).

David Walsh. *Selling Out America's Children: How America Puts Profits Before Values and What Parents Can Do* (Minneapolis: Deaconess Press, 1994).

Marie Winn. *The Plug-In Drug* (New York: Penguin Books, 1985).

National Coalition on Television Violence; www.nctvv.org

ON DOING WITHOUT TV

Ruth and Steve Bennett. *365 TV Free Activities You Can Do with Your Child* (Holbrook, Massachusetts: Bob Adams, 1991).

Frances Moore Lappe. *What to Do After You Turn Off the TV* (New York: Ballantine Books, 1985).

Marie Winn. *Unplugging the Plug-In Drug* (New York: Viking, 1987)

TV Turnoff Network: www.tvfa.org or www.tv-turnoff.org; (202) 518–5556. The official TV turnoff website.

MEDIA LITERACY WEBSITES/ORGANIZATIONS

Center for Media Education: www.cme.org; (206) 628–2620. Works to create quality electronic media for children and youth.

Center for Media Literacy: www.medialit.org; (310) 581–0260. Great resource for media literacy curricula.

National Institute on Media and the Family: www.media andthefamily.org or www.mediafamily.org; (888) 672–5437. Website includes movie, TV, video game, and computer game content ratings—go to "Free Family Resources" and the "Kid-Score" section.

The New Mexico Media Literacy Project: www.nmmlp.org; (505) 828–3129. Go to "Free Resources" for more information on how to "talk back" to your television and other media.

The Northwest Media Literacy Center: www.mediathink.org; (503) 244–7109.

OTHERS

Center for the Prevention of School Violence: (800) 299–6054; www.ncsu.edu/cpsv

Children's Defense Fund: www.childrensdefense.org; (800) CDF–1200. Information and advocacy on a variety of topics affecting children, including causes of violence.

Alan Reder, Phil Catalfo, and Stephanie Renfrow Hamilton. *The Whole Parenting Guide* (New York: Broadway Books, 1999).

10

❦

Coping with Peer Pressure and
Creating Community

I remember peer pressure well. It was the driving force behind
my obsession with the Monkees in the sixth grade. It was certainly responsible for that cigarette I smoked in St. Frederic's
girls' rest room in seventh grade. I can't think of any *other*
reason I would have worn "go-go" boots and hip-hugger
skirts in junior high.

And it still hounds me—as it does, to some extent, all of us.

We're all subject to peer pressure; yes, even you downshifters. Peer pressure operates whenever we allow the beliefs
or actions of those around us to influence our behavior, whenever we unquestioningly accept their interpretation of the
world.

For downshifters in North America, living in this most
acquisitive of cultures, surrounded by peers with ever more
materialistic lifestyles, simplifying can be particularly difficult. If peer pressure is hard to resist when you're just doing
the normal American things, it can be doubly difficult when
your family has chosen to live "outside the norm," as simplified families do.

The need to belong and to identify with a group is particularly strong as a child is growing up and it becomes nearly overwhelming in early adolescence. Unfortunately, this compulsion to conform doesn't end when we become grown-ups. Dealing with our own peer pressure—and helping our kids deal with theirs—is essential to living a simple, authentic life.

Tactics for Adults

You probably thought that this chapter would primarily address helping our kids cope with peer pressure. It does do that, but first I'm going to deal with *adult* peer pressure. Because if, as adults—the assumption being that we're mature, self-confident, and self-directed individuals—we cannot resist the impulse to "keep up with the Joneses," there's not much hope for our kids. And it will be extremely difficult to "communicate your convictions and practice what you preach" (see Chapter 7) if your beliefs and behavior are excessively impacted by those around you.

From my vantage point, it also seems that the pull of peer pressure is stronger for those with kids than for those who are childless. I didn't have kids until I was thirty-five, so I spent many years as a "child-free" adult. As a parent, I've encountered peer pressure more often than I did as a single person, perhaps because parents are bombarded with child-targeted marketing or because we're surrounded by our kids' friends' parents who may have differing value systems. Besides, it's particularly important for those of us with children to resist the pressure to conform: Our ability to follow that distant drummer—joyfully!—is imperative as we model and teach simple values to our kids.

Many of the wonderful parents I interviewed for this book really struggled with the peer pressure issue. They were painfully honest with me about their feelings, about their self-doubts and misgivings about being different. I understood exactly what they were saying. A few times I blurted out, "I wish you were my neighbor!" And I meant it. I wished that we could daily give each other support.

Lisa Cunningham, the Peace Corps volunteer, says that peer pressure hit her hard when she returned from Botswana. She shared these thoughts: "It seemed like everyone drove two big SUVs, had their kids in lots of activities, ate out, had big beautiful houses. I kept thinking, 'How do they do it? Why can't I have that? That should be me.' "

Shelby Pawlina still has those "odd man out" feelings when she's around coworkers. "My strong ideas about recycling, being outdoors on vacations, and especially my disassociation from media and my desire to create a broader community than my nuclear family, don't resonate with most folks I work with," she says.

"In general, I feel a little 'out of the loop,' " Shelby continues, "as I'm not hip to the new fashions, television shows, or what's happening to the movie stars."

Rather than ignore the fact that peer pressure exists, here are some strategies adults can use in dealing with societal and group pressure to conform to a materialistic lifestyle.

COMMITMENT TO THE CAUSE

The soul searching described in Chapter 2 is essential for each person attempting to downshift in our consumer culture. Without articulating your real beliefs and having a foundation of what your true values are, it will be *very* hard to turn your back on our culture's peer pressure.

Patti Idrobo notes that she feels peer pressure not from any one individual or group but from society generally. "Just knowing how 'everyone' does things [exerts] peer pressure—not to 'deprive' my children, not to be cheap, not to be an extremist."

Still, Patti is able to resist it. Her commitment to living

simply overshadows the pull of peer pressure. "I just feel too strongly about it," she explains.

Linda McDonough's dedication to simple living helps her in these situations too. "I try to remember that [those questioning my lifestyle] aren't mean, they just don't understand. I believe this stuff strongly enough that I am able to hold firm."

SELF-ESTEEM, SELF-KNOWLEDGE

My comment earlier about adults being mature, self-confident, self-directed individuals was given tongue-in-cheek. It's not at all clear that most adults have these qualities. You really have to wonder when you see "grown-ups" adopting all the latest trends.

Even those, like myself, who've wholeheartedly embraced simplicity, have misgivings. Not questions about the integrity of the movement, but those illogical self-doubts that pop up when you're doing something that's perceived as different from the mainstream. Heck, you can have these when you're a veritable clone of middle-class America, so when you're not following the crowd, they inevitably occur more often.

So a hardy self-esteem, even a thick skin, is a valuable asset for downshifting adults. The combination of having a decent self-image along with knowing what you really believe in makes for a strong foundation for a simple lifestyle.

How do adults acquire self-esteem? Certainly having a solid understanding of their values and knowing that they're living them is a good foundation. Beyond that, it seems that many of those tactics that we can use with our kids, which I address later in this chapter, can help us too.

I don't mean to imply here that parents with less self-confidence can't simplify. That's not the case. They may, however, need to rely more on support systems, like those mentioned below.

COMMUNITY: USING POSITIVE PEER PRESSURE

Doing things differently takes a lot of courage. And for most people, even those with solid egos, it takes some kind of support system. "We tend to become like those around us," Cecile Andrews, author of *The Circle of Simplicity*, explains.

"Consumerism is based on the premise that we're alone; that we don't need people but rather more stuff. It's part of our 'wrong thinking,' that we can go it alone," says Andrews. "But it's really hard to do it all on your own. You'll inevitably feel 'weird.' I really feel strongly that support is needed."

I see it when I visit the Internet simple living discussion boards. Time and time again people write in asking, "Am I the only one who feels this way?" Often they're frustrated because their relatives are giving the kids inappropriate—or just too many—gifts. Maybe they've decided to "make do" with only one car and are feeling a bit "out of it." Or they're simply baffled by a world with so much stuff and so little meaning. Gayle Dixon, a mother of two from Golden, Colorado, describes this dilemma poignantly: "Sometimes, I cannot say what I think because many people think it's weird to want a simpler society and lifestyle."

Finding or creating a community of like-minded peers is about taking the peer pressure concept and using it for positive outcomes. Instead of feeling forced to behave against your convictions, you feel supported to act in accordance with your beliefs because those around you accept and value them.

A note here: Communities both support simplicity and are *supported by* simplicity. The communities of "simple" people that we create or join, obviously, support us in our quest for simplicity. On the other hand, our communities— our neighborhoods, groups of friends, churches, schools, et cetera—are enhanced and made stronger when people live more simply, have more time for each other, and rely more on each other. Creating community is, in fact, one of the common values of those within the simplicity movement.

VIRTUAL SUPPORT GROUPS

One method of finding support and community is through simple living discussion boards on the Internet. Lisa Cunningham, who found a traditional support group difficult to keep going, has developed a longstanding relationship with "an on-line community of women" she met on the discussion boards at parentsoup.com.

"A few people there were interested in talking about simplicity, the environment, and other issues beyond parenting, and so we spun off our own discussion group on onelist.com," explains Lisa. Her virtual support group has been going strong now for over two years with about twenty members. "We're all on different parts of the path to simpler living, but it has been wonderful to know that there are others out there on the same journey."

These on-line support networks can be found at www. simpleliving.net, www.newdream.org, www.mothering.com, www.unschooling.com (for home schoolers), and www. parentsoup.com.

TRADITIONAL SUPPORT GROUPS

Traditional—"real"—support groups and "simplicity circles" are another way to connect with simpatico types. Creating these groups is a bit more involved than logging on to the Internet, but the rewards are well worth the effort.

You can find other like-minded individuals in a number of ways. One is to visit www.simplicitycircles.com or www.simpleliving.net and list your group information and hope that folks will contact you. You can also approach your church about starting a simplicity circle. Other organizations—for instance, your child's school or preschool, your

SIMPLICITY CIRCLES

Simplicity circles are a specific type of support group. Based on a Swedish model, these support groups have sufficient structure to keep them going yet are informal enough to allow for individual differences and group spontaneity. Cecile Andrews, who directs the Simplicity Circles Project for Seeds of Simplicity, describes how to start and maintain one of these groups in *The Circle of Simplicity* and at the simplicity circles website—www.simplicitycircles.com.

Lilly and John Lombard, who live in the Takoma Park, Maryland, area, are part of a simplicity circle that meets every other week and has been going strong since November of 1998. Every quarter the members meet to come up with topics for the next twelve weeks.

The group has explored many simplicity-related topics including decluttering, vegetarianism, eco-friendly homes, envy and deprivation, building community, rituals, practicing mindfulness, responsible investing, transportation alternatives, and, not surprisingly, raising children simply.

Each meeting has a nominal facilitator, who typically does some sort of research on the topic, perhaps preparing a handout or finding a speaker. The evening starts with the same icebreaker: Each member shares one thing they did to simplify their lives or one thing that was in alignment with their values since the last meeting. The facilitator then introduces the evening's topic. But, Lilly notes, the group doesn't need a lot of facilitating beyond this. Partly because they know each other so well and due to their shared interests in the topic, Lilly says, "It just works."

An added plus to the Lombards' group, according to Lilly, is that all of the eleven members live within a radius of a mile or two of each other. "We all share the same community interest and involvement." Those shared interests in part explain the group's regular gatherings *in addition* to their circle meetings.

(continues)

> *(continued)*
>
> The group has participated in several volunteer projects, such as bringing meals to elderly neighbors, trash pickups, and organizing an alternative gift fair—as well as enjoying game nights, potlucks, weekend retreats, home canning demonstrations, "pizza and poetry nights," and winter solstice rituals.
>
> "We feel so lucky to have this group," concludes Lilly. "It feels like a big family."

mother's support group, or your book group—are likely places to start.

Sometimes you can find support group members through organizations that you don't even belong to. One Internet poster found group members by attending events at Waldorf schools—private schools with many simple living values—even though her kids weren't enrolled there. You can also take out ads in alternative publications or post a notice at a bookstore, coffee shop, food co-op, or other location that might be frequented by simplicity types.

Many support groups evolve out of simplicity study groups. Anne Felker's group started when her church sponsored a *Your Money or Your Life* (YMOYL) study group. (Contact the New Road Map Foundation, www.new roadmap.org, for more information on starting a YMOYL study group.) You can also check with the Northwest Earth Institute (www.nwei.org) about their voluntary simplicity course. Janice Arnold's group in a small town in eastern Texas evolved after the NWEI's course.

"It's a wonderful antidote to the sense of isolation in this culture that is so centered on buying and spending," says Anne of the support she receives from her group.

COHOUSING COMMUNITIES

Finding support for our simple lifestyles would be made much easier if all of us had a support group like the Lombards' (see "Simplicity Circles" on page 151) or if, say, *all* of our neighbors had simple values. Families who've opted to live in cohousing communities, many of which hold simplicity as a core value, often find themselves in the latter situation, surrounded by simple living households.

This is the case for Joanne Delmonico and John Summer, parents of Lily, age four, who live at Trillium Hollow, a cohousing community in Portland, Oregon. Joanne says Trillium Hollow has a pretty typical cohousing arrangement: There are twenty-eight private, self-contained condominiums clustered around a large "common house"—the site of communal meals, meeting rooms, a library and lounge, even a rumpus room for the kids. Joanne points out that other parents living at Trillium Hollow are pretty much "on the same page" with her and her husband on many simple living parenting issues. "Living in a cohousing community definitely sustains and supports our simple values," she adds.

The cohousing concept got its start in Denmark in the 1970s; there are now about fifty cohousing communities across the U.S. Visit www.cohousing.org for more information.

COMMUNITIES OF FAITH

Many of the parents I interviewed felt that their churches and faiths provided needed support for simplifying. In addition to religious teachings, churches often offer simplicity study groups. And if your church has yet to do so, you can organize one yourself. You can even, as a nonmember, approach a church about facilitating a simplicity group.

Anne Felker has found support within her Quaker community, which, she points out, embraces simple living as a core belief. Paul Wilson and Linda Farris have had the same experience with their Quaker meeting, and regard their church as their community more so than their neighborhood. Linda McDonough receives encouragement and motivation through her Episcopalian congregation. Kathleen Murphy's Catholicism has been a great support for her. She's also found an e-mail discussion group of like-minded Catholics at the Caelum et Terra (Latin for "heaven and earth") website—www. caelumetterra.com.

Other folks have mentioned their frustration with their religious communities, pointing to the ostentatious lifestyles of members, even the ministers! Some eventually seek other, more sympathetic congregations. In larger communities it's possible to "church shop." But you can also, perhaps, be the trailblazer, the one who persuades the rest of your average American churchgoers to consider simplicity. You may find that they were hungering for it.

ECOTEAMS

The Household EcoTeam Program, better known simply as EcoTeams, is offered through Global Action Plan. Eco-Teams are essentially neighborhood environmental education groups. They're discussed in detail in "Show You Care: Start an EcoTeam" on page 68. They cover many simplicity topics and can also develop into simplicity support groups. Another simplicity-related offering of Global Action Plan is the Livable Neighborhood Program, which focuses on building community. Visit www.globalactionplan.org for details.

Adult Peer Pressure "Hot Buttons"

The simple living families I interviewed mentioned several recurring themes concerning adult peer pressure. Here are two primary ones:

RELATIVE SUPPORT—OR LACK THEREOF

Dealing with the reactions of relatives—from parents and siblings to ex-husbands, even current spouses—can be daunting at times. Differences arise particularly during the holidays (see Chapter 16) but may occur year-round if you live close to relatives and see them frequently. The types of issues that come up vary, but from my informal survey of simple families, the major offenses involve inappropriate gifts—war toys, battery-operated toys, Barbie, televisions—or just too many toys purchased by relatives. Another is the relative allowing your kids to watch too much TV or unsuitable movies. Junk food is also a frequent bone of contention.

Simple living families are nearly unanimous in their advice to "be firm." For example, Tara Strand-Brown claims she's had to be "very stern" with her mother regarding gifts to her son, Tevon: "Sometimes I have to risk a scene to stay true to my values and give back inappropriate gifts. The occasional big plastic toy she gives, I simply tell her, 'Okay, but it must stay at your house.' "

Talk with your family and let them know how you feel about the situation. Sometimes one discussion will be adequate, but often it will be an ongoing issue. It will depend upon your relationship with your relatives and the importance of the issue in question as to how you handle recurring problems.

That thick skin I spoke of earlier is sometimes needed: Janice Arnold notes that her siblings sometimes "poke fun at us for having holey socks, that sort of thing." She sticks to her guns, keeps explaining, and "hopes our example speaks for itself." Lenora Ridgard says, "I've been labeled as extremely picky in my family—when I request no war toys, for example. I'm willing to take that label."

Some parents feel that they must take what might be considered drastic actions, like the mom on the Internet discussion board who began to routinely open her daughter's gifts before her birthdays and at Christmas to see if relatives had ignored her requests *not* to buy GameBoys and Barbies for her child. It's your prerogative to do this—they are, after all, *your* kids. But also keep in mind that these relatives really do love your kids—and that they love you too, most likely.

Give the relatives ideas for acceptable toys along with the suggestion of "adventure gifts," like going out for tea, a trip to a museum, a picnic, a hike or other outing, and similar special experiences.

Laural Ringler points to a positive aspect of the problem of unsupportive relatives. She says she and husband Tom Caldwell have been modeling "less is more" for the last decade. "We're converting our families to the fun of it!"

THE BIRTHDAY PARTY PUZZLE

"Over the top" kids' birthday celebrations are another big peer pressure issue for many simple families, particularly those living in high income areas. I heard on National Public Radio about a child's birthday party where guests were invited to a sleepover *at an FAO Schwarz store.* Along with party games, food, and toy demonstrations, each guest received a pound of candy and a $100 gift certificate to spend at the store (the birthday kid's "take" was even higher). The party cost thousands of dollars.

Whoa! While the folks in Patti Idrobo's neighborhood aren't quite that ostentatious, she still laments the excess. In her town in New Jersey, Patti says, "The custom seems to be that every child, every year, has a party, often in a place like a gymnastics school, bowling [alley], zoo, Chuck E. Cheese, et cetera, serving pizza or another meal. If there is anyone who does not do this, they are 'invisible'—I have not seen them." Often the child's entire class is invited, resulting in way too many gifts. And extras—like clowns, magicians, even ponies!—are common.

"I just don't think such extravagance is necessary to

show children how special they are to us," says Patti. "If it is not necessary, then why do it—what will they expect for an encore?"

Her response has been to stick to her guns. This year Patti threw backyard parties for her two daughters, with cake and ice cream—and lots of fun. The guests decorated cloth bags that Patti had assembled, turning them into "snack bags" for school. (The kids at her daughters' school are required to have midmorning snacks brought in a separate bag; Patti figured she'd give them an environmentally friendly alternative *and* a fun activity in the process.)

Several of the parents I interviewed mentioned the ever-expanding expectations regarding gifts for the birthday kid. It's not uncommon, they say, for the gifts to be valued at twenty dollars—and up. The kids who bring the more reasonably priced presents inevitably feel a little awkward. And certainly the birthday boy or girl doesn't really need all of this excess.

Brook Thornton of Yorktown, Virginia, points out another birthday party aspect that many downshifted parents detest—"goody bags." "Why do kids need to have a present because they went to a party? Isn't being invited enough?" queries Brook.

Patti Idrobo is trying to spark a dialogue with a goal of downscaling these annual events. She's begun to talk with other like-minded parents about offering an alternative for those who are tired of elaborate gatherings but feel pressured to continue them.

So far, Patti has called her concept "Celebrations of Value—Honoring People and Their Values," which she envisions working like this: Those families wishing to participate would send invitations that indicate, "This is a 'Celebration of Value' Party." The invitations would then state, "The birthday boy (or girl) requests no gifts. If you feel you'd like to provide a gift, please consider a donation to a worthy organization." The gatherings themselves would be scaled-down, cake-and-ice cream affairs, with a focus on homemade fun versus laser tag and pony rides.

(Note: Adults can also participate, as I did on my last birthday. Not everyone honored my request but several did and I had the honor of sending in almost $200 in donations to my favorite overseas relief group.)

Obviously, participating in a "Celebration of Value" would require a heart-to-heart talk with your children. Not all kids would be interested, but some would. And that's where you start . . .

Patti's proactive efforts provide a prototype of how simple living parents can handle societal forces that undermine simple living. She's not just dealing with the cultural peer pressure issue herself, she's joining with others to help them—and all parents—address the birthday party issue. Bravo, Patti!

Tactics for Our Kids

Everything said in the adult tactics section could be repeated here, but with this significant caveat: Most kids are essentially bystanders—even spectators—in our efforts to live simply. They're not living simply, for the most part, because they've made the decision that it's the right thing to do—we've *told* them that it's the right thing to do. We hope they're adopting our perspective as they grow, but their values and worldviews are not fully formed. So they likely haven't nearly the commitment to the cause that many of us parents have.

Your family's values and those emerging values of your children are nonetheless crucial in responding to peer pressure. This is a recurring theme among parenting experts. The very definition of peer pressure—to allow others to dictate our goals and values and therefore our actions—implies that the strength of the family's values is pivotal. Performing the values clarification asked of you in Chapter 2 is crucial, then, in helping your kids deal with the compulsion to conform. Having your children participate in that effort is also important.

Communicate your values to your kids and help them to discern their own beliefs, but don't forget that they're still *kids*. Especially as they get older—during those adolescent, "separating from Mom and Dad and becoming my own person" years—they will feel a strong pull from their peers. (See "The Teen Years" on page 165.)

HELPING OUR KIDS TO KNOW, AND LIKE, THEMSELVES

Authentic self-esteem is one of the most important tools we can help our kids acquire: authentic, meaning it's not false—for example, based on wearing the latest clothes, owning a PlayStation 2 or a color-coordinated cell phone—but rather, based on the child's own intimate understanding of himself. Jan Anderson, a simple living mother of five from Clearview, Washington, says that "the more comfortable the child is with himself, then the more he's able to deal with peer pressure and cultural influences." True for adults; true for kids.

Rhonda Ramos is a simple living mom who happens to have a master's degree in child development. Rhonda says that children need to have an "internal dialogue that says 'do the right thing.' If a child does not have this self-esteem, the voices of doubt about themselves will win out and they will be willing to engage in behaviors that are unhealthy, to see if it makes them feel better about themselves."

Self-knowledge is another trait we can help our kids acquire. Kathleen Murphy gives this example of how her six-year-old's self-knowledge helps her deal with peer pressure: "I asked her if she felt any need to get Barbies or Pokémon because the other kids have them, and she looked at me as if I were nuts. Her response: 'How can I want something if I don't like it?' "

I love this example! To me it goes to the heart of the peer pressure issue. Alison's response, "How can I want something if I don't like it?" says it all: If your child knows herself well enough and trusts herself, that self-knowledge will support her through many peer pressure situations.

Karen Schneider-Chen's teenage daughters tell her that they don't really feel peer pressure. When I asked Karen why, she said, "I really believe it's because they have a strong sense of themselves, of what they like and what they don't like. That self-confidence girds them against outside influences."

How do we help our kids acquire self-esteem and self-knowledge? Rhonda Ramos says both of these traits are cultivated by teaching kids autonomy and by fostering creativity. Autonomy, according to Rhonda, "is more than the ability to do a task; it is the attitude of 'I can do it!' as well. Children need as much autonomy as is developmentally appropriate for them."

Creativity, says Rhonda, comes from allowing children "to bloom in their own way and to express themselves uniquely." Give them plenty of "open-ended" art supplies— not coloring books, notes Rhonda. She also recommends that kids be allowed to solve problems on their own, using their own logic, without adult direction. She adds that kids need "time and space to contemplate in order to know who they are becoming."

Simplicity is a giant step in the right direction. By eliminating much of the excess—particularly commercial excess— from our lives and our kids' lives, we're setting the stage for their journey of self-discovery. We can give them the "time and space" they need to really know themselves. As part of that unstructured time, we can foster their creativity through art, music, dance, and drama. See Chapters 11 and 12 for more information on these tactics.

ACCEPTANCE OF SELF—AND OTHERS

By modeling and talking with our kids about self-acceptance, we help them acquire this important trait. This means that *we parents* need to accept ourselves first. Be good to yourself! Enjoy your life as a downshifter! This will have a *huge* impact on your kids.

How we treat others also greatly impacts our kids. If they see us treating others according to their social status, they'll pick up on it. And the message we'll be sending is the opposite of the one we want to give. We'll be telling our kids that they *are* how much money they make, the profession that they practice, the house they live in, the car they drive. Go out of your way to treat others fairly, regardless of their outside appearances. Your kids will absorb the important value that all human beings deserve respect, themselves included.

DISCUSSION AND ROLE PLAYING

Unless you plan to raise your kids on a deserted island, they will occasionally encounter peer pressure. Forewarned is forearmed. Talk with your children about what peer pressure is and how they can deal with it.

Lisa Cunningham's two daughters seemed immune to peer pressure until they began school. Then, Lisa says, she began to see "the effects of commercialism creep in," like the Furbies and Barbies kids brought for "show and tell." (Good grief! Shouldn't teachers say *no* to that one?)

"My main line of defense," says Lisa, "has been to talk, talk, talk about it—why it is that I reject most commercial messages—and hold the line."

Brenda Scearcy put her daughter off when she wanted one of those robotic dogs that were introduced a while back. Instead, Brenda asked daughter Larkin to report back to her on how long her friends who had similar toys actually kept playing with them. "She confirmed that [these toys] sit in their closets now," says Brenda, "and she was glad she hadn't wasted her birthday wish on one of them."

Patti Idrobo actually "role-plays" the typical peer pressure scenarios with her kids. She asks them how they would react if . . . "I might say to them, 'What would you do if someone said to you your sneakers are not as good as theirs because theirs are brand name sneakers?' Then we talk about it."

Role-playing is a wonderful tool for helping kids anticipate and prepare for awkward peer pressure moments. If this technique works as a therapy technique and as a training tool for executives, we can certainly employ it informally to help our kids.

Another—major—factor in peer pressure is the impact of television viewing. Television and its impacts are addressed in Chapter 9.

COMMUNITIES FOR KIDS

A community of like-minded—and like-valued—peers is important for kids, just as it is for adults. Sending your child to schools that will complement your simple values is a huge help in combating peer pressure. As with the support groups and simplicity circles mentioned above, the peer pressure at these schools can become a positive force. "Sending kids to alternative schools is the biggest thing in having them adopt those [simple] values," claims Cecile Andrews. Her kids attended Orca Elementary in Seattle, Washington, which Andrews describes as focusing on the arts and the environment. The values taught there of simple living, respect for the earth, and an emphasis on art made a lifelong impression on her kids: They still live simply at ages thirty-one and thirty-two. Other parents send their kids to private Waldorf or Montessori schools, both of which have teachings that are in keeping with many simplified families' values. See "The Montessori and Waldorf Philosophies" on page 244.

Home-schooling (or unschooling) your kids is another primary way in which simple families avoid many peer pressure issues. Sara Robinson cites peer pressure as the main reason she decided to home-school her two kids. Her daughter was in second grade at the time, and Sara recalls that her "girlfriends' main topics of discussion were: who was on a diet, who was prettiest, who had the coolest clothes, whose parents were richest. At the age of seven!" Michael Fogler, whose son Ben, thirteen, is unschooled, notes that "he has far less peer pressure than kids who go to school." Educational choices are discussed in greater detail in Chapter 15.

If a school where simple values are taught is not a possibility for you, and home schooling doesn't work for you for whatever reason, you can find alternative groups that complement your simple lifestyle. Often, simple living parents join churches precisely because they want their kids exposed to some simple values. If you're a member of a church, you can take the initiative to start a youth group that emphasizes environmental and simple values. Other parents find that scout groups, particularly with their focus on nature, can be a reinforcement for simple values. Volunteer opportunities are also good ways to connect with like-minded folks.

Some schools have opportunities such as the Roots and Shoots program through the auspices of the Jane Goodall Institute. (See Chapter 14 for more information.)

Parents can and should lobby for schools to include courses in simplicity, media literacy, and the like, helping to create some of that positive peer pressure.

Kids can also log on to www.generationfix.com for "virtual support" from the forums provided there. This site was created by Elizabeth Rusch, author of *Generation Fix: Young Ideas for a Better World,* and is geared to kids ages 8 to 16 who want to do something about problems they see in their communities and across the globe. Topics covered include many simplicity-related themes including the environment, hunger, and homelessness.

Family Study Circles

Cecile Andrews believes that if the parents are part of a simplicity circle, the very existence of that group will impact the kids positively. "The kids may be off to the side but they're hearing the grown-ups talk, even if there's no separate program for the kids," she says, sort of an osmosis approach.

She also feels that if simplicity circles work for adults, they can work for families too. Your own nuclear family could be the setting for a "family simplicity circle." Andrews recommends that parents use *The Family Virtues Guide* by Linda Kavelin Popov as the basis for a study circle with the kids. Janet Luhrs, author of *The Simple Living Guide,* has used this approach with her two kids, holding weekly "virtues meetings" at which she and the kids discuss different virtues like kindness, compassion, and honesty. "It gives the kids a grounding," Luhrs believes.

Participating in a family simplicity circle reinforces those beliefs contained in your Family Values and Vision Statement. As noted above, experts agree that this strategy is crucial in combating peer pressure.

Varied Peer Groups

Another important facet of communities for kids is that they not be entirely composed of peers of the same age, ethnicity, and socioeconomic status.

Connecting with grandparents and other older relatives is one example. By such contact, children learn—or are reminded, as they get older—that senior citizens have much to offer, including their time, patience, and knowledge of "the way things were." With these multigenerational communities, kids have a separate reference group besides their school friends with which to identify.

Exposure to other cultures is another way to broaden a child's peer base. Some simple families live in diverse communities; others attend local cultural festivals; a few are able to travel.

A fantastic opportunity for families is to take a "volunteer vacation." Sponsored by groups like Habitat for Humanity and the Sierra Club, these trips combine doing good with fun, travel, family bonding, and exposure to other cultures. One simple living family I spoke with signed up for a three-week stint with Global Volunteers, helping to construct a bridge in Costa Rica. Their son was thirteen at the time and had started to pick up some of his peers' attitudes. His volunteer experience made a huge difference. According to his mother, "he became more conscious of what he had and what he took for granted."

Age minimums for children vary with the organization and the specific project; there are more opportunities as kids get older. See the "Resources" section for more information.

If travel is not feasible, pen pals are a fun way for kids to learn about and appreciate other cultures, and to understand their own better. One possibility is the Children Just Like Me Penpal Club. Another is the Kids Media Club. See "Resources" for details.

THE TEEN YEARS

Peer pressure and adolescence are nearly synonymous. All of us can recall teenage fads, and just plain juvenile *behavior,* that we succumbed to. My examples at the beginning of this chapter—Monkee mania, wearing "go-go" boots, smoking the cigarette—all occurred once I'd hit adolescence.

So here's the warning: Just because you live simply—even if you start when your kids are in (cloth!) diapers and do "all the right stuff"—you may likely feel deep frustration once your kids become teenagers, or even preteens, when "fitting in" becomes painfully important. Our kids *will* be pressured to blend into our materialistic culture. A large part of that "fitting in" will be of a commercial nature.

I interviewed a number of families with teens and older children. Almost all indicated that the teen years were challenging and that watching their kids become more and more influenced by commercialism was particularly agonizing. Even parents of kids who'd been home-schooled found this to be true. Michael Fogler, who home-schooled son Benjamin, discovered that at age thirteen his son began asking for Nintendo, cable television, and other consumer items. "These notions just seem to be in the water," admits Michael.

But here's the good news: I didn't find any of these parents to be completely pessimistic about what the ultimate outcome would be for their kids. David Sweet, father of two teenage sons, was typical: "It's hard for kids to see the whole picture, how it's all related. It's a rare teenager that pulls it all together." He acknowledged the setbacks but voiced optimism: "My feeling is that they'll come to see the value of simplicity eventually." Michael Fogler feels similarly: "My prediction is that our example will have some lasting impression."

I also spoke with several of the teenagers of simple living families, and it was clear that they had assimilated many of their parents' simple values. For example, Kat Wilson, age sixteen, says that among her values are "respecting every being's right to pursue happiness" and "living with minimal impact on the planet." Travis Rhoad, a fourteen-year-old from Texas, is another simple-valued teen. Travis noted that his parents "are not big into owning a lot of things. They don't care what the neighbors have that we don't have. I learned from them about wants versus needs. If I really want something, I save for it and buy it." Another teen, Suzanna Chen, sounded to me like a mature, simple living adult when she said, "It's important to live up to your own standards, not those of other people."

Having noted these encouraging results, I need to add here that your child may not end up adopting simple values. After all, they are their own people and they'll ultimately need to make those decisions for themselves. Fortunately, growing up in a simple family will have a huge impact on them. Our kids are very likely to adopt our values, particularly when those values are articulated and made clear and when the family actually practices what it preaches—an admittedly rare event in our culture.

We won't really know, however, until they're adults. In the meantime, here's advice from the teen trenches:

1. REMEMBER THAT YOU ARE IMPORTANT TO YOUR TEENS

Child development specialist David Elkind notes in his book about the teen years, *All Grown Up and No Place to Go,* that "parents are the single most powerful, nonbiological influence on their children's lives." It's easy to forget this fundamental truth during the teen years. Especially during early adolescence, when conforming seems to be the number one rule of conduct, we may overlook our very important roles as our children's mentors, teachers, and spiritual counselors. This is the period when our children bridge the gap between childhood and adulthood—and they really *do* need our guidance. Our involvement really *does* make a difference.

2. KEEP ON DOING WHAT YOU'VE BEEN DOING, ADJUSTED TO THE CHILD'S AGE

All of the tactics mentioned throughout this book about bringing kids along on the simple route apply to teens too— for example, communicating and modeling, helping your kids acquire self-knowledge and self-esteem, and acceptance of self and others.

An example of adjusting a tactic to your kid's age is, instead of reading picture books to them, to leave simplicity-related newspaper articles, magazines, and books lying around. One mom mentioned that she subscribes to *Adbusters* magazine (see "Resources" at the end of Chapter 8) and that her kids often pick it up and browse through it. *Utne Reader* and *Mother Jones* also come to mind as likely candidates for strategic placement, unbeknownst to your teens, on the coffee table or in the breakfast nook.

Another example is to elevate the discussion of commercialism and continue modeling and teaching media literacy. For example, tell your kids what you think of your city's plan to rename the municipal stadium after one of its corporate sponsors—and ask what *they* think. Continue to critique and comment on advertisements and other commercial presences. Simple living mom Rose Marie Cordello says: "Teens need to be able to deconstruct this consumer culture to make sense of it."

3. KEEP FAMILY VALUES AT THE FOREFRONT

Your teens will encounter situations where their internal compasses on what is right and wrong will be tested. Their ability to "do the right thing" will depend upon the strength and clarity of their family's values.

Taking the time to formulate a Values Statement (Chapter 2) and then periodically reviewing it is crucial. Continuing to observe family rituals like Family Night (see Chapter 12) is also important. And modeling a life that is in sync with your values is essential. Teens need this values foundation to help them make the right decisions.

4. FIND SUPPORT FOR YOUR TEENS
AND THEIR SIMPLE LIFESTYLES

If your teens attend a mainstream public school or a heavily commercialized private school, consider helping them find communities of similarly valued peers—through church groups, Roots and Shoots programs, your own family—as explained in this chapter.

5. ENJOY YOUR SIMPLE LIFE

"It seems cliché," says Rose Marie Cordello, "but if your teenagers see you happy, then they're going to understand simplicity better." Rose Marie adds that she feels this was an important factor in her own daughter adopting a simple lifestyle as an adult.

6. HELP YOUR TEENAGERS
FIND THEIR "PASSION"

One of the fulcrums of living simply is finding something that you love to do. This is true for kids too. Help your kids discover their passion—music, art, sports, math, animals—whatever it might be. This is a major factor in a child acquiring self-knowledge and self-esteem; having those traits will assist your teen in resisting negative peer pressure.

7. REMEMBER THAT THIS TOO SHALL PASS

Several parents pointed to an encouraging sign. They discovered that, while middle schools and junior highs are hotbeds of peer pressure, by high school kids often "find themselves" a bit and are less influenced by the materialism around them. One mom said, "Walk down the halls of a middle school and *everyone* looks the same. Conformity is king. By high school they've begun to follow their own lead more."

The bottom line, say many of these parents, is that you have to do the best you can—and hope. The strategies outlined in this chapter will assist you in helping your kids cope with negative peer pressure while creating positive, supportive communities. It will then be up to them to determine how they'll live their lives.

Resources

COHOUSING

The Cohousing Network: www.cohousing.org. General information on cohousing and directory of cohousing communities across North America.

Chris Hanson. *The Cohousing Handbook: Building a Place for Community* (Point Roberts, Washington: Hartley & Marks Publishers, 1996).

Kathryn McCamant, Ellen Hertzman, and Charles Durrett. *Cohousing* (Berkeley, California: Ten Speed Press, 1993).

HELP FINDING TRADITIONAL SUPPORT GROUP MEMBERS

www.attachmentparenting.org: (615) 298–4334. Attachment Parenting International; coalition of individuals and organizations advocating attachment parenting methods; has support group startup assistance.

www.simpleliving.net

www.simplicitycircles.com

PEN PALS

Children Just Like Me Penpal Club, DK Publishing, 95 Madison Avenue, New York, NY 10016.

E-Pals: www.epals.com. Classrooms can register here for "cyber pen pals."

Kids Media Club: www.kidsmc.com. Pen pals from around the world.

SIMPLICITY STUDY COURSES/RESOURCES

Cecile Andrews. *The Circle of Simplicity: Return to the Good Life* (New York: HarperCollins, 1997).

Mark Burch. *Simplicity Study Circles: A Step-by-Step Guide* (Philadelphia: New Society Publishers, 1997).

Global Action Plan: www.globalactionplan.org; (845) 679–4830. EcoTeam website.

The New Road Map Foundation: www.newroadmap.org; download group study guide for *Your Money or Your Life* or order print copy for $5.00.

The Northwest Earth Institute: www.nwei.org; (503) 227–2807. Voluntary Simplicity and Deep Ecology courses among others. (NWEI also has fourteen different "sister earth institutes" around the country.)

SIMPLICITY-RELATED PUBLICATIONS
Mother Jones, 800/439-6656; www.motherjones.com
Utne Reader, 800/736-UTNE; www.utne.com

VIRTUAL SUPPORT GROUPS FOR KIDS
www.generationfix.com. Website for kids ages 8 to 16 who have "ideas for a better world." Includes discussion boards and live chats on subjects ranging from hunger and homelessness to violence and discrimination.

VIRTUAL SUPPORT GROUP WEBSITES
www.caelumetterra.com. Simple living support for "counter-culture" Catholics.
www.ipj-ppj.org. Parenting for Peace and Justice website. Includes discussion boards along with other information.
www.mothering.com
www.newdream.org
www.parentsoup.com
www.simplcliving.net
www.unschooling.com; for homeschoolers.

VOLUNTEER VACATIONS
Cross Cultural Solutions: www.crossculturalsolutions.org; (800) 380–4777, ext.300.
Earthwatch: www.earthwatch.org; (800) 776–0188.
Global Citizens' Network: www.globalcitizens.org; (800) 644–9292.
Global Volunteers: www.globalvolunteers.org; (800) 487–1074.
Habitat for Humanity: www.habitat.org; (800) 422–4828, ext. 2549.
Sierra Club Outings: www.sierraclub.org/outings; (415) 977–5522.

Bill McMillon. *Volunteer Vacations* (Chicago: Chicago Review Press, 1998).

OTHERS

David Elkind. *All Grown Up and No Place to Go* (Cambridge, Massachusetts: Perseus Books, 1998).

Linda Kavelin Popov. *The Family Virtues Guide* (New York: Plume, 1997).

11

Human Beings—or Human Doings?

In 1981 the first edition of *The Hurried Child* was published. Written by child development expert David Elkind, *The Hurried Child* warned parents of the problems associated with hurrying our kids, expecting them to grow up too fast by over-scheduling them with a wide range of classes, sports practices, and games; exposing them to age-inappropriate media, music, and clothing; and subjecting them to repeated testing at ever younger ages. Elkind "outed" the problem of the pressure on kids for early intellectual and physical achievement and the consequent failure to give kids a childhood.

Twenty years later Elkind is back with his third edition of the book and he warns us that the problem has worsened. "Parents are under more pressure than ever to overschedule their children," he reports. He also emphasizes that overtesting in public schools, media pressures, and the marketing of violence to kids have all escalated.

I'm sure you know what Elkind is referring to. You see it everywhere. A classic example for me was the mother I spoke with recently who was lamenting about having failed to sign her child up for a particular gymnastics class that had then filled. It was taught by a noted professional, she pointed out, and would have been a great opportunity for her youngster. She was psychologically kicking herself for having lost the opportunity, and wondered if she was a bad parent for failing her child in this manner.

The saddest part about this little anecdote is that the child in question was only two years old.

Many parents reading this will recognize the scenario as one they've witnessed—or perhaps even been a party to—countless times. The problem of overpressuring and over-scheduling has reached crisis proportions for some American families. I know of a family who has their child signed up for two different sports (with practice and game nights), music *and* dance lessons, and an art class—all taking place weekly—plus monthly scout meetings. Not only is it unlikely that this is a good thing for the child in question, but as more and more parents overbook their kids, it leads other parents to question whether—by *not* scrambling to sign their kids up for every activity offered—they're somehow neglecting them and ensuring that their future college applications will be rejected.

It becomes a vicious cycle, so much so that Elkind added a section in his 2001 edition of *The Hurried Child* on "peer-group parent pressure," noting that parents feel forced to enroll their kids in sports and other classes partly just to guarantee that they'll have playmates.

Many of us thirty-something and forty-something parents look back at our own childhoods and think, "Whoa, have things changed!" Growing up in the sixties, I recall virtually no sports offerings for girls, outside of P.E. I did take piano lessons, I was a Brownie and then a Girl Scout for a few years, and I used to drop in at the local parks department summer "arts and crafts" sessions. But that was the extent of it. I never even went to summer camp.

I think I can truthfully say that maybe a little more "enrichment" could have done me some good. Ours was a small town, and exposure to the arts, literature, and culture was limited. I might have discovered some things about myself that have taken me decades to unearth.

But now, it seems, we've gone to the other extreme. Even the limited amount of formal extras my kids have had thus far in their lives is well beyond anything that even the most over-scheduled kids of the sixties and seventies were exposed to in our little hamlet. Today's kids have access to a seemingly unlimited smorgasbord of camps and classes, not just in the summer, but year-round. The temptation, particularly for parents who work full-time, is to sign them up for everything without ever really considering the consequences.

"Successful" Kids—and Parents

A major force in the endless pushing of our children is our country's obsession with success, and, indeed, our very definition of success. Most parents have never truly considered what success means for themselves or their kids, but have blindly accepted a materialistic American version of this concept. Our eyes are on the prize as we parent—and the prize is the "best" college and, ultimately, a plum, high-paying, executive or professional position, rather than the reward of raising happy, well-adjusted, caring, and responsible individuals, without regard to their social status. (Isn't it interesting that this major cause for our hurrying of our kids goes to the very heart of why folks are choosing to simplify?)

Many parents are so focused on their children getting into a prestigious university, or perhaps being the next Tiger Woods, that they start priming them for their college applications in preschool and buy them pint-size golf clubs at age three. By the time they're freshmen in high school, they're taking their first—of several—college admissions tests, and soon afterward they're signing up for SAT prep classes to the tune of several hundred dollars. Kids are viewed more as products to be improved upon than children that need our love, guidance, and unhurried time to develop.

Here's more evidence that we're too focused on producing "successful kids": According to a recent *U.S. News & World Report* article, more than 40 percent of the school districts in the country have either dropped recess or are considering doing so. Why? The pressure to find more instructional time to boost achievement scores. Fun is out; achievement is in.

In her book *Creating Balance in Your Child's Life*, Beth Saavedra calls upon parents to resist this temptation to "commoditize" their kids, to instead help them keep their "core identities" intact. She reasons that "if our children's identities

WHAT IS CHILDHOOD FOR?

Rhonda Ramos, the mother of two with a master's degree in child development, feels that childhood should be a "safe harbor," a period to grow and learn those things needed for adult life. "Childhood should be a time to feel safe and nurtured," she says, "so that the child's self-esteem is built up to the point of the child being ready for the world in which they live."

Hurrying our children—pushing them to take on more than they're developmentally ready for—is anathema to this goal. It runs counter to the "safe harbor" idea, that childhood is a time for nurturance, protection, and education.

By not sheltering children from adult information—from television and movies to music and websites—and by imposing nearly adult expectations on them, we've transformed our kids' early years into a kind of hybrid child/adulthood. One need look no further than the current explosion of elementary school–age Britney Spears look-alikes to understand this phenomenon. Childhood is no longer a unique period, according to some experts. We've put adultlike pressures on our kids that they're not yet equipped to handle.

and feelings of self-worth are too closely tied to performance and externally measurable success, their true selves will be obscured, and, over the long run, they may lose sight of who they are, inside."

Parents need to keep their "core identities" intact too, to help them resist the temptation to become adult human doings. Otherwise, they can become obsessed with pursuit of "success, American style"—putting in long hours, resulting in the need for their kids to be occupied. Our overscheduling of ourselves then becomes both a cause and a separate problem.

This pressure to "overdo" is bad for adults—and worse for kids. "Overscheduling is developmentally inappropriate for children and can cause them a great deal of stress as well," Rhonda Ramos emphasizes. Furthermore, when we overschedule our kids "we run the risk of obscuring their individual identities with an overabundance of activities, and the child can become lost," according to author Beth Saavedra.

Downshifting parents acknowledge the temptation to "overdo." Cathy Harris is a mother of three who is trying to simplify but finding that her kids' activities have almost taken on a life of their own. "Overscheduling is a problem," she says. "The kids end up feeling tired, stressed, and unhappy, just like an adult would, when they have way too much to do and not enough time for themselves."

Diana Wright of Thetford, Vermont, has also struggled with the lure of after-school activities for her two girls. "We're trying to figure out the dance between providing our kids with new things and not becoming chauffeurs," she says.

Ten Tips for Handling Hurrying

Resisting the temptation to become a human doing takes effort in our culture. Here are a number of methods that downshifted families employ to "unhurry" both parents and kids.

1. CUT BACK YOUR WORK HOURS

This approach is, of course, the simplicity sine qua non for adult members of the family. Cutting back work hours can take many forms: reducing your commuting time, switching to a flextime work schedule, saying no to overtime and to promotions that mean more time and pressure, not taking work home, working fewer hours, even quitting to work from home as an independent contractor/freelancer.

Whether you're able to cut back your hours will depend upon the unique circumstances of your family and your occupation. The details on how to do this can be found in a number of books. *Your Money or Your Life* is a good place to start, as is Michael Fogler's *Un-Jobbing: The Adult Liberation Handbook*.

2. MINDFULLY LIMIT OUTSIDE ACTIVITIES

Limiting your kids' activities is the equivalent of cutting back their "work hours." As you make decisions on which activities to allow and which to drop, you'll need to ask yourself if the sport or lesson in question is in keeping with your beliefs and your child's needs. This may be a time when you'll want to refer to your Family Values and Vision Statement. Ask yourself: "Is this activity in sync with my values? Will this program help develop those values I hope to encourage in my kids? Is this how I want my family to spend its time? Is my goal for my child to foster an interest in a subject or skill or to push her to overdo, to overachieve?"

Linda McDonough's six-year-old daughter wanted to take a dance class, but Linda wasn't sure she wanted a traditional dance experience for her with the requisite costumes and recitals. Linda wanted to keep it simple. She searched and found one without those extras. "I want our extracurricular activities to add to the quality of our lives, not take away from them," says Linda. "So far they have."

LITTLE LEAGUE BLUES

Questioning the wisdom of Little League seems, on its face, almost un-American. But a growing number of experts are doing just that. David Elkind believes that Little League, and other organized sports for kids, with their adult-imposed schedules and rules, can take the joy out of playing.

Opting out of organized sports can be difficult if most, or *all,* of your children's friends are signed up. If your decision is to participate, get involved and lobby for a relaxed approach, for example, one practice and one game a week, and a "have fun" versus a "let's win" attitude. If you decide to forgo the organized play route, look for other like-minded families for "pick up" games. Finding a sport that the whole family can enjoy, like tennis, biking, or badminton, is another option.

The very least you can do is *mindfully* contemplate why you're signing your children up. Experts also recommend that you consider waiting a few years, say until second or third grade, before suiting Junior up in cleats and jockstraps. Finally, think long and hard about opting for "classic" or "premier" soccer, a costly and competitive year-round version of that sport complete with professional coaches, multiple practice and game nights, and, often, cross-state travel.

Most downshifted families have a rule of one or two activities—sports, music, dance, et cetera—at a time or per "season." Often this rule will go from one to two as the child gets a bit older. By limiting the number of outside activities your kids—and you—engage in, you're both safeguarding family time and ensuring that all members of your family won't become overwhelmed. Lynne Cantwell notes, "I have always limited my kids to two activities at a time. It keeps us all sane!"

Rusty and Kate Rhoad of The Woodlands, Texas, also restrict their three kids' extracurricular activities. "All three take piano lessons and they can each participate in one sport at a time," says Kate.

Recognizing that adults can get overscheduled too, Kate and Rusty are vigilant about not overextending themselves. Kate points out that "not having so much going on in our lives frees up a lot of time."

Janet Luhrs, author of *The Simple Living Guide* and mother of two teenagers, falls back on the concept of "conscious balance" when making decisions about extra activities for her kids and herself. "Conscious balance means that I am fully aware of my motivation for making choices," she says. "If the choice is based on insecurity, I look hard at the insecurity." The general rule—for *all* family members—adopted many years ago is that they only schedule activities before dinner, except occasionally. Decisions on extra activities are made based upon whether the activity is important enough—and in keeping with their values enough—that it should override their value of having time together as a family.

It should also be noted that kids don't necessarily have to take a class to learn about a subject. Sometimes Mom or Dad or another relative or friend may have expertise, or just an interest, in a topic and they can help the child learn more. Or the child can take the issue on as a research activity. Visiting museums and historical sites can also substitute for formal classes. You'll have time to do more of these things for and with your child if you've simplified.

3. LISTEN TO YOUR CHILD

When trying to decide which classes and how many sports or other activities to sign your kids up for, follow your child's lead. This seems to be a no-brainer, but many parents really do push their kids to do things that they're not inclined to do. Many times this is well intentioned, as in, "I know they'll love it if they just try." Certainly in some circumstances it might make sense to prod a kid to take a class, say, if a counselor or teacher advises it. But generally speaking, kids will know what they want.

Debbie Newman, who has two children, follows "the

kids' leads as to what interests them, and we don't pressure them to always have something going on."

The "limit activities" rule (number 2, above) can sometimes conflict with the "listen to your child" rule. My thinking is that the "limit activities" rule should take precedence. We violated our own activity limit rule one spring when we allowed one son to sign up for both soccer and baseball—and we regretted it. Between practice and game nights for both sports, and soccer for the other son, Sunday became our only sports-free day. We won't make that mistake again.

4. MODEL AN UNHURRIED LIFESTYLE FOR YOUR KIDS

This is related to the first two strategies—that is, it's easier to have a relaxed approach if both parents aren't working full-time and overextended with other activities. If you're working many hours, make efforts to leave your work at the office and to find unstructured time for yourself and your family. Parents must also ensure that they have adequate quiet and downtime for themselves (see tips 7 and 8). By doing so, you'll model these practices for your kids—and keep your sanity in the process.

HELP YOUR KIDS FOCUS MORE ON LIVING, LESS ON ACHIEVING

John Andersen, a simple living dad of two, tries to model a deliberate pace for his kids. He urges parents to encourage their kids to put less emphasis on achieving.

"We need to find ways to help our children think more in terms of enjoying life rather than feeling they always need to achieve something," he says. "The achievement mentality can open doors, but it also has a very negative downside. I see far too many adults who let it get the best of them. They forget how to play, to relax, to take in the grandeur of each and every moment. That's no good in my book."

Nor in mine.

5. USE A LARGE, PROMINENTLY DISPLAYED CALENDAR TO RECORD ALL FAMILY AND INDIVIDUAL COMMITMENTS

Neither my husband nor I are superorganized types. That's why the enormous monthly calendar on our refrigerator is so valuable. We're able to keep track of everyone's activities pretty painlessly.

But it's also a great help in seeing when we've overcommitted. Having a visual reminder of how crowded a week looks amounts to a warning system that we need to slow down.

6. GUARD FAMILY TIME

One of the commitments you'll want to note on your calendar is special family time. Many simplified families designate one night weekly as Family Night; others set aside an entire day each week as Family Day.

Your special family time may instead be your practice of eating together every night, taking walks after dinner, or enjoying Saturday morning pancake breakfasts. Rituals help to protect precious family time and make it special and important for children. Chapter 12 has more information on how to integrate rituals into your family life.

7. PROVIDE QUIET TIME

All of us, kids *and* adults, need more peace and quiet. Amen! But developmentally, kids are in even greater need of solitude. Jane M. Healy in *Endangered Minds* says that a developing brain "needs time and quiet space in which to develop the ability to manage itself . . . a child's mind should be furnished with some pieces of quiet thought, not the tacky trappings of constant noise."

Make sure that your schedule includes these quiet moments. My younger son's first-grade teacher had a daily

SQUIRT period: **S**uper **Q**uiet **U**n**I**nterrupted **R**eading **T**ime. We adopted this ritual a few years back, designating a half hour (almost) every weeknight as a peaceful reading period.

8. SUPPLY AMPLE "DOWNTIME"

In addition to actual quiet, we need "downtime," time to "chill," pet the cat, gaze at clouds. Jill Jordan, who has two young sons, Chris and Thomas, wisely explains that "kids need 'downtime,' time to dream and play and just 'be.' So do adults! All this pressure to 'do' stuff leads to the misperception that you're not really living unless you are 'producing' all the time. But so much busyness leads to overconsumption and no time to savor the intangibles, such as relationships."

Those relationships can flourish with enough downtime. When we slow down with our kids, we relax, our tempo decelerates to an unhurried "kid pace," and we acquire the time and patience to *really* listen to them. This is good for us; after all, stress is related to all kinds of medical and emotional problems. It's good for our children too. They feel valued and important when they are truly heard and respected. Their confidence and self-esteem blossom.

9. PROMOTE BOREDOM—AND CREATIVITY!— WITH "DO NOTHING DAYS"

Lisa Cunningham expresses another reason why it's important for kids to have unstructured time: "A certain amount of boredom is good, it leads to creativity."

Lisa is right: Boredom is often a catalyst for creativity. To be truly creative, one can't be rushed. This is true for both kids and adults. In fact, a large body of psychological research concludes that downtime is needed for the three "i"s: inspiration, imagination, and innovation.

These unstructured blocks of time occur naturally, particularly in the summer, if you've cut back on other commitments. If yours is a busy family or you just want to ensure some uninterrupted hours, you may need to actually schedule a "Do Nothing Day," or at least a "Do Nothing" afternoon, occasionally. Pencil it in on your family calendar. You could use the morning for chores/errands and then parents and kids are free to do . . . nothing. Family members may end up actually doing *something*, for example, reading, playing catch, or tackling a jigsaw puzzle, but doing nothing is completely acceptable. "Activities" like lounging on the porch swing or hammock, peering off into the distance, and daydreaming are to be encouraged. (It goes without saying here that television viewing, web surfing, and the like are, however, *not* acceptable.)

Home is the best place for a "Do Nothing" event; familiar surroundings will help you and the kids relax.

According to author Beth Saavedra, these unstructured blocks of time can lead to a sort of *focused* downtime that she calls "real time," when creativity, among other conditions, can flourish.

Real time encompasses presence, attention, and authenticity. Real-time activities vary greatly, says Saavedra. She notes that artistic expression, playing music, arranging flowers, prayer circles, even rocking in a chair, can all involve real time. She describes real time as "anything that brings you and your children's attention to a one-pointed focus."

If you must require *some* productive element to downtime, "Do Nothing Days," and "real time," consider this: Creativity often precedes academic achievement. Studies indicate that both listening to music and performing it stimulates spatial intelligence and synaptic development in children. Schools that focus on the arts routinely produce academically excellent students. Art programs even reduce dropout rates.

10. LET THEM BE KIDS

The bottom line is that we must allow our children to have full and happy childhoods. This rule is especially pertinent when it comes to age-inappropriate fads and activities, such as letting young girls dress like mini-adults and permitting preschoolers to watch R-rated movies. In fact, limiting unsuitable media is a means and an end in allowing kids to just be kids: They'll be exposed to less junk and they'll be less likely to mimic what they *don't* see and hear. (See Chapters 8 and 9 for a full discussion on this.)

Shelby Pawlina, a preschool teacher and mother, eloquently sums up the antidote to hurrying: "Contrary to popular belief, young children do not need extra classes, computers, television, or fast-tracked schooling. They need time to play with natural things, with real people, in fresh air. Everything follows from there."

Resources

William J. Doherty. *The Intentional Family: How to Build Family Ties in Our Modern World* (Reading, Massachusetts: Addison-Wesley Publishing, 1997).

William J. Doherty and Barbara Z. Carlson. *Putting Family First* (New York: Henry Holt, 2002).

David Elkind. *The Hurried Child* (Cambridge, Massachusetts: Perseus Publishing, 2001).

Michael Fogler. *Un-Jobbing: The Adult Liberation Handbook* (Lexington, Kentucky: Free Press, 1997).

Jane M. Healy. *Endangered Minds: Why Children Don't Think and What We Can Do About It* (New York: Simon & Schuster, 1990).

Janet Luhrs. *The Simple Living Guide* (New York: Broadway Books, 1997).

Neil Postman. *The Disappearance of Childhood* (New York: Vintage Books, 1994).

Beth Saavedra. *Creating Balance in Your Child's Life* (Lincolnwood, Illinois: Contemporary Books, 1999).

Putting Family First Website: www.puttingfamilyfirst.us. Putting Family First is a group of citizens "building a community where family life is an honored and celebrated priority." Includes information on how to start a "Putting Family First" movement in your area.

❦

12

Simple Pleasures and Family Rituals

When my two sons were about preschool age, my family began a practice that would end up as an endcaring family ritual.

The idea took hold one evening during a fall storm when the power went out. We brought out the candles and kerosene lamps, lit a fire in the fireplace and drew close around the flames, playing board games and reading by the firelight. When the power came back on, the boys didn't want to use the electricity, they wanted to continue our "low tech" experience. So we did—and "Pioneer Night" was born.

After that, every few months my husband or I or one of the boys would say, "Let's have a Pioneer Night!" On Pioneer Nights we don't use any electrical devices; the phone goes unheeded; dinner might be sandwiches or hot dogs roasted—with an eye to safety—over the fire; and candles are de rigueur.

Simplifying allows families to regain control over their time and to choose what activities they really want to participate in. Many families find that the simple activities bring the most pleasure. They also discover that creating family rituals or traditions—like my family's Pioneer Nights—brings the family together in ways that are both enjoyable and memorable.

Simple Pleasures

Simple pleasures are those activities that typically cost no money (or very little) and yet inevitably provide the most genuine delight, the greatest joy.

You know just what I mean: watching clouds go by, gazing at the stars, making snow angels, observing a hill of industrious ants at work, sitting on the porch on a summer's eve while sharing stories, laughing with your best friend over coffee . . . Simple pleasures don't involve high technology, frequently have something to do with nature, and always result in a bit of bliss or a lot of laughter.

In fact, my conclusion is that most simple pleasures are those that people have enjoyed since the beginning of time. I imagine our distant ancestors—cave guys and gals—clustered around the evening campfire, yukking it up, sharing stories they'd heard while hunting and gathering that day.

Simple pleasures are at the core of many downshifted families' daily lives. Roger Meyer, a simple living dad from St. Paul, Minnesota, says that he doesn't believe his daughter, Olive, will feel deprived someday because the family didn't focus on acquiring the latest toys for her. "It's not the *stuff,* the *things* in your life, that you remember when you grow up," he concludes, "it's the people and relationships and fun."

I think Roger is right. I grew up in the sixties as the youngest in a blue-collar family of seven. The other day I sat for a while and tried to remember some of the "stuff"—toys, clothing, et cetera—from my childhood. My mind could only draw a few images to the surface: a chemistry set I asked for and received one Christmas; a "Chatty Cathy" doll, one of the first to talk, by pulling a string; my Scholastic book collection. That's about it.

What I do remember are a host of simple pleasures:

- Huge birthday parties where my mom and aunts made dozens of corn dogs while countless cousins played hide and seek, "swing the statue," and canasta.
- Our pets. We lived on an eight-acre plot a few miles outside of a small town. We had several cats, dogs, bunnies, chickens, and cows. All were important members of our family.
- Playing in our barn.
- Scavenger hunts. (Remember these? Adults prepare a list of common household items, for example, an egg, the newspaper "funnies," an ashtray, a curler, an envelope. Kids team up in groups of two or three and then fan out into the neighborhood, knocking on doors to ask for items. The first group to collect all of them and return home wins.)
- Sliding down the Big Hill on our property—in the winter, on sleds; in the summer, on flattened cardboard boxes.
- A makeshift tree house that my siblings and I built.
- Putting on plays with my sister and my cousins.

It seems that all of my best memories are of simple pleasures. I'm not alone in this! For their book *The Secrets of Strong Families,* authors Nick Stinnet and John DeFrain surveyed 3,000 families. They asked participants to close their eyes and think back to their childhood and recall their happiest memories. Inevitably, their recollections were of doing things with their families, rituals like bedtime stories, family get-togethers and vacations, working on the farm with Dad, playing the piano and singing together.

One of the biggest perks of having kids is the ability to

tap into some of these forgotten joys of childhood, all the while creating lasting, beloved memories for your kids. As with so many aspects of simplicity, it's a win-win situation.

THE NEED FOR PLAY

I just overheard my younger son on the phone with a friend. "Can you come over to play?" he asked.

I love hearing these words! So much so that I've borrowed my sons' lines. I've started asking my friends if they'd like to play. After all, though we cloak our requests as invitations to dinner and suggestions to have a cup of coffee, what we really want and need to do—kids *and* adults—is *play.*

In *The Hurried Child,* David Elkind urges parents to allow their children to play more. "Perhaps the best evidence of the extent to which our children are hurried is the lack of opportunities for genuine play available to them," he says. His concern is that we're forgetting what childhood is really for—a time to nurture and teach our children but also to allow them to be kids—and that we're turning childhood into, in essence, a corporate training ground.

For example, Elkind points to the evolution of summer camp from a generic opportunity to spend some time in the woods to a big business, offering training in nearly every subject imaginable. A recent "summer camp" edition of our local parenting magazine contained these "themed" camps: equestrian, computers, various sports, ballet, gymnastics, theater, even a camp for kids who wanted to learn about the stock market! Elkind notes that this "reflects the new attitude that the years of childhood are not to be frittered away by engaging in activities merely for fun."

More's the pity, he says, because play—that "frittered" time of our lives—is really the antidote to the hurrying of childhood, which causes stress in our kids. Elkind wisely calls play "nature's way of dealing with stress for children as well as adults."

One of our responsibilities as parents, then, is to ensure that our kids have ample opportunity for play—and that we do too. Here are a few of the many ways simple families play together:

Card and Board Games

There are those perennial card game favorites like poker, Crazy Eights, and Go Fish—but the range and diversity of games that can be created from a few decks of cards is staggering. We've used a book called *The Book of Cards for Kids* for new card game ideas. It seems every family we know also has a number of card games to share that we've never heard of.

Board games are another possibility. Again there are those old standbys, like Monopoly, Clue, and Life, among others. Many simple living families find these competitive board games not in keeping with their family values. Others would just appreciate some new options.

Luckily there are alternatives. One source is Family Pastimes (see "Resources" at end of chapter). My family has spent many evenings cooperatively trying to solve mysteries with Family Pastimes' Eagle Eye Detective Agency board game. Another possibility is People of the Planet Game, available through www.realgoods.com. We've also found other "mind games" to be a lot of fun, particularly Taboo (manufactured by Milton Bradley) and Apples to Apples (see "Resources").

Parties, Get-Togethers, and Celebrations

In her book *The Shelter of Each Other,* Mary Pipher says that celebrations protect families. These include the obvious—birthdays and anniversaries—and the not so obvious, like a child learning to ride a bicycle or your nephew going to the state swimming finals. "I don't think a family can overcelebrate," says Pipher. She notes that these celebrations can contain speeches, plays, songs, and writing. There really are no rules except to have fun!

COOPERATIVE GAMES

When most folks hear "games," they think Milton Bradley and Parker Brothers. But simple living families know that there are dozens of games that can be played indoors or outdoors, with no (or few) props needed; just add people. Karen Schneider-Chen has been teaching workshops on cooperative games— and playing them with her family—for many years. Here are a few of her recommendations (see "Resources" section for more ideas):

Try Not to Laugh (or "Muk")

Players sit in a circle. One player is "it" and starts the game by saying, "Muk!" All conversation and smiling stops when "Muk" is called. The player designated as "it" tries to make another player in the circle talk or smile. Anything goes, *except* no touching and no averting of eyes.

Command Performance

One player leaves the room. The rest of the group decides on a pose that is specific but not too detailed. The "poser" returns and begins striking poses. The group signals hot or cold until the poser strikes the correct pose.

Fictionary (kids should be independent readers for this one)

You'll need a good dictionary, paper, and pencils.

Each player is given a piece of paper and a pencil. One player, designated as the referee, picks an unusual word from the dictionary and then pronounces and spells it aloud for the group. (If someone in the group already knows the word, the referee must find another.) The referee writes the word and its definition down on a slip of paper (it helps to paraphrase the definition a bit so it won't sound like it came from the dictionary). Everyone else tries to think up a definition for the word

(continues)

(continued)

and writes it down on their piece of paper. The referee collects all the definitions and reads them aloud, and the rest of the players try to guess which is the real definition.

Song Chain (great car trip game)

One player begins singing a song he or she knows, while the other players listen carefully. When another player hears a word that she knows to be in a different song, she breaks in, singing the new song. The original singer stops and the new singer continues, until another member of the group breaks in with a new song.

Humor

I think that the greatest simple pleasure for my family—and many others—is finding the humor in life, just sitting around talking and laughing about *whatever*. We don't necessarily tell jokes, although all of us have been known to do so. Often it's the joy of sharing those oddball observations of life, like how a tomato we've picked looks like a snowman or guessing out loud what the cat is really thinking as he dashes from room to room.

Laughter is sorely needed by all of us, says simple living mom Karen Schneider-Chen. Karen recently became certified as a "laughter leader" by the World Laughter Tour organization. She points to studies that indicate that the average preschooler laughs 400 to 500 times a day. By the time that child becomes an adult, she's laughing only seven to fifteen times daily. The paradox, according to Karen, is that laughter may be more important for adults "because it decreases the hormone that causes stress." "We pay a high price for growing up," laments Karen.

Karen's family makes a conscious effort to incorporate

humor and laughter in their daily life. She also uses humor in her part-time job as a jail outreach worker, holding weekly "laughter club" meetings for inmates.

Laugh with your kids whenever and wherever you can. As Karen notes: "It really is the best medicine."

OTHER SIMPLE PLEASURES

The following simple pleasures involve some elements of play—and just pure joy.

Connecting with Nature

Rachel Carson, who gave us the insight of *Silent Spring,* said, "If a child is to keep his inborn sense of wonder, he needs the companionship of at least one adult who can share it, rediscovering with him the joy, excitement, and mystery of the world we live in." I wonder if, in her wisdom, Carson urged adults to accompany children on this nature journey as much for the adults' benefits as for the kids.

Kids truly can help us see the beauty and wonder of nature. When my youngest was seven, we took a trip to eastern Oregon and stopped at an overlook of Hell's Canyon, the deepest river gorge in the country. We'd been driving for quite a while, the mercury had hit 100 degrees, and I was tired and hungry and not really in the mood until my little guy said, with genuine awe in his voice, "What a beautiful sight!" He was right—as he so often is. It was spectacular, and I would have missed it without him along.

Children are typically better connected with nature than adults. They don't have to wade through other stuff—"to do" lists, job concerns, what to make for dinner—to be fully present and enjoy whatever natural phenomenon is presented to them at any point in time. Luckily for us, their observations and obvious fascination with nature are contagious.

Nearly every simple living family I queried mentioned nature-related simple pleasures, particularly those with very young kids. Amie Averett of Killeen, Texas, is a good example. She and her son Taylor, two, enjoy watching birds, studying bugs, catching frogs, and looking for bats and butterflies. They also take family walks every other night, which are peppered with frequent stops, initiated by Taylor, to investigate nature a little further.

Stargazing is another nature-related activity mentioned by several families. You don't need sophisticated equipment—not even binoculars—and you don't need to drive anywhere special to do this. Just walk outside after dinner on a clear night and start looking. Even if you live in the city—and hence have a considerable amount of "light pollution"—you'll still be able to see quite a bit.

Many families also mentioned bird-watching, a great way to get your kids to take hikes when they don't really want to. Bird watching is, after all, a hike *with a point.* Call your local parks department for bird viewing destinations in your area. Checking out a field guide or "bird book" for your region from the library is also a good plan: The kids will enjoy trying to identify their feathered friends. If you have several pairs of binoculars, take all of them along. Pack a snack—and you're off.

Camping is another tried and true simple pleasure. After all, nearly all kids *love* camping. A few days in the woods with the family has these additional perks: It costs very little, is light on the earth, provides quiet moments and lots of downtime, teaches survival skills, and gets the kids away from the boob tube. In short, it makes a nearly perfect simple living vacation. See the discussion about camping in the rituals section later in this chapter.

Storytelling

Back when my parents were children, storytelling was a major source of entertainment. Today we've substituted television, movies, radios, computers, Nintendos, and CD players. Unfortunately, the messages learned from these electronic authorities are often not the ones we're hoping to communicate to our kids. And there certainly isn't much chance for family bonding or creativity if the source of all of your family's stories is an appliance.

All of us have stories to tell! I didn't truly realize this until my youngest, several years ago, started to make this simple request: "Mom, tell me about when you were a kid." I've found the best tales to share involve those aspects of my youth that are different from my kids' lives. I grew up on a small farm; they're city kids. This one fact gives me plenty of material.

Some stories rise to the level of "family folklore" and are told over and over again. There's the one, for example, about my husband's pole vaulting career. At a high school track meet, the school's lone pole vaulter was a "no show," so the coach asked my husband, then sixteen, to step in. Suffice it to say, it wasn't as simple as it looked. Or his story about the time he was accosted on the golf course by a rabid squirrel, complete with his maniacal squirrel impersonation. Or the time all four of us went for a hike and had not one, but two, flat tires on the way home.

This last example demonstrates that kids can tell their stories too. They love to do this; it gives them an important role as the sharer of information, and they value the story in a special way when they retell it.

Grandparents are wonderful resources for family folklore–type tales. They'll enjoy recalling their youths, while the kids will delight in hearing about their beloved Grandma and Grandpa's childhoods, learning a bit about "the way things were," and just listening to a good yarn.

Both factual and fictional storytelling are powerful methods for relaying morals and values. So not only is yarn-spinning entertaining, it's also good for our kids.

And it's good for us. It's amazing how therapeutic it can be to recall some of your childhood's special memories—how you handled some bizarre predicament, how a relative or teacher was involved in your life, or just some wacky mo-

STORYTELLING 101

The stories you tell can be either fact or fiction. If you feel intimidated by the prospect of creating tales, follow these tips from Chase Collins's book *Tell Me a Story*.

First come up with a hero or heroine—this could be your child, an animal, a kid from another century, an alien! Example: "Once upon a time, Sara lived with her mom, dad, grandma, and two little brothers on a farm . . . " Next, create a conflict or challenge (this often involves the need for the heroine to set out on a journey). Example: "During a blizzard, the power and phones went out. Sara's parents were gone and her grandmother was sick. Sara needed to get to the doctor's house, three miles away." Then have the hero resolve the conflict: "Sara tried to walk but kept falling through the deep white drifts. How could she keep from sinking through the snow? Then she had an idea: She would strap two tennis rackets to her feet . . . " Which leads, of course, to a happy ending.

It's an added plus if you can incorporate morals into your story; they'll usually pop up anyway. For instance, in the above example, Sara showed resourcefulness, creativity, perseverance, responsibility, and love for her grandmother. Ask your kids what the moral or message of the story is.

ment. Perhaps if we told more stories we'd need psychologists less.

The Arts

Art is an important simple pleasure. As noted in Chapter 10, art and creativity are prime methods for kids to develop self-knowledge and self-esteem. Parents intuitively know this. When I queried simple living parents about the best toys they'd ever purchased for the kids, nearly every one of them mentioned arts and crafts supplies.

The beauty of art is—well, that it doesn't have to be beautiful. *Utne Reader* recently ran a story about a group of friends who hold weekly "bad art" nights during which the participants are encouraged to create for the sake of creating, with no expectations and no standards.

I love this idea! While we haven't adopted this practice, we have engaged in bad art sprees with the kids. We have two walls of art in the living room of our home to show for it. Most of it is the kids'—and certainly the *worst* of it is the adults'.

"The Arts" aren't, of course, limited to painting and sketching. Music, dance, and theater are other simple pleasures that many families enjoy. Whether you're making music or merely enjoying it, you're experiencing a simple pleasure. The same is true for dance and theater. Patti Idrobo of Livingston, New Jersey, often puts on music and dances with her daughters Marlena and Elisa. Other times the three will stage a homemade play.

Kids love the added dimension of recording the play for posterity—and for their friends to watch. You don't need cutting-edge technology either; our twelve-year-old camcorder has performed entirely adequately as the recorder of these works of art. I've watched kids cooperate on plots, cobble costumes together, write elaborate scripts, even add musical scores when they know they're going to be part of a "home movie." It seems to bring out the hidden dramatic flair in even the most reserved kids. And it's fun!

Many simple families try to take in free and low cost concerts and other art events. But your home can be an arts center too. You can, as noted, engage in "bad art" sessions. You can create or listen to music at home, you can dance with your kids to the oldies station, you can put on plays for relatives and neighbors, or for yourselves. As with most artistic endeavors, the possibilities are limited only by your imagination.

Volunteer Work

Volunteering with your kids could be the ultimate win-win simple pleasure scenario. You get to have fun, do a good deed, be with your family, expose your kids to those less fortunate, teach lessons in social justice and community, and pass along some of your values—simultaneously.

And then there's the "helper's high." In *The Healing Power of Doing Good: The Health and Spiritual Benefits of Helping Others,* authors Alan Luk and Peggy Payne note that 95 percent of volunteers surveyed in a national study reported that personally helping on a regular basis gives them an immediate, physical feel-good sensation, which the authors term a "helper's high." Other benefits include less pain, fewer colds, and overall greater well-being. The greater the frequency of volunteering, the greater the health benefits.

It's important to get a good match of volunteer opportunity for your family, particularly the ages of your kids. It's nice when you can coordinate your kids' interests with the activity too: for example, volunteering at the Humane Society for an animal lover.

But unless you live in a very small town or rural area, there should be opportunities for your family at each stage. Call your local volunteer bureau—or the social service agency directly—for more information.

The Sky's the Limit

Here are some additional ideas for simple pleasures practiced by downshifted families:

- Indoor picnics in front of the fire in the winter
- Lemonade and cookie stands in the summer
- Teaching life skills, like cooking, sewing, carpentry, gardening, and auto mechanics
- Flying kites
- Treasure hunts (clues lead the kids to each successive clue until they find the "treasure," a small treat for everyone); indoors in the winter, outside in good weather
- Playing hopscotch
- Working on a family project together, like creating a birdhouse

- Watching planes land and take off at the airport
- Throwing a Frisbee around, or just playing "catch"
- Attending local cultural festivals
- Reading to each other—even after the kids are reading on their own

These are only a few of the countless types of simple pleasures families can enjoy. (You'll find other ideas in "Alternatives to TV Viewing" on page 134.) The possibilities for play are limited only by the imagination. Try some of these or think up your own, perhaps borrowing some of those activities you enjoyed when you were young.

Family Rituals and Traditions

Rituals are those acts or observances one repeats with regularity. When most folks use the term "family ritual," they're referring to one of these recurring family practices that has special significance to them.

Rituals can be as minor as the piggyback rides you give your kids from their bedrooms to the kitchen each morning. Or the fact that you *always* chant "Home again, Finnegan" when you pull into the driveway.

Rituals can also be relatively elaborate affairs, like the equinox and solstice rituals of Shelby Pawlina and her family. On these days, the family wakes up early, before dawn, and hikes up a small mountain near their home. Together they watch the sun rise. Then they read an inspirational passage and "offer water to the gods" (by spitting) in the four directions. "It's a beautiful and inspirational family time together," says Shelby.

Other examples of family rituals abound: bedtime stories, walking the kids to school, doughnuts on Sunday mornings, weekly visits to the grandparents. Indeed, just about any of the simple pleasures referred to above can become a ritual if it is meaningful for family members and performed on a regular basis.

I'm not sure when a family ritual becomes a tradition. Perhaps it has to cross that generational line, metamorphosing into a tradition when you transport it from your childhood to your adulthood or when your children adopt the same practice. Many of my own family's customs are not in the strictest sense traditions but we like to think of them that way.

THE IMPORTANCE OF RITUALS

In her book *The Shelter of Each Other,* Mary Pipher urges families to establish rituals. Why? "Family rituals protect time," says Pipher, and family time is, of course, essential for bonding and connection. Pipher adds that rituals are important for children: "Children like to be able to predict events. It gives them a sense of control."

Michelle Eaton, a mother of two from Utah, agrees. "Rituals ground kids and make family time special and sacred," she says. In fact, rituals make the family *itself* special; they imprint upon all members the uniqueness of the family. Besides, Michelle adds, they're fun! Linda McDonough eloquently concurs: "Rituals and stories, work and love, are what make a family. Family rituals are the liturgies that celebrate our families and our love for each other."

Put this way, those practices of reading to your children every evening or starting each morning with a hug and a kiss take on new meaning, added importance—they become sacred. We'd be wise to look at them this way.

In researching the book *Ask the Children,* author Ellen Galinsky asked kids about their feelings on a number of topics related to their family lives. Galinsky says that "children mentioned family rituals as being especially memorable in a positive way. Children talked about the made-up bedtime stories such as an ongoing story about a cow, a pig, and a chicken that went on night after night. Children talked about taking a walk every evening with a parent, or always singing 'Michael, row your boat ashore' in the car."

Galinsky goes on to report that family rituals and traditions aren't just pleasant experiences for kids, they're pivotal in their development. She notes that studies conclude that rituals and traditions are "important components in children's school readiness and school success."

COMMON RITUALS OF SIMPLE FAMILIES

Simple families have many endearing family rituals. Some are those that close families everywhere share—reading together, bedtime stories, saying grace before meals. Others are unique. Here are a couple that perhaps a majority of simple living families have established.

Eating Dinner Together

This accepted practice of years past has resurfaced as a tradition for some families. While studies show that only 54 percent of all families eat together five or more days a week, my unscientific research reveals that a far greater percentage of simple families make a habit of sharing meals daily.

Eating together regularly is an important tool for staying in touch with your kids and, indeed, for family sanity. Simple living mom Jan Anderson says of this ritual, "It unifies the family, gives us a core." Surveys reveal that teens who eat dinner with their families on a regular basis feel a direct correlation between this family activity and feelings of satisfaction and personal well-being. According to a recent report by the National Center on Addiction and Substance Abuse, teens who *don't* eat meals with their families are twice as likely to use drugs as those whose families do eat together every night. And, a few years ago, I read that the single commonality among National Merit Scholars is that their families ate dinner together regularly.

Simple living families ensure that family dinners lend themselves to discussions and fun by banning distractions like phone calls and reading at the table. Many simple living families also add a special dinnertime ritual to their evening meal together. Some designate one or two nights a week when the kids plan and cook the evening meal. Jan Anderson's family blows out a candle and then pauses for thankfulness at each meal.

Several families mentioned the "highlight-lowlight" ritual. During the evening meal, each family member shares the high point and low point of their day, a practice that keeps families connected and triggers further conversation.

Shelby Pawlina's family makes a point of eating both breakfast and dinner together. At breakfast they sing "Oh, How Lovely Is the Morning" (adapted from "Oh, How Lovely Is the Evening") in a round. "At dinnertime," says Shelby, "we hold hands, and go around the table hearing what each person is thankful for. When everyone has shared, we hold up our connected hands and say, 'Good Life!' I love the positive focus of that ritual."

Family Day—or Night

Establishing one day of the week as Family Day when no one schedules anything else is a great way to protect family time. Many simple families have established this ritual, most as a Family Night. (See "Family Night" on page 10.)

A number of the simple living families I interviewed designated one evening a week as video night, even if the family otherwise watches no television at all. My family does this too. Friday night is "pizza and movie" night at our house, and *all* of us look forward to it. I *never* have to think of what to fix for dinner that night and yet I know everyone will be happy with the meal and that we'll all relax afterward with a good movie.

The Rhoad family of The Woodlands, Texas, has been observing "Crazy Fridays" for many years. On Friday nights the family dines on pizza, they give each other washable tattoos, watch a movie, and get to go to bed late without brushing their teeth! "Every kid in the neighborhood wants to do this!" says Kate Rhoad.

What kinds of movies do these families watch? Many of them choose to watch what I call "message movies," films that have some lesson of morals or values that viewers can soak up all the while they're being entertained.

Here are a few video recommendations for your family's own "Movie Night" (you'll want to consider your child's age/maturity on some of these):

To Kill a Mockingbird	*The China Syndrome*
October Sky	*Mr. Smith Goes to*
Goodbye, Mr. Chips	*Washington*
Gandhi	*Driving Miss Daisy*
The Long Walk Home	*Remember the Titans*
The Education of Little Tree	*Contact*
The Miracle Worker	*Apollo 13*
Mr. Holland's Opus	*Babe*
Cry Freedom	*Fly Away Home*
Chicken Run	*Searching for Bobby*
Iron Will	*Fischer*
The Grapes of Wrath	*The Good Earth*

RITUALS BEYOND THE IMMEDIATE FAMILY

Experts note that family rituals should also involve those outside the nuclear family. Connecting with grandparents and other extended family members is particularly beneficial for children. These multigenerational rituals allow kids to bond with people who love and cherish them, and it exposes them to their heritage and ancestry.

Reunions—where several generations come together to visit, eat a good meal, and laugh—are common extended family rituals. If you're fortunate enough to be a member of a family that "reunites," you'll notice that many of the activities that occur at these events are simple ones. At our (almost) annual extended family reunions, folks "catch up" with each other, play cribbage, dine on pot luck. We'll usually have an intergenerational game of softball, and the kids always manage to play "hide and seek."

One of Linda McDonough's family's traditions is an extended family ritual, a yearly camp-out with aunts, uncles, cousins, and grandparents in attendance. My family observes a similar annual practice. Every summer my extended family—three of my siblings and their families along with my own family—goes "yurting," that is, we stay in yurts at state parks. Yurts are a cross between a teepee and a cabin, feature futons, bunk beds, and electricity, and are ideal for the Pacific Northwest, where you're never quite sure if the camping weather will be glorious or if you'll spend the weekend in your rain slicker, huddled under a tarp. Even my folks—in their eighties—stay at a nearby motel and visit during the day. We've been observing our yurting tradition now for six years and it's among my kids' very favorite summertime activities. We swim, boat, fish, hike, and sing (really!) around the campfire while eating those perennial favorites, S'mores. Cribbage and Taboo games are also big hits.

You don't, of course, have to stay in yurts to make a memory out of an annual intergenerational camping trip. Camping en masse with your extended family, however, truly does make the event memorable. We always divvy up the meal-making duties: Each family is responsible for one evening meal and one breakfast; you're on your own for lunches. If you plan ahead, you'll also avoid each family having to bring *everything*. One family can bring the Coleman stove, another the lantern, another the tarps. It's a testament to the bonding power of community, family, and nature.

Intergenerational contact should be encouraged at all of these gatherings—and in everyday life too. Kids who have frequent contact with extended family gain, in essence, a similarly valued group to belong to and identify with, another way for them to combat peer pressure.

Grandparents and grandchildren have a special relation-

ship, and rituals surrounding them should also be encouraged. Sunday dinner with grandparents, special sleepovers, or
regular trips to the zoo are all ways to keep this connection
vital.

Cherished rituals can also involve community connections such as block parties and neighborhood garage sales,
fun for all concerned.

FIND THE TIME AND INSPIRATION FOR CREATING FAMILY RITUALS

Parents may wonder where they'll come across the time for
these new practices. A significant method of unearthing hours
to devote to family is to turn off your TV (see Chapter 9).
Mindfully limiting outside activities will also free up time for
rituals (see Chapter 11). Another strategy is to build on those
family observances you already have in place. For example,
everyone has to eat. Make a point of dining together and
adding a simple ceremony, like lighting a candle. When it
comes time to do chores, put on a favorite family CD and sing
together.

How you introduce rituals to your family will depend, in
part, on the ritual in question, the age of your children, and
your family's style. Most experts recommend that, rather
than unilaterally declaring the adoption of a new practice,
you take a gradual and somewhat democratic approach to the
initiation of a new ritual, particularly with older kids. If your
family holds regular household meetings, add the idea of a
new (or improved) ritual to your next agenda. The family can
adopt the ritual and then evaluate it at a later family meeting.
You can also use a more spontaneous "let's try this" approach. For example, you could simply schedule a Family
Night as an experiment (make it a lot of fun!) and then ask
the family if they'd like to continue it.

Families don't need to look far for inspiration regarding rituals. They can reminisce about those childhood rituals
they cherished—and then continue them. They can borrow

from the ideas of others or they can research the customs of other cultures. Many families also create completely unique practices.

Original rituals come in all categories and classes. Shelby Pawlina's family's practice of never wrapping gifts is an example. "Instead," says Shelby, "we hide them in places where the recipient would find them on a typical day—in the medicine cabinet with the toothpaste, under a pillow, or with the bag of garlic heads."

Linda McDonough's family has also created their own very unique traditions. One is St. Clare's Day. Daughter Molly's middle name is Claire, so Linda thought she'd like to share her patron saint's feast day with others. For their August 11 celebration, they invite anyone with Clare in their name—even Clarences are welcome, although they've never had any show up. Their list of Clares now numbers about twenty; about half attend each year. They make candles, because Clare means light, and for every guest who arrives, Molly Claire buys a can of food to donate to the local food bank. The feast includes Italian food and wine, and always ends with a fitting dessert—eclairs!

The McDonough family's St. Clare tradition demonstrates how creative, fun, and special rituals can be. However you come up with your own family's rituals and traditions, you will treasure them forever.

Resources

BOARD GAMES
Family Pastimes, RR 4, Perth, Ontario, CAN K7H 3C6; (613) 267–4819.

Out of the Box Publishing: (608) 244–2468.

Real Goods: www.realgoods.com

RITUALS/TRADITIONS
Elizabeth Berg. *Family Traditions: Celebrations for Holidays and Everyday* (Pleasantville, New York: Reader's Digest, 1992).

Meg Cox. *The Heart of a Family: Searching America for New Traditions That Fulfill Us* (New York: Random House, 1998).

William J. Doherty. *The Intentional Family: How to Build Family Ties in Our Modern World* (Reading, Massachusetts: Addison-Wesley Publishing, 1997).

William J. Doherty and Barbara Z. Carlson. *Putting Family First* (New York: Henry Holt, 2002).

Cindy MacGregor. *Family Customs and Traditions* (Minneapolis: Fairview Press, 1995).

Carolyn Pogue, editor. *Treasury of Celebrations* (Northstone Publishing, 1987); available through Alternatives for Simple Living, (800) 821–6153.

SIMPLE PLEASURES

Chase Collins. *Tell Me a Story: Creating Bedtime Tales Your Children Will Dream On* (Boston: Houghton Mifflin, 1992).

Terence Dickinson. *Nightwatch: A Practical Guide to Viewing the Universe* (Toronto: Firefly Books, 1998).

Jane Drake and Ann Love. *The Kids Summer Games Book* (Toronto: Kids Can Press, 1998).

Roxanne Henderson. *The Picture Rulebook of Kids' Games* (Chicago: Contemporary Books, 1996).

Jacqueline Horsfall. *Play Lightly on the Earth: Nature Activities for Children 3 to 9 Years Old* (Nevada City, California: Dawn Publications, 1997).

Dale N. LeFevre. *New Games for the Whole Family* (New York: Perigree Books, 1988).

Sambhava and Josette Luvmour. *Everyone Wins! Cooperative Games and Activities* (Philadelphia: New Society Publishers, 1990).

Gail MacColl. *The Book of Cards for Kids* (New York: Workman Publishing, 1992).

Jack Maguire. *Hopscotch, Hangman, Hot Potato and Ha Ha Ha: A Rulebook of Children's Games* (New York: Prentice Hall Press, 1990).

John Mosley. *Stargazing for Beginners* (Los Angeles: Lowell House, 1998).

VOLUNTEERING WITH KIDS

Call your local volunteer bureau or a service agency directly. Or visit www.citycares.org. City Cares is a network of volunteer clearinghouses in thirty cities across the country, linking volunteers with appropriate nonprofit agencies.

Alan Luk and Peggy Payne. *The Healing Power of Doing Good: The Health and Spiritual Benefits of Helping Others* (New York: Fawcett Columbine, 1991).

OTHER RESOURCES

Rachel Carson. *Silent Spring* (Boston: Houghton Mifflin, 1962).

David Elkind. *The Hurried Child* (Cambridge, Massachusetts: Perseus Publishing, 2001).

Ellen Galinsky. *Ask the Children: What America's Children Really Think About Working Parents* (New York: William Morrow, 1999).

Mary Pipher. *The Shelter of Each Other: Rebuilding Our Families* (New York: Grosset/Putnam, 1996).

Beth Wilson Saavedra. *Creating Balance in Your Child's Life* (Chicago: NTC/Contemporary, 2000).

Nick Stinnet and John DeFrain. *The Secrets of Strong Families* (New York: Little, Brown, 1985).

Lenore Terr. *Beyond Love and Work: Why Adults Need to Play* (New York: Scribner, 1999).

13

⟨⟨⟨

Teaching Your Child
Money Management

One of the most important responsibilities for simple living parents is to teach our kids how to manage their own money. Because those of us within the movement know that getting control over our finances is a crucial factor in simplifying, we realize that helping our kids acquire this skill will make a huge difference in their lives.

And where else will kids get this financial savvy? At the same time that the culture is busy inundating all of us with consumeristic messages, it simultaneously imparts no knowledge on how we should responsibly budget and pay for these purchases. That would obviously be counterproductive to the bottom line message of spend, spend, spend. Our schools aren't picking up the slack; the JumpStart Coalition for Personal Financial Literacy estimates that 90 percent of high school graduates receive no personal finance education. It's up to us.

What I Hope My Children Learn About Money

My wish for my children is that early in life they learn the meaning of financial intelligence, financial integrity, and financial independence—the "FI3" popularized in the book *Your Money or Your Life*. (See "Your Money or Your Life" on page 76.) I hope that they'll make the connection between unnecessary purchases, resource depletion, and environmental degradation. I want to help them understand that, as Americans, the world's most voracious consumers, they particularly need to grasp the concept of "enough," and that by doing so, they can play an important part in preserving the earth. When they do make purchases, I want them to make *mindful* purchases, determining that what they're buying is important to them now and will still be important to them later. I want them to internalize the wisdom of the saying "Money can't buy happiness," and with that knowledge, I hope that they'll focus on people and causes rather than acquisitions.

I also want them to learn about the social responsibility involved in spending money, that by consuming consciously they can make a difference in the lives of countless others. Sometimes these "do's" and "don'ts" get fuzzy. For example, my family generally buys only from union stores, because we believe strongly in workers' rights. But we also want to support local businesspeople, and that sentiment can conflict with our union support. We want to marshal our money efficiently; but we also know that the price of an item doesn't always reflect its *cost* in human and environmental terms. The ability to weigh the pros and cons of various purchases is part of the financial intelligence and integrity I'd like my children to acquire.

Along the same lines, I want them to know the power of sharing their money with those less fortunate and with causes that can make a difference. They can give more to others who need it more than they do, if they've wisely limited their own expenditures.

I also hope that my sons ultimately choose to work in a field that they feel strongly about, that they "follow their passion," no matter what it pays. I know from my own experience that living simply can allow you to have that kind of freedom.

RAISING SAVERS

Another significant aspect of teaching our children about money is to help them, early on, get into the habit of saving. Luckily, this coincides with our efforts to help them discern what is "enough."

Clearly, as a nation, we're pretty inept when it comes to "putting away for a rainy day." A recent survey by the Employee Benefit Research Institute and the American Savings Education Council revealed that almost one-fifth of all American workers had saved nothing for retirement, and half had saved less than $50,000. According to finance expert Neale S. Godfrey, Americans have the lowest rate of savings of any developed country.

It's really no wonder that Americans are such abysmal savers. It's not that most of us are living hand to mouth. But instead of saving—surprise!—we're spending. In fact, we're spending more than we make. According to the Federal Reserve Board, personal debt reached an all-time high in April of 2001, with credit card and consumer loans reaching $1.58 trillion. Our already low savings rate has declined from 8.6 percent in 1984 to –0.6 *percent* (yes, that's a negative number) in the first quarter of 1999. As seen in Chapter 8, we're constantly bombarded with messages to buy this or that gadget—now! now!—and pay—later! later! All of that advertising is incredibly effective.

Communication

Not surprisingly, many of the techniques for teaching money management skills are similar to those needed to teach kids about simple living generally and about standing up to the consumer culture in particular. For one thing, you can simply talk with your kids about financial matters. Telling them about your own financial decisions, perhaps even even allowing them to be involved in those discussions if appropriate, can be both educational and enlightening. Explaining your purchases—why you comparison shop and check unit prices at the store, why you get three quotes if the water pipe breaks, why you don't buy heavily packaged foods—will help your kids understand your decisions and will teach them the mechanics of "living on less" simultaneously.

The "needs" versus "wants" analysis is a central theme in communicating money management to your kids. My kids and I have had quite a few conversations about whether potential purchases involve necessities or, in truth, luxuries. Americans generally live so far beyond "needs" that it's difficult to discern what *is* a true need and what is an extra, or in essence a culturally based need. The question "Do I really need this item?" is very often answered in the negative.

We've concluded over time that we, like many, many other Americans, have much more than we need, and that the goal is to keep those "extras" in check. So parents have to take the analysis a bit further and answer—and at the same time help their kids answer—a second question: "How much is enough?" Simplicity advocate Vicki Robin has observed that those who can discern how much is enough for themselves have a "sense of purpose" that directs them; they are, essentially, in touch with their values. Refer back to your Values and Vision Statement and ask yourself, as *Your Money or Your Life* recommends, "Is this expenditure in alignment with my values?" Ask yourself this question *out loud* so your kids will hear it. Let them listen as you and your spouse deliberate this issue. Kids learn how to answer the "How much is enough?" question for themselves when they hear their parents discussing it. Ask the other *Your Money or Your Life* query also: "Did I receive fulfillment, satisfaction, and value in proportion to life energy (money) spent?"

The next step, of course, is to have your kids ask themselves these questions when they spend money. Particularly for younger kids, the "Is this expenditure in alignment with my values?" question is a stretch. But the second query—about fulfillment, satisfaction, and value—works at all ages. Sara Robinson poses several prepurchase queries to her two kids, ages ten and eight: "Don't you already have one like that? How long do you think you're going to enjoy playing with that? If you buy that, will you still be able to afford that skateboard you've been saving for? Where are you going to put it in your room?" Sara adds that her kids have heard the questions so many times, they've started to ask them of themselves, without prompting.

Lynne Cantwell performs postpurchase analyses with her two teenage daughters. She'll ask them, "Do you feel like you got your money's worth? Would you spend your money that way again?" This evaluation has helped her girls think twice before the next similar purchase.

Modeling
....

Communication efforts will have little impact if Mom and Dad aren't practicing what they preach. The American Savings Education Council conducted a survey of 1,000 parents in January 2001. The results indicated that 82 percent of parents felt they were doing a good or excellent job of managing their money and believed that they were imparting good financial habits to their kids. But less than half of those surveyed paid off their credit card balances each month and only 45 percent had a budget and followed it most of the time. The survey concluded that parents overestimate what they can teach and underestimate the influence of their own behavior.

Be aware, then, that your kids will pick up more on what you *do* than what you *say*. Demonstrate the "hows" of cost cutting every day by giving your kids many chances to witness financial sanity in action. My kids learned one of the prime simplicity purchasing rules—"Buy used"—through my husband's example. He wanted a Foosball table for our basement, and the kids watched him check the "thrifties" ads—your local daily newspaper probably has something similar—for several months before he found a good, reasonably priced (recycled!) table, instead of running out to buy a new, expensive one.

My husband's lengthy search for a Foosball table also modeled "delayed gratification" for our kids, an extremely valuable lesson. We have a rule in our house that anyone who wants a nonessential item costing over ten dollars must wait at least twenty-four hours before purchasing it. (Note: While this is a family rule, it's almost always triggered by one of our kids' desires.) The twenty-four-hour delay is useful in at least two ways: It puts some time between the "stimulus" and "response" in the instant gratification formula, teaching us patience. It also, quite often, results in the child simply forgetting about the item he felt so strongly about the day before.

You can model delayed gratification, patience, and the priceless lesson of enjoying what you have every day for your kids. They'll see you *not* go to the mall. They'll witness you *not* wasting time and money shopping solely for the sake of shopping. They'll observe you being perfectly happy with less. You can "walk your talk" and teach your kids in the process.

Allowances

Nearly every parent I interviewed for this book has an allowance system for his or her kids. Why? Well, more of that adult peer pressure, for one thing. We give our kids allowances because it's a culturally expected thing to do. I doubt that many kids in third world countries are getting a weekly allotment of mad money.

Most parents also believe that, properly handled, allowances help kids learn money management. They teach them about issues like budgeting, comparison shopping, and saving.

Linda McDonough describes how daughter Molly learned several lessons with one purchase, her "excellent Furby acquisition adventure." Molly, age six, wanted a Furby, and Linda decided to let her save up her allowance money until she had the eighteen dollars to buy one. It took Molly ten weeks. "Several moms said, 'I would have *given* you all our Furbies,' but I wanted her to have the experience of saving and then deciding if it was worthwhile," recalls Linda. She also notes that, after Molly made her purchase, "she found another Furby at the thrift store for one-tenth the price, and that was a good lesson too." In addition, Molly discovered that Furbies need batteries, and she had to pay for those too.

"I made lots of mistakes with my money as an adult," explains Linda. She feels that allowing Molly to have these experiences—saving, budgeting, and sometimes making bad decisions—will help her learn to handle money early on.

ALLOWANCE AMOUNT

Several experts recommend that you pay your child his or her age each week in dollars—for example, five dollars weekly for a five-year-old—and from my extremely informal survey of simple living parents, most folks follow this rule of thumb. I think this "rule" is a lot like the rule about making the number of kids invited to your kid's birthday the same as his age: arbitrary. Besides, it seems to me that it will depend not only on your financial situation, but also on what you expect your child to use the money for. Will they be buying bon-bons and Barbies with it? Or will they have to cough up their lunch

"WORK FOR PAY" VERSUS "NO TIES" ALLOWANCES

There is no one cast-in-stone method for handling allowances. There are clearly, however, two schools of thought on how allowances work. Most experts subscribe to the no-strings-attached approach. Under this theory, kids should receive an allowance that is unconnected to the performance of chores. The thinking here is that working around the house is part of being a member of the household and should not be compensated for. Mom and Dad do chores and don't expect payment; neither should the kids. Allowances are "allowed," not earned.

Others believe that a child's weekly ration of cash should be tied to chore performance. These "work for pay" advocates believe that allowances should be earned. If the child fails to complete prescribed household tasks, allowances are withheld.

One expert, Neale S. Godfrey, recommends a modified "work for pay" approach. Godfrey feels that there are certain chores that a child shouldn't be paid for—those involving personal maintenance, like going to bed on time and brushing teeth, and what she calls "citizens of the household" expectations—general housekeeping chores that everyone in the family is expected to chip in and do. These are differentiated from Godfrey's "work for pay" chores, to some extent arbitrarily, by the parent. For example, "citizen of the household" tasks might include setting the table, putting away laundry, and loading the dishwasher. "Work for pay" might include changing the cat's litter box, watering the garden, and cleaning bathrooms. Once kids are of school age, Godfrey adds a third category of odd jobs—those more irregularly occurring needs like car washing or lawn mowing, again for pay. (All of these chores are adjusted to be age appropriate for the child.)

"No ties" families simply make chores and allowances completely separate subjects. Kids are expected to do their

(continues)

(continued)

chores. And parents hand out allowance weekly—or monthly or biweekly—regardless of chore performance.

A frequent accompaniment to either approach is to allow kids to earn additional money for odd jobs, such as bathing the dog and cleaning out the attic. Sometimes these exceptions and add-ons make the two schools blur.

And that's okay. Remember, there are no rules! You decide what makes sense and what's best for your family.

Both of these schools of thought, incidentally, view allowances as a primary method of teaching children money management skills like budgeting, saving, comparison shopping, and the like. The "work for pay" system might also more heavily teach the value of "no free lunches."

money too? My husband and I came to the conclusion many years ago that our kids should get their age in dollars each *month*. We require them to pay for very little at this point in their lives. We'll revisit the allowance amount question if their needs change.

Your job is to figure out what *you* think is the right amount, depending upon your family's financial situation and the requirements put on the allowance money. As you'll see below, many families give their kids more money as they get older but also add to those items that must be paid for with allowance money.

SIMPLE ALLOWANCES

While most experts advocate a "no strings attached" approach, most families apparently want to instill the work ethic. In one survey by Merrill Lynch, 97 percent of teenagers receiving an allowance said they have to perform duties to earn it.

Simple living parents, rebels that they are, seem to buck

this trend. My unscientific survey found that most simple families are "no strings attached" folks. But beyond this similarity, simple families seem to devise their own systems.

Kate Rhoad adheres to the dominant theory. "We pay an allowance that's not tied to the work that they do. They're citizens of the household and they need to help and they do." The kids' allowances are divided up: 65 percent to spend, 25 percent for savings, and 10 percent for giving.

Linda McDonough has a "no ties" allowance for her kids. Ten percent goes to their church and the remainder is divided one-third to "red light" money (long-term savings, college, house, et cetera), one-third to "yellow light" money (short-term savings, birthday and Christmas presents), and one-third to "green light" money (for discretionary spending, souvenirs on trips, candy, et cetera).

My kids also have a "no ties" allowance, with 10 percent designated for charity, 20 percent for college savings, and the rest for spending. Mom and Dad also "match" the charity and college amounts, which has frequently resulted in the kids' putting more than the minimum toward those efforts.

Michelle Eaton's family has a more elaborate setup. Her two kids have regular chores and receive a regular allowance. If they want extra money, they can earn "kid cash." Michelle explains: "Extra chores have set 'dollar' amounts. The kids turn in an 'expense sheet' once a month, and we figure out their earnings. Kid cash can be exchanged for special privileges (like having friends sleep over or eating at McDonald's) or it can be traded for cash," the exchange rate for which, Michelle adds, is slightly less than fifty cents on the dollar. This may sound elaborate, but Michelle notes that once you've set the system up, it takes relatively little time to operate.

A few of the downshifted parents I interviewed did employ "work for pay" systems. One simple mom, Judy Laquidara of Owensboro, Kentucky, gives Chad, her thirteen-year-old, a dollar per year of school per week. He's in seventh grade, so he gets seven dollars weekly, or $1.40 for each weekday. Chores, which must be completed by 8:00 P.M., are listed on a chart in her son's bedroom. Judy checks them off then. "On Friday," she says, "he gets his full seven dollars if he's done the chores for the whole five days. If not, he gets $1.40 for however many days he did his chores." Again, it depends on you, your goals, your family, and your situation.

Sara Robinson, although she noted that chores are not linked to pay, added that "if I have to do someone's chores for them because they flake out, then I do insist on being paid a fair wage for my labor—and that comes out of the allowance." I might have to make use of this concept occasionally. . . .

As far as when to begin allowances, again it seems that this is up to the individual family. Neale S. Godfrey believes that three years old is not too early to begin allowances. Other experts say first grade is a good beginning point. Some parents find that waiting as long as possible is the preferred method. Again, it's up to you.

Cecile Andrews, whose children are grown, adds that, however the no-strings versus work-for-pay issue is handled, she would encourage families to work together. Put on an "oldies, goldies" station and sing while you work! Or just talk about life. This may well turn into one of those beloved family rituals.

Miscellaneous Money Management Rules for Kids

Several of the simple living families I interviewed ask that the kids keep track of what they spend—à la *Your Money or Your Life*. This is often a bookkeeping essential *and* a significant educational tool. My sons are required to do this. On several occasions, as they looked at their month's expenditure list,

I've heard them say, "I think I'll quit spending so much on [whatever they'd been overbuying]."

Many families also help their kids open savings accounts at banks or credit unions, a first step to instilling that savings habit in your child. A few parents agree to "match" any amount put into savings, as an incentive. Urging kids to save takes on added meaning when you show them how savings can grow over time. Show them a compound interest chart, available on-line at www.coop-bank.com/savecalc.html. My kids were astounded when I did this, illustrating to them that if you start with $100 invested at 6 percent, and add only ten dollars monthly, you'd have almost $1,200 after seven years, almost $5,000 after twenty.

Perhaps a majority of simple living parents require the child to pay, out of their allowances, for amounts in excess of what the parents think is reasonable for clothing and other essentials. Basically, Mom and Dad pay for the "need," the kids pay for the "want." Lenora Ridgard says that if daughter Ariel asks for the "brand name" item, Mom puts up the money for the basic item and Ariel kicks in the difference. For example, when Ariel was three she wanted Barney shoes. Lenora had Ariel chip in the extra five dollars for the shoes with the purple dinosaur on the side. It was a good lesson. Lenora says that now when Ariel is faced with spending her own money, she often says, "Never mind."

My husband and I take this approach too—and it works very well. The kids turn into shrewd consumers when they're faced with parting with their own money—or they conclude that the "want" isn't so important after all.

AS THEY GET OLDER

Often, allowances evolve as kids get older. For example, Lynne Cantwell's daughters, Kathryn and Amy, get more now that they're teens—fifty dollars monthly for Amy and sixty dollars for Kathryn—but Lynne expects them to buy school supplies and to pay for many activities, and to put 10 percent aside for savings. "I'm trying to both limit the drain on my checkbook and teach the girls how to manage money," says Lynne.

Gerald Iversen, National Coordinator of Alternatives for Simple Living, and his wife, Rita, instituted a "family allowance" program when the kids were fifteen and ten, respectively, some fifteen years ago. All family members were given an annual allowance of $500. From that amount, they had to purchase all clothing, entertainment, and incidentals. Gerald says it was a great educational tool: "The children learned quickly to economize." The kids are grown now, but Gerald and Rita continue this approach.

Jan Anderson says her job as her kids get older is "creating the awareness." When her sixteen-year-old, who works at a part-time job, wanted to buy a class ring and letterman's jacket (total cost, $580!) Jan had her figure out how many hours she'd have to work to pay for it. "I took the *Your Money or Your Life* approach," says Jan. "I asked, 'How much of your life energy are you spending?' " When her daughter said she still wanted the items, Jan let her earn the money to buy them.

Janet Luhrs, author of *The Simple Living Guide,* says that, despite the family's simple lifestyle, "as soon as my daughter hit high school she wanted to shop and buy clothes. She's a classic teenager." Luhrs's approach has been similar to Jan Anderson's—building an awareness about financial responsibility and communicating that simplicity is not about deprivation, but choices. Daughter Jessica receives an allowance and, Luhrs says, "if she wants to spend all of it on one sweater, then that's that, she knows I'm not going to bail her out." Luhrs adds that she talks to both her kids "endlessly" about debt, which is, as noted above, an American epidemic.

As your children get closer to that leaving-the-nest age, the "pay as you go" message becomes increasingly important. Talk with them about how credit, debit, and ATM cards work. Let them watch you write checks for the *full balance* of your credit card each month and tell them that paying interest on that balance is pure insanity.

The early teen years might be a good time to show your kids how the compound interest concept works in reverse. For example, a $1,000 credit card balance, with no additional purchases, financed at 20 percent—a common credit card rate—would take 109 months, *over nine years,* to pay off, assuming twenty dollars is paid each month. Ten-dollar monthly payments would not even cover the interest portion of the debt; the $1,000 would *never* be repaid at this rate.

Having these talks with your adolescents is pivotal! According to a Merrill Lynch study, more than two-thirds of teens have never discussed responsible credit card use with their folks. Make sure your kids aren't in that majority.

The early teen years are also an optimum time to expose your kids to Lynne Cantwell's study guide for middle school–age kids based on the book *Your Money or Your Life.* In her guide, Lynne takes middle schoolers through the nine steps of YMOYL and applies them to "real life" middle school hypotheticals. (The study guide is described in more detail in Chapter 8.)

BEYOND ALLOWANCE, BEYOND THE NEST

Lynne's guide was recently made available as a download at www.simpleliving.net. Its impact won't be known for a while.

There can be no doubt, however, that it—and other programs like it—are needed. According to the Center for a New American Dream, from 1990 to 1997 college students' average credit card debt jumped 250 percent from $900 to $2,250. University administrators now cite "financial mismanagement" as a crisis among college students.

Perhaps with the time and energy that simple living parents devote to help their children acquire money management skills, along with the efforts of folks like Lynne Cantwell, we can reverse this trend and raise a generation of financially adept young people.

Resources

Lynne Cantwell. *Your Money or Your Life, Study Guide for Middle Schoolers*. Available as a download from www.simple living.net or www.newroadmap.org.

Joe Dominguez and Vicki Robin. *Your Money or Your Life* (New York: Viking, 1999).

ALLOWANCES

Neale S. Godfrey. *A Penny Saved* (New York: Simon & Schuster, 1995).

Neale S. Godfrey and Carolina Edwards. *Money Doesn't Grow on Trees* (New York: Fireside, 1994).

ORGANIZATIONS/WEBSITES

Consumer Reports' Center for Kids Online: www. zillions.org. Helps kids eight and up "evaluate products, see through ad hype, be money smart, and think for themselves."

JumpStart Coalition for Personal Financial Literacy: www. jumpstartcoalition.org. A nonprofit with the goal of making teenagers financially competent by the time they leave high school.

www.coop-bank.savecalc.html. Website with compound interest chart examples.

14

◁▷

EcoFamilies, Frugal Families,
Healthy Families

The beneficial consequences of simple living—its win-win nature—are probably most pronounced, most visible too, when it comes to the environment. Simple living—living lighter on the earth—is, by its very definition, a vote for the planet.

This ripple effect goes further than the environment, as Ernest Callenbach's Green Triangle theory demonstrates. In Callenbach's model, the points of the triangle are Health, Environment, and Money, and his hypothesis is that what benefits one of these three typically benefits the other two. A good example is riding your bicycle more. Good for your health (exercise), good for your pocketbook (savings on gas, parking, maintenance), and good for the earth (less pollution, less resource depletion).

Those of us who embrace simple living believe that Callenbach's Green Triangle can easily metamorphose into a square, a pentagon, even a hexagon and beyond. In addition to Health, Environment, and Money, we can add Community, Happiness, Economic Justice, Compassion, and other virtues. The point here is that most actions that are good for the earth, our health, and our finances also contribute to greater community, to increased individual and family happiness, and even to world peace.

So whenever a simple living family acts in an environmentally friendly manner, they're almost certainly having a positive impact on all of these other areas. Doing the "green thing" is doing the right thing, all the way around.

Consuming Less

The primary way simple living families care for the earth is by using less of its precious resources. There are countless ways that these families consume less.

USE IT UP, WEAR IT OUT, MAKE IT DO, DO WITHOUT

This Depression era motto pretty much sums up the approach that Brenda Scearcy and her family—husband Jim Loewenherz and daughter Larkin—take with regard to consumption. The family shops—almost exclusively, according to Brenda—at secondhand and consignment shops for clothes and toys. "We never buy new clothes," she says, "and we almost never buy something before the old one is worn-out or outgrown." In addition, they take excellent care of their possessions and resell them back to the consignment shops or donate them.

Brenda feels strongly about the issue of taking care of belongings, whether they're clothes or cars. "I realize that maintenance is labor-intensive, but it's worth it," she says. "This is one of the most important things for me to pass on to my daughter."

Brenda points out that some of her low consumption efforts may appear to complicate her life—for example, using cloth diapers versus disposables, or buying bulk carrots and parceling out school-lunch-size portions rather than buying the prepackaged snack sizes. But she emphasizes that she looks at their long-term simplicity versus their short-term convenience. "They simplify environmental cleanup for coming generations, who will have to deal with landfill issues, but they're more work for me," elaborates Brenda. "I think I've simplified my decision-making process by asking a single question to decide how or whether to do something: 'How much environmental damage does it do?' "

Laurie Cohen's family—husband Marshall and daughters Sarah and Abigail—is another example of a low-consumption household. Along with frequenting thrift stores and buying other used items, Laurie avoids products packaged in nonrecyclable materials, and even takes reusable containers to use as "doggy bags" when the family dines out.

FRUGAL FAMILY TIPS

General Strategies: Simplified families adopt several overall cost-cutting principles:

- They make mindful purchases, asking themselves: Do we need this item? Is this purchase in sync with our family's values? Consequently, they consume less.
- They buy used whenever possible.
- They comparison shop and get at least three quotes on large purchases.
- They have better things to do than to "go shopping."
- They borrow—and share—items like rarely used tools and appliances, crowd-size punch bowls, and turkey roasting pans, even trucks for moving days.
- They reuse, repair, restore, refurbish . . . you get the picture.
- Their egos and self-images are not dependent upon the type and amount of their possessions.

(continues)

(continued)

- They *don't* try to keep up with the Joneses.

Specific tips: There are literally thousands of individual ways that simple living families cut costs. A number are mentioned in this chapter. Here are a few additional cost savers that many simple families implement:

1. Use the library. Our local library is our "one stop education and entertainment center." Here's a partial list of what we've been able to access gratis: videos, music CDs and tapes, magazines, DSL Internet access, juggling and magic shows, books on tape, poetry readings, storytelling and puppet shows, concerts, lectures by well-known authors, plays, dance performances, and—almost forgot—books!

2. Entertain at home. This applies to everything from dinner parties to kids' birthday bashes to coffee with your best friend. The cost is minimal—and you can kick your shoes off and sprawl on the couch.

3. Eat at home. This is a corollary of the above entry. The average American now eats 30 percent of his meals away from home, meals that cost more but deliver less nutrition. Simplified families have the time to prepare home-cooked fare—and they're healthier for the effort.

4. Form a "clothes pipeline." Simplified mom Yolanda McVicker's family participates in this informal exchange of kids' clothing with several other families. A total of over a dozen kids of varying ages and sexes pass clothes along to the others as they outgrow them. Hand-me-downs rule!

5. Opt for cloth diapers and wash them yourself. By buying inexpensive "rag" diapers from a local diaper service—ones the diaper service felt weren't quite pretty enough to continue to use—and then washing full loads after soaking them, I calculate that I saved *thousands of dollars* over my five years of diaper duty, and trod lightly on the earth in the process.

6. Think cooperatively. Babysitting co-ops are one example

(continues)

(continued)

of this strategy. Member families agree to watch the other members' kids, typically earning "credits" when they babysit, which they, in turn, can "spend" when they need child care. Cooperative preschools—where families commit to helping in the classroom and actually run the school—are another example, as are indoor play cooperatives, where younger kids can gather to have fun together. Ask other parents or at local churches about these groups.

7. Take light-on-the-earth, light-on-the-pocket vacations. Camping is a favorite simple living holiday. As one downshifted mom told her kids, "We can either spend a few days at Disneyland or three weeks camping, which would you prefer?" The kids chose days of exploring the outdoors and eating S'mores.

8. Get it free. Your local daily newspaper probably has a classified section devoted to inexpensive articles for sale. Ours is called the "thrifties." Every week at least a dozen *free* items are also listed there. Along with the omnipresent kittens, we've seen the following offered: couches, tables, washers and dryers, campers, firewood, refrigerators, microwaves, chickens and rabbits, even hot tubs! It's truly amazing what folks will give away, if you're willing to pick it up.

For more ideas, check the books listed in the "Resources" section at the end of Chapter 1.

EATING LOWER ON THE FOOD CHAIN

Another significant environmental practice for the Cohens is their vegetarian diet. By not eating meat, they are lower on the food chain than their carnivorous peers, resulting in less environmental impact—less water used and less land devoted to grazing. This also means that *all* of the family's food waste can be composted, which it is.

The Cohens also eat primarily organic foods. They're able to save money on their organically grown produce by belonging to a Community Supported Agriculture (CSA) farm.

CSAs involve arrangements between consumers and small, local, organic farms. Households like the Cohens' sign up with a CSA farm as a member or shareholder (the terminology varies) and pay a prescribed amount up front to share in the harvest. They become, in essence, partners with the farmers, reaping windfalls in "bumper crop" years and sometimes receiving less if nature fails to cooperate. Laurie likes the fact that CSAs support farmers who don't use pesticides and that they connect consumers with the land. For more information about CSAs in your area, see "Resources" at the end of this chapter.

Tara Strand-Brown of Occidental, California, used to belong to a CSA until she and three other households in her rural neighborhood formed a community garden on land owned by one of the families. Tara says that this effort has been a great community builder and amazingly hassle-free. "Our goal is to keep it simple," she says. The group comes together for a handful of days to till and plant, and then each household waters once or twice a week and weeds as needed. When harvesting time comes, "we just sort of feel it out," she says. "It really just works."

Anne Felker of Nazareth, Pennsylvania, grows much of her own food and tries to buy the balance at local organic farms. "We seldom go to the grocery store," she says. "It's worth it to us to pay a little more for organic."

HOUSEHOLD UTILITIES AND WATER USAGE

Here are just a few of the methods that Laurie Cohen's family uses to reduce their use of utilities and water: They've switched to compact fluorescent lights—which fit into regular incandescent bulb sockets yet use 70 percent less electricity—in several "high use" areas, and are careful to turn off lights in empty rooms. Their home is well insulated. They've turned their water heater down to 120 degrees. They keep the thermostat at 62 degrees in the winter and throw on a sweater.

They run the dishwasher and clothes washer only with full loads. They've fixed leaky toilet and drippy faucets. They've installed "low flow" shower heads and take short showers. And they don't water their lawn, let alone use any chemicals on it. "We've tried to learn to love dandelions," quips Laurie.

All joking aside, Laurie reasons that if every household in America made even a small effort, it would add up to a huge impact on the environment. "The whole environmental issue seems so huge," she adds, "it's nice to know that we as individuals can make a difference."

TRANSPORTATION

For many environmentally minded people, the big transportation offender is the car. Brenda Scearcy, huband Jim Loewenherz, and daughter, Larkin, are a one-car family—as are many simple living families. And they drive that one car as little as possible. Larkin and her mom walk to school each day, over a mile, no matter the weather. "We're committed [to it]," says Brenda. Besides, she points out, the walk gives them a chance to connect with nature, with each other—and some good exercise.

Kathleen Murphy's family has gone a bit further. Three years ago they sold both of their cars, and they now travel solely by public transit (and the occasional car ride with an acquaintance). "People really seem to think we must be horribly inconvenienced," says Kathleen. "But we honestly and truly enjoy taking the bus. I am continually amazed at how good it has been to be car-free. We like to sit at the back of the bus where the three of us can face each other, and we talk and play games and fool around in ways that could not happen in a car." Kathleen adds that, although their original motivation was to save money, they continue to live car-free because of the amount of quality family time they've found while using public transportation.

The Murphy family lives in Ottawa, Canada, which has

an excellent public transportation system. Families in more rural settings or in cities with mediocre transit setups will find a carless existence more challenging. But it's certainly something to strive for.

The least we can do is be more conscious of our car dependence and try to cut back whenever possible. Laurie Cohen quit making the thirty-five-mile round trip to her daughters' private school each day, instead signing them up for a transportation service "bus." Consciously combining errands is another way the Cohens have cut down on car use. (Use this as one of those "teachable moments": Allow the kids to plot your errand route so as to use the least amount of fuel.)

My own family designated Sunday as a car-free day several months ago, at my younger son's urging. Except for emergencies—and we haven't had any yet—we walk or bike to our destinations, or simply stay home. Making one day a week car-free also piggybacks nicely with Family Day, when Mom, Dad, and the kids devote twenty-four hours to "hanging out" together. See Chapter 12 on Family Rituals.

RECYCLING

Recycling is, of course, the *last* action mentioned in the environmental trilogy: *Reduce, Reuse, Recycle.* By buying and consuming less and by reusing and repairing items, there is much less left to recycle.

But recycling is, obviously, important. Simple living families recycle religiously, whether their municipalities provide recycling services or not. The Cohen family's *low* consumption habits and *high* recycling efforts have resulted in the family producing only about seven pounds of garbage weekly, less than a tenth of what their seventy-gallon trash can holds. (Laurie only has to put her garbage out once each month.)

RECYCLING RULES!

1. Call your local sanitation department and ask what recycling services are available. Many cities now provide curbside recycling. If so, get details on what items are recyclable and how they should be sorted for pickup.

2. If your city doesn't provide curbside services, find out what items are recyclable locally and where you can bring them (your sanitation department should know). Talk with your neighbors about working out a cooperative schedule where a different household transports recyclables to recycling destinations each week or every other week. (Don't forget to advocate for curbside recycling too!)

3. Establish a household recycling center. Find a convenient location—ours is in a large cabinet in our kitchen—and set up bins or bags for those materials that are recyclable—typically, glass, tin, aluminum cans, paper, cardboard, plastic containers, newspapers, and magazines.

4. Compost all nonmeat food leftovers. A couple of good concise books on this subject include *Backyard Composting* and *Let It Rot!*

5. Get rid of junk mail by writing to Mail Preference Service, Direct Marketing Association, P.O. Box 9008, Farmingdale, NY 11735.

6. "Precycle." Remember that you only have to recycle those items you don't consume or reuse. Cut down on your recycling needs by "precycling." Here are a few "precycling" examples: buying items with little or no packaging; purchasing quality products made to last; reusing items whenever possible; bringing cloth bags to the grocery store for carrying purchases; opting for cloth napkins, dishcloths, dust cloths, and diapers; and using your own coffee mug when buying "to go" drinks.

The True Cost of "Stuff"

Some may argue that many environmentally correct products cost more than their less earth- and people-friendly alternatives. It's true that organic vegetables generally cost more than "regular" produce. Similarly, sheets made with organic cotton are pricier, and other products made from recycled materials can cost more. Products that are made in sweatshops and those sold at nonunion megastores are often "bargains."

There are ways to avoid paying many of these higher costs, primarily by buying and consuming less, but also by actions like joining a CSA farm, growing your own vegetables, and eating less or no meat. But it is true that sometimes you'll pay more for items like organic fruit and fair trade/shade grown coffee.

You may pay more, but the actual "cost" or burden on the earth and on the lives of our brothers and sisters around the world will be less. Some simplicity advocates have suggested that all products should include an individual "EIS"—environmental impact statement—or "true cost" label, which would reflect the harm to the earth *and* to low wage workers around the world due to such practices as sweatshops, worker exposure to pesticides, and other human rights abuses.

You can, of course, watch for "certified organic" labels on many food products and the "fair trade certified" stickers on coffee and tea. You can join Co-op America (see "Resources") for information on companies that are socially and environmentally responsible and those that aren't. Unfortunately, that still leaves many items without any real environmental cost/social justice impact disclosures.

Until we have those universal "true cost" labels, we can remember the question that Brenda Scearcy asks when she is deciding whether to buy an item—even when she's thinking of hopping in her car to run an errand: "How much environmental damage does it do?" You can ask: "How much 'people damage' does it do?" too. And then act accordingly.

EcoTeams: Environmental Support Groups

Laurie Cohen's family wasn't always so earth-friendly. While Laurie always considered herself to be conscious of environmental concerns, she learned many new conservation actions when she participated in an EcoTeam in 1999. The EcoTeam Program is a project of Global Action Plan (GAP), a nonprofit group dedicated to educating citizens on how to live more lightly on the earth. With the help of their neighborhood EcoTeam group, Laurie and her family learned new ways to conserve water and energy, discovered additional recycling and low consumption habits, and committed to driving their car less.

True to the Green *Hexagon* theory, there are other benefits to EcoTeams. Llyn Peabody, GAP program manager, notes that "after completing the program, participants often tell us that the aspect of EcoTeams they enjoy most is the sense of community building it brings to the neighborhood." According to Peabody, neighbors taking the EcoTeam program together often end up sharing tools, car pooling, exchanging child care, and participating in other community oriented activities.

EcoTeams are municipally sponsored programs in several communities around the country, but individuals can spearhead their own group by contacting GAP. See "Show You Care: Start an EcoTeam" on page 68 for more information.

Growing Green Kids

All of the methods for helping your kids embrace simplicity work in guiding them toward a love and respect for the earth. Communicating your convictions, teachable moments, and, above all, practicing earth-friendly habits are key. (See "Earth-Friendly Explanations on page 88 and chapter 7 generally.)

John Davis, a simple living dad from Greensboro, North Carolina, uses all of these methods: "I talk about [the environment] every chance I get. I show [my son] that spiders are good, that dead leaves shouldn't be thrown away, that nothing, really, can be thrown 'away,' that walking instead of driving is an opportunity to be cherished, that pollution doesn't stop at man-made borders."

A recent posting on a simple living discussion board brought some additional ideas to mind. The writer was deeply concerned that her pessimism about the future of the planet was impacting her kids. I empathized immediately. It's been especially frustrating since the current administration took office.

As usual, this poster's virtual friends had great ideas. I found two suggestions particularly helpful in this regard. One was to look for family projects that make a difference to the earth, even a small part of it. Cleaning up your street, participating in an Earth Day celebration, and volunteering with an environmental group are all possibilities. Joining an EcoTeam is another project that families can undertake together.

The other idea supplied by the Internet posters was to get out and enjoy nature. This is, of course, one of the fulcrums of growing a green child. Imbuing a love of nature in your child will result in a respect for the planet. Hiking, camping, and bird-watching all come to mind.

Gardening with kids is another of these "environmental connection" strategies. Kathleen Murphy and her six-year-old daughter garden together. "Seeing Alison's beaming smile when she harvested 'her' peas for the first time was well worth any efforts made in weeding and watering," says Kathleen. Your kids are also much more likely to eat their (organic!) vegetables if they had a hand in growing them.

OLDER KIDS

The success you have in bringing your kids along can vary greatly depending upon their age.

Younger kids will sometimes turn into "ecopolice," hounding you to turn the water off or to recycle every scrap of paper. On the other hand, the preteen and teenage years—when their peers' values of consumerism can kick in—can be more difficult.

Which is not to say that you should give up on your teens. Keep using the same tactics you've used all along, adjusting the information to the age level of the child. (See "The Teen Years" on page 165 for more details.)

You can also look for help from environmental support and education groups for kids. Roots and Shoots, for instance, a program of the Jane Goodall Institute, is available for all age groups—preschool through college. These groups can be formed as part of the school curricula, as after-school efforts, or separately, and have a focus on the environment, animals, and the human community. Groups sponsor local projects like establishing bird sanctuaries, setting up recycling programs, and volunteering at soup kitchens, and are also involved in international efforts with other Roots and Shoots groups. There are branches in every state and over fifty countries worldwide. For more information, visit www.jane goodall.org.

Youth for Environmental Sanity is another organization for high school and older kids. Started by two teenagers in 1990, it now has branches in forty-five nations. Visit www. yesworld.org.

A SUSTAINABLE FUTURE

All of your efforts to preserve the planet—and to help your kids become environmentalists—will result in a greater likelihood that the earth can survive and flourish for your children and grandchildren. GAP's Llyn Peabody agrees. "If each of us takes good care of our share of resources," she reasons, "we'll have a beautiful, bounteous world to pass on to our kids."

Resources

Michael Brower and Warren Leon. *The Consumer's Guide to Effective Environmental Choices: Practical Advice from the Union of Concerned Scientists* (New York: Three Rivers Press, 1999).

Stu Campbell. *Let It Rot! The Gardener's Guide to Composting* (Pownal, Vermont: Storey Books, 1998).

Rachel Carson. *Silent Spring* (Boston: Houghton Mifflin, 1962).

Karen Christensen. *Home Ecology: Simple and Practical Ways to Green Your Home* (Golden, Colorado: Fulcrum Publishing, 1990).

Catriona Tudor Erler. *The Frugal Gardener* (Emmaus, Pennsylvania: Rodale Press, 1999).

Richard Heede et al. *Homemade Money: How to Save Energy and Dollars in Your Home* (Snowmass, Colorado: Brick House Publishing, 1995).

Linda Mason Hunter. *The Healthy Home* (Emmaus, Pennsylvania: Rodale Press, 1989).

John Jeavons and Carol Cox. *The Sustainable Vegetable Garden* (Berkeley, California: Ten Speed Press, 1999).

Beth Richardson. *Gardening with Children* (Newtown, Connecticut: Taunton Press, 1998).

John W. Roulac. *Backyard Composting* (Ojai, California: Harmonious Press, 2001).

John C. Ryan and Alan Thein Durning. *Stuff: The Secret Lives of Everyday Things* (Seattle: Northwest Environment Watch, 1997).

Linda Tilgner. *Let's Grow: 72 Gardening Adventures with Children* (Pownal, Vermont: Storey Books, 1988).

BOOKS FOR KIDS

Jacquelin Horsfall. *Play Lightly on the Earth: Nature Activities for Children 3-9 Years Old* (Nevada City, California: Dawn Publications, 1997).

John Javna and the EarthWorks Group. *50 Simple Things Kids Can Do to Save the Earth* (Kansas City, Missouri: Andrews & McMeel, 1990).

David F. Marx. *Earth Day* (New York: Children's Press, 2001).

Bobbe Needham. *Ecology Crafts for Kids: 50 Great Ways to Make Friends with Planet Earth* (New York: Sterling Publishing, 1998).

David Suzuki and Kathy Vanderlinden. *Eco-Fun* (Vancouver, British Columbia, Canada: Greystone Books, 2001).

Kim Michelle Toft. *One Less Fish* (Watertown, Massachusetts: Charlesbridge, 1998).

DECREASING JUNK MAIL

Write to Mail Preference Service, Direct Marketing Association, P.O. Box 9008, Farmingdale, NY 11735.

ENVIRONMENTAL WEBSITES FOR FAMILIES

Canada's Earth Day website for kids: www.ecokids.ca. Includes environmental facts, games, and downloads for children.

The Environmental Defense Fund's website on pollution in your community: www.scorecard.org

The Environmental Protection Agency's Explorer's Club: www.epa.gov/kids/. Fun, environmentally related stuff for kids.

Field Trips Site: www.field-guides.com. Virtual field trips.

Global Action Plan: www.globalactionplan.org; (845) 679–4830. EcoTeam program website.

Institute for Earth Education: www.eartheducation.org; (304) 832–6404.

National Wildlife Federation's field guides site: www. enature.com

The Northwest Earth Institute: www.nwei.org. Voluntary simplicity and deep ecology courses.

Roots and Shoots program: www.janegoodall.org/rs

Youth for Environmental Sanity: www.yesworld.org

INFORMATION ON CO-OP AMERICA

Co-op America is a nonprofit group dedicated to (1) educating its members about how to use their spending and investing power to bring the values of social justice and environmental sustainability into the economy, (2) helping socially and environmentally responsible businesses to emerge and thrive, and (3) pressuring irresponsible companies to adopt socially and environmentally responsible practices. Visit www.coopamerica.org or call (800) 58–GREEN.

INFORMATION ON COMMUNITY SUPPORTED AGRICULTURE

You can request a listing of CSAs in your area from Bio-Dynamic Farming and Gardening Association, (800) 516–7797; or go to their website, www.biodynamics.com, and click on "CSA" for a listing of CSAs and lots of good CSA information. General information on CSAs is also available at the Appropriate Technology Transfer for Rural Areas website, www.attra. org, under "Publications—Marketing and Business." CSAs and related cooperative farming organizations are also featured at www.growingformarket.com and at www.csacenter.org.

INFORMATION ON ECOTEAMS

Contact Global Action Plan at P.O. Box 428, Woodstock, NY 12498; (845) 679–4839; www.globalactionplan.org

❧

15

Education Matters

For my mother and father, raising a family of five children in a small town during the fifties and sixties, making educational choices for their kids was a pretty simple proposition. As devout Catholics, there was no question that we would all go to the local parochial school. And with, at most, one class per grade (some grades were combined), even the question of which teacher to jockey for was a nonissue for them.

Had we not been Catholic, the choice would also have been simple, because the local public schools and the Catholic grade school were the only options. There were no private schools—not that we could have afforded them—and no magnet schools (public schools with focused curricula in arts, et cetera) nor other special programs within the public schools.

Flash forward thirty or forty years and—oh my!—how times have changed. The public schools alone are a maze of possibilities in most cities. In Portland, Oregon, where we live, in addition to the neighborhood schools, there are magnet schools for the arts, Spanish and Japanese immersion, environmental studies, and science, among others. And the number of private schools has increased dramatically in recent years, from conservative Christian schools to Waldorf and Montessori, and myriad other choices. The alternative of home schooling has nearly become mainstream too.

I've tried to put my finger on the reason for this explosion of educational options. Certainly, increased affluence has allowed many parents to pull their kids out of public schools when class sizes have risen or test scores have dropped. And parents and administrators within public schools have worked hard to develop programs that attract and keep students.

But it also has to do with parents generally taking a more "hands on" approach to their kids' educations. This is especially true of simple living parents. Many have thought long and hard about where and how to educate their kids, attempting to ensure that the educational environments their children experience will complement the parents' simple living values. Simplified families are much more likely to home-school or "unschool" their kids—an approach allowing older kids to design their own curriculum—than parents generally. Many also send their kids to private schools; others opt for public schools.

While they may end up making different choices, most simple living parents have carefully analyzed the options. They are also very involved in their kids' schooling. That's obvious if they're home-schooling or unschooling. And for those who send their kids to public and private schools, simplifying allows them the time to volunteer and to supplement their kids' educations when needed.

Just which educational option makes sense for your family will depend upon a number of factors:

- The quality of the public schools in your area and the availability of special programs within them
- How strongly you feel about the philosophies of various private schools
- Your opinion on the benefits of home schooling

- The extent to which your local public schools have allowed commercialism to invade the halls
- Your interest in giving your kids a school environment with racial, ethnic, and income diversity
- Your inclination to send your children to a religious school
- Your financial situation

Here is how different simple families have resolved these issues for their own families:

Private Schools

The Montessori educational approach attracts many simple living parents. Debbie Newman has chosen this option for her two kids. Her reasoning? The Montessori philosophy of learning for learning's sake. "They're learning because they choose to, not because they're going to get a piece of candy for doing it," says Debbie. "We also appreciate the support our school provides against commercialism and in favor of global citizenship." In addition, the school reinforces the family's concern for the environment, as is demonstrated in the school's lunch policy: "We are not allowed to send any food for lunch in containers that are not reusable," she says, which means no Ziploc bags or disposable, individual size servings. The school composts waste too.

The Waldorf philosophy of cherishing childhood and prolonging it was mentioned by a few families. The simple values of no toys, no logos, no sweets at school, and discouraging families from exposing kids to TV and other media make Waldorf a good match for downshifted families. Tara Strand-Brown, who has no television by choice, felt that the Waldorf approach complemented her family's values. She enjoys a rare situation: Her son attends a Waldorf charter school—a free, public institution with Waldorf philosophies.

THE MONTESSORI AND WALDORF PHILOSOPHIES

Many simple living families choose Montessori or Waldorf schools for their children—and for good reason. Here's a look at each schooling method:

Montessori

Dr. Maria Montessori (1870–1952), founder of the Montessori method, believed that "education is a natural process spontaneously carried out by the human individual." Her advice was to "follow the child." The premise at Montessori schools is that children teach themselves, that they have an innate passion for learning. The role of the teacher is to provide a "prepared environment" and opportunities and activities for the child to progress at his or her own individual pace.

There is a deep respect for the child as a unique individual in the Montessori environment. The child's social and emotional development is also central. The natural world is emphasized by providing children with "hands on" experiences. Classes are usually of mixed age.

Waldorf

Rudolf Steiner (1861–1925) developed the concepts behind Waldorf education and believed that children become fully absorbed in the learning process when they connect what they learn to their own experience. Consequently, Waldorf schools emphasize experiential learning with a focus on art, music, gardening, and other "hands on" learning activities. The curriculum is geared to the child's stages of development, and it attempts to balance academic, artistic, and practical work; hence the Waldorf principle of educating the whole child— "head, heart, and hands."

Teachers often "loop up" with their classes for several years so they can grow and learn together with their students. Testing and grading are limited, and competitive activities and electronic media are discouraged.

Shelby Pawlina sends her daughter to a private school where class sizes are small and the curriculum is experience-based. There is no testing, says Shelby, but rather, authentic assessment of each child, with teachers who strive to understand each student's learning styles and strengths. She adds that creating a loving and respectful community among all living things is a focus too. "It just feels like a place that will support some of the values we're working hard on at home," she says.

Home Schooling and "Unschooling"

When I asked one "unschooling" dad, Paul Wilson, what "unschooling" was, his response was to ask me a question: "If you, as an adult, wanted to learn about a subject, what would you do?" I told him the obvious—read books, contact experts, make observations, maybe search the Internet. "That's what 'unschooling' is," Paul said. "That's what kids who are 'unschooled' do."

Paul's answer explains why many parents begin, with younger children, by home-schooling them with prepared curricula. Then, when the kids are a bit older, the parents allow the children to unschool—in essence, permitting the children to prepare their own curricula, deciding for themselves what and how they wish to study.

Once again, the reasons many simple living parents choose the home schooling/unschooling option has much to do with their simple lifestyles. Many don't want their kids exposed to the commercialization and peer pressure that often come with a public school education. Others feel that, between overcrowding and an "institutional attitude," their public schools can't provide a quality education.

Michael Fogler says it well when he explains his reasons for unschooling his son, Benjamin: "First, there's the grading, ranking, tracking, competing stuff, which I didn't like.

Then, there's the notion that learning is imposed upon someone by only certified experts who tell you exactly what should
be learned, when it should be learned, and how it should be
learned. Then, there's the whole increasing focus on career
preparation being practically equivalent to education."

Couple these concerns with a simple lifestyle that allows
one or both parents to be home, and you've created the ideal
environment for home schooling. For more information on
home schooling and unschooling, see "Resources" at the end
of this chapter.

Opting for Public Schools

My husband and I concluded that our local public schools
would work well for our two boys.

To be honest, we never considered home schooling or private schools, primarily because we believe strongly in supporting the public educational system, but also because we're
blessed with relatively good public schools in our area. And
the fact that public schools are free certainly didn't hurt.
These two factors—free, quality education—convince many
downshifted families to send their kids to the local public
school.

My own family's big decision was choosing among the
many options available throughout our school system. When
our oldest was ready for kindergarten, we visited seven
different grade schools and finally settled on a very small—
two-hundred-student—kindergarten through third grade
school one neighborhood over from ours. It was a tough decision!

Public schools offer another educational element I consider important: diversity. Few private schools can boast the
racial, ethnic, and socioeconomic mix that the public schools
can. I wanted my kids to grow up with people of varying
backgrounds, and they are, something that I certainly didn't

experience when I was a kid. Several of the families I interviewed mentioned this benefit of public schools. I believe this interest in diversity stems from simple living parents' views on global citizenship (see "Raising Your Child to Be a Global Citizen" on page 58) and their desire to understand other cultures and live in harmony with all races and nationalities. Understanding and harmony are precursors to justice and to peace, and all are values that simple living families hold dear.

Linda McDonough, a single mother with two kids, articulates her decision to send her girls to public schools this way: "I cannot afford private schools, and I work so I can't homeschool. I also try to support the public schools—if they aren't good enough for my child, they shouldn't be good enough for anyone." She also loves the diversity. The school her oldest attends—and her youngest will attend later—has forty-one different nationalities represented among its 390 students!

In larger cities, families can avail themselves of magnet or alternative public schools, some of which have many simple values. Simplicity leader Cecile Andrews sent her two kids to Seattle's ORCA Elementary, which emphasizes the arts and the environment. Andrews feels that the decision to send her kids to an alternative school was pivotal in helping her kids embrace simplicity. The combination of a environmentally focused curriculum and classmates with similar simple values was a potent antidote to negative peer pressure.

Occasionally you can find these options even in smaller communities. Tara Strand-Brown sends her son, Tevon, to a charter (public) Waldorf School near her rural home in Occidental, California.

ADVOCATE FOR GOOD PUBLIC SCHOOLS
AND SIMPLICITY CURRICULA

A little shameless plug here: Even if you decide not to send your children to public school, please support adequate financing for these institutions. More and more parents are choosing to opt out of public schools at the same time that their funding is becoming more precarious. The end result is that those left within the public school system will be hurt by larger classes, fewer support services, and a growing proportion of kids with special needs. Many of those "left behind" will be from poor and/or disadvantaged families. They need help at every stage, and a meaningful education is a big piece of the puzzle for many of these children. Supporting public schools adequately would also help the growing problem of commercialization of schools (see Chapter 8).

Here's another radical idea: "All schools should teach something about voluntary simplicity because of its connection with the environment," says Cecile Andrews. While most schools now integrate environmental themes in the curricula, "living on less" is rarely explored. See Chapter 14 for information on environmental curricula/programs for kids. Chapters 8 and 9 contain details on efforts to include media literacy in schools.

The High Cost of College

Most friends recite obligatory congratulations when you first tell them you're pregnant. But the response we received from one acquaintance upon hearing that we were expecting again when our first was barely walking caught us off guard.

"Oh no! You'll have two in college at the same time!"

The thought had never crossed my mind.

If you look simply at the numbers, my friend's concern was well-placed. Four years at a public institution already averages over $40,000. The cost for many private colleges is currently around $100,000, much more if an Ivy League school is part of the plan. These prices are expected to keep rising at about 5 to 7 percent annually.

With inflation factored in, this means that the college cost for your kindergartner could easily approach $100,000 for a public college and upward of $200,000 for a more prestigious private school. Oh yes, you also need to multiply these figures by the number of children you have.

If you let them, these totals can send you into "sticker shock" and cause you to throw your hands up in despair, concluding that there is *no way* you can possibly pay for your children's higher education and retire before your eightieth birthday.

Fortunately, there are a number of ways to make college more affordable for your kids. Living simply will help you.

PRELIMINARY MATTERS

There are at least two ways to avoid *any* cost for your children's college education. One is to not help your kids pay for college at all, telling them that they're on their own.

Not many of us come to this conclusion, however. While we may have footed the bill for college ourselves, it's a different story for the next generation. Both my husband and I are in this boat, having financed our own educations through savings, loans, part-time jobs, grants, and scholarships. But when I was in college, tuition at my four-year alma mater (a state university) was an astoundingly low $500 annually; today that same state institution charges $4,098 for in-state undergraduates, $14,000 for out-of-state tuition.

That expense can be a ball and chain, particularly acquired so early in life. Gerald Iversen, father of two grown children, says, "I feel strongly that parents are responsible for their children's education, that debt is the 'enforcer' of overconsumption. Children are more likely to get into the work-spend-work-spend death cycle if they have accumulated debt." Viewed from this perspective, not helping your child with college costs seems almost inhumane.

The other method of avoiding any college expenses is if your child doesn't attend college. Most of us college-educated, middle- or upper-middle-class Americans shudder at this thought, but ultimately it's your child's choice. Cecile Andrews's son didn't attend college; he makes a living as an artist, and Andrews is rightly proud of him.

Linda McDonough, a single mother of two daughters, one of whom is adopted, has a different perspective on the "college or not?" question. When I asked her how she would handle her girls' college expenses, she said: "When I talk to others of adopting another child, this is the most common 'reason' why I shouldn't. 'How will you put them through college?' they ask. They seem to feel that it is better for a child to live without love and a permanent home than to jeopardize anyone's chance to go to college. I feel that love, food, and parents are necessities. People stress about paying for four years of a child's life that are far less significant than the first four years. Let's stress about that a little more and worry less about earning enough to put our kids through college."

Food for thought!

One final idea was conveyed by several downshifted parents. Kids—and adults!—appreciate something more when they've had to earn it, or at least part of it. Something else to think about.

For those who can and want to finance all or a portion of their kids' higher education, here are some tips:

HELPING WITH COLLEGE COSTS
THROUGH SAVINGS

One observation at the outset: Living simply is a tremendous boost toward the goal of saving for your kids' educations. If you've been able to scale down to the point where you're saving 50 percent or more of your income, stashing some of those savings away for college funds is much more "doable" than if you're spending frivolously on flashy cars and big screen TVs. Another factor: Hopefully you've imparted some of your simple ways to your offspring. If they're willing to forgo the cell phone, Palm Pilot, and cutting-edge laptop computer, their college bill won't include so many "incidentals."

On the other hand, it's also true that part of your simple living plan may be for one or both parents to work part-time—or not at all—in order to spend more time with family. After all, the ultimate goal of voluntary simplicity is to enable its practitioners to be involved in those elements of life that matter most to them. For families, time with each other is often number one.

Consequently, you may not be planning to foot the entire bill for your kids' higher education. This is the approach most simple living families take. They hope to save and pay for a portion of each child's college costs.

Each family will approach the task of saving for college differently, depending upon their income level, number of kids, expectations about higher education, and help from other sources—such as grandparents and scholarships. Here are a number of methods that can assist families in saving the needed funds, cutting the cost of college, and finding financial assistance.

SAVING AND INVESTING

Saving should be second nature to downshifters. What to do with that money, assuming you'll use it for your kids' college expenses, is another issue. The experts note that how you invest those funds for college should be based upon the number of years you have to allow those savings to grow.

Generally speaking, these experts recommend that you choose more aggressive—or "growth"—mutual funds, the younger your child is. So if you have a newborn, they would counsel you to put most of those savings in index or similar mutual funds. Simple living parents will probably also want to consider the social responsibility of the fund. The Social Investment Forum, www.socialinvest.org, offers detailed information on socially responsible investing and includes a mutual fund screening chart.

Kalman Chany, author of *Paying for College Without Going Broke*, recommends that "gradually, as your child gets closer to college, adjust your asset allocation so that more of your account is in fixed assets"—investments like certificates of deposit (CDs), money market funds, bond funds, and U.S. Treasury securities. The same advice applies if you're only starting to save at, say, middle school age. "Avoid the temptation to start day trading to make up for lost time," warns Chany. By the eleventh or twelth grade, he says, the bulk of your assets should be in fixed income accounts.

Chany also counsels parents, "If you have any hope of financial aid, never put money in the child's name." Why? Because college financial aid departments consider up to 35 percent of a child's assets available for college expenses, whereas they view only about 5 percent of the parents' assets to be available. "You could save some on taxes," elaborates Chany, "only to lose more later in financial aid."

ALTERNATIVES TO THE HIGH COST OF COLLEGE

Simplifiers pride themselves on their creative approaches to cost cutting. Here are a few ways that simple living parents recommend for keeping college costs down.

Consider the community college–state university approach

My husband lived at home, attended a local community college, and then switched to a public university in town, and in the process saved thousands of dollars. In 1999–2000, the average tuition for a community college was $1,627—much more affordable than the $32,000-plus price tag at an Ivy league school or even the average state university tuition of $10,000 annually.

(continues)

(continued)

Have the kids live at home while they attend college

If you're lucky enough to live in a city with a good university, this could be a big cost cutter for you. But you'll want to weigh this approach against the benefits of a campus college life experience. It will depend upon your child, your home situation, and, again, your finances.

Have Mom or Dad get a job at a college

Many colleges and universities provide free or reduced tuition for the children of their employees. This obviously won't work for everyone, but it's something to keep in mind if you have some flexibility.

Cooperative education

Almost 1,000 colleges around the country allow students to attend college full-time between stints of working full-time in their field of study. Kids usually spend alternative terms in college and then at work with both private companies and the federal government. For more information visit www.co-op.edu.

Running Start

Jan Anderson's seventeen-year-old participates in a program called Running Start, in which high school seniors take courses at the local community college. The college classes qualify both toward high school requirements and toward college credit. Contact your school district to inquire about similar programs in your area.

Equivalency or "challenge" tests

Some colleges allow you to "challenge" a course by taking a test. You then receive the credit for the class. While you pay a fee for the test, it's typically far less than tuition. Contact your college for more information.

(continues)

(continued)

ROTC

My niece received her B.A. from Notre Dame by joining ROTC—the Reserve Officer Training Corps—and, boy, was my brother glad. The downside is that you have to commit to four years of active duty plus two more years in the Reserve. My niece hasn't minded too much; her husband was in the ROTC program too. It might not work for everyone but it's another option. Call (800) USA–ARMY.

Head Start, Peace Corps, VISTA

If a young person is so inclined, joining one of these social service organizations will result in the federal government forgiving at least some of your college loans. Visit www.peace corps.gov.

AmeriCorps program

You can also earn up to $4,725 yearly in educational grants—which you can use to repay school loans—by joining this program where you work for minimum wage with educational, environmental, police, elderly, or homeless groups. Call (972) 490–1776 or visit www.americorps.gov for more information.

Think twice about "status schools"

Many parents urge their kids to apply to private, prestigious universities, without really questioning why they're pushing their kids in that direction.

If you're one of these parents, ask yourself: Is the private institution worth the extra cost? Is this purchase in keeping with my values? Why am I pushing my kids to go to a private college? This analysis goes to the essence of simplifying. If your conclusion is that a private university fits your child's situation, then living simply will help you pay those higher costs.

(continues)

(continued)

Some families decide to save enough for their child to attend a public university. If the kid then wants to go to a private college, he or she has to pick up the difference.

Assistance from relatives

Grandparents help out in a lot of cases. Ever since our kids were born, one set of grandparents has given them savings bonds at each birthday and Christmas. We *really* appreciate those bonds—and the kids will too someday.

APPLY FOR FINANCIAL AID—EARLY AND OFTEN

Everyone should take the time to apply for aid, no matter their circumstances, according to Kalman Chany. The help that's available includes needs-based grants, scholarships—which are merit-based but also frequently take need into consideration—work-study money, and loans.

Along with the FAFSA (Free Application for Federal Student Aid) available at high schools and on the Internet, many colleges also require the financial aid Profile form, and some private schools also have their own forms. Ask early in your child's senior year—or, preferably, in the spring of her junior year—for all of these documents. You should also contact schools that your child is applying to for more information.

Find out as much as you can about aid and scholarship programs. "The more you understand about the process, the more likely you'll get money," explains Chany.

There are literally thousands of scholarships out there that are available to high school students. A good comprehensive source is *The Scholarship Advisor* by Christopher Vuturo. This resource lists over 100,000 (!) scholarships that are available to students, and not just the straight A, all-state football star. There are scholarships for the visually impaired, for those of Polish and Norwegian descent, for P.K.'s (preachers' kids), for children of disabled veterans and union members, for students who've worked part-time in restaurants, for kids who have a pilot's license, even for students who are "from a peanut producing family." The criteria for these awards also varies greatly and, along with academic performance, often includes financial need as well as community service, character, essays, and school activities.

Starting early is imperative. With scholarship money, the early—and persistent!—bird catches the worm.

Resources

FINANCING COLLEGE

Kalman Chany with Geoff Martz. *Paying for College Without Going Broke* (New York: Princeton Review, 2002).

Cooperative Education Colleges: www.co-op.edu

Dr. Jerry Ice and Dr. Paul Jay Edelson. *The Complete Book of Distance Learning Schools: Everything You Need to Earn Your Degree Without Leaving Home* (New York: Princeton Review Books, 2001).

Benjamin Kaplan. *How to Go to College Almost for Free* (Gleneden Beach, Oregon: Waggle Dancer Books, 2000).

Christopher Vuturo. *The Scholarship Advisor* (New York: Princeton Review, 2001).

Americorps: www.americorps.gov

Peace Corps: www.peacecorps.gov

ROTC information: (800) USA–ARMY.

HOME SCHOOLING

Rhonda Barfield. *Real Life Homeschooling: The Stories of 21 Families Who Teach Their Children at Home* (New York: Fireside, 2002).

John Gatto. *Dumbing Us Down: The Hidden Curriculum of Compulsory Schooling* (Philadelphia: New Society Publishers, 1992).

Kathy Ishizuka. *The Unofficial Guide to Homeschooling* (Foster City, California: IDG Books Worldwide, 2000).

Elizabeth Kanna and Rebecca Kochenderfer. *Homeschooling for Success* (New York: Time Warner, 2002).

John and Kathy Perry. *The Complete Guide to Homeschooling* (Los Angeles: Lowell House, 2000).

HOME SCHOOLING WEBSITES

www.holtgws.com: Growing Without Schooling; (617) 864–3100. Home schooling curricula and resources.

www.homeschool.com: "Your Virtual Homeschool." Extensive information on home schooling along with message boards, support groups, and other resources.

www.homeschoolnewslink.com. Website for *The Link,* a bimonthly home schooling newspaper available free by calling (888) 470–4513; good basic home schooling information.

www.unschooling.com. Detailed information on the unschooling option (sponsored by *Home Education* magazine).

MONTESSORI AND WALDORF SCHOOLS

The American Montessori Institute: www.montessori-ami.org

The Association of Waldorf Schools of North America: www.awsna.org; (916) 961-0927.

The Montessori Foundation: www.montessori.org; (800) 655–5843.

16

Simple Holidays

I asked my mother, who had an *involuntarily* simple childhood, as I mentioned earlier, to tell me what Christmas was like when she was growing up during the 1920s and 1930s in a small town in northern Minnesota.

Christmas Eve, she says, was very special. "Neighbors began to stop by around five or six to visit, maybe for a little Christmas cheer." By eight or so, family and friends had arrived, and the evening was spent decorating the tree, singing Christmas carols, and catching up.

By eleven o'clock everyone, Catholic or not, prepared to walk to midnight mass, which back then actually took place at midnight. The town, blanketed in snow—we're in Minnesota, remember?—looked like a scene from Currier and Ives.

Mom remembers one Christmas particularly well. An ice storm had caused a temporary power outage. The town was serenely quiet as the group trudged the half mile to the small church, and, without streetlights, the stars lit the way. Mom thought of the three Magi, how a star guided them too.

The church where they gathered was decorated with pine boughs and lit with dozens of candles. Mom vividly remembers the music that night. The choir director was the high school music teacher, and his family brought their viola, cello, and violin to accompany the voices. The combination of scents, sights, and sounds has stayed with my mother for seven decades. "I can remember the fragrance of pine, the children's voices, the beauty of the candlelit altar, and feeling that I was surrounded by those I loved. It was a magical evening," my mother recalls.

The magic continued as the group traipsed home through the snow, anticipating the next event—for the evening was far from over. The tradition after midnight mass was to sit down to a festive meal, with a once-a-year treat, a French dish called *tortiere* (meat pie) and all the trimmings.

After a leisurely dinner, presents were opened. But Mom emphasizes that "the gifts weren't the highlight, it was really the whole evening.

"We didn't have a lot of money then so gifts weren't very big. But I think we enjoyed the holidays more then than we do now," Mom laments. "Christmas was a time that we had special foods, did special things. Now we have that stuff all year long."

From Christmas to "Crassmas"

My mother's description of her childhood Christmases along with her comments on why the holidays were so special then really tell it all. Christmas, once a magical time for focusing on family, friends, and faith, has degenerated into a commercialized and frenetic ordeal. The simple holiday memories that my mother treasures—emphasizing people, spirituality, and endearing traditions, with gifts as nearly an afterthought—are, in fact, the very things that folks now yearn for.

According to a 2000 survey by the Center for a New American Dream, 84 percent of Americans would prefer a less materialistic holiday, with more emphasis on the things that money can't buy. More than three-quarters feel that excessive holiday advertising and marketing to kids is taking the joy and meaning out of the season. Jo Robinson and Jean Coppock Staeheli, authors of *Unplug the Christmas Machine*, note that "virtually all the people we've talked to . . . [long] for a simpler, less commercial, more soul-satisfied celebration." When participants of their workshops were asked to fantasize about their perfect Christmas, Robinson and Staeheli found that what most people envision is a simple holiday. Their common fantasies involved "simple gifts, natural decorations, a fire, traditional food, leisurely schedules, music, time spent out of doors, and an emphasis on family activities." Sure sounds a lot like my mom's Christmas memories.

The Mega-Consumer Microcosm

The more I research the subject of holiday excess and the more I actually experience Christmas chaos each year, the more I see the period from Thanksgiving (and earlier!) through New Year's as a nearly perfect microcosm of our year-round struggle with materialism.

How so? The modus operandi of our culture is to overconsume throughout the year. During the holiday season, we obviously have to "up the ante." The ostensible reason is to "celebrate" the season. But it's really just another marketing maneuver with the ultimate goal of ringing up sales. Indeed, almost everything said in this chapter could be applied to life in our consumer culture generally.

According to studies, a solid majority of families would like to simplify the holidays; they would likewise prefer simpler living year-round. The types of activities that are truly meaningful during the holidays are the same as those that we hold dear generally—family time, get-togethers with friends and relatives, walks, music, and other simple pleasures connecting us with each other and nature. All of those things that make my mother's holiday memories so dear.

In fact our greater dissatisfaction with Christmas probably relates to the fact that Christmas represents our normal consumeristic society magnified—multiplied exponentially!—and consequently we sense its meaninglessness on a larger scale. "For many of the people we talk to," say Robinson and Staeheli, "Christmas is often just a little bit more of the things they are used to all year-round—more food, more people, more material goods."

The irony, of course, is that the interval between Thanksgiving and New Year's *should* be a natural ally of the simplicity movement. Christmas is about the ultimate simple birth of a child in an animal's stable, a child who eventually implored his followers to give up all of their worldly belongings and follow him. Perhaps due to this paradox, our annual Christmas obsession with too much stuff and too much to do is seen for what it truly is during the holidays—misguided and meaningless. An attempt to buy happiness gone horribly wrong.

HOLIDAY HYPE

Almost everything said in this chapter can also be applied to those other December holidays, Hanukkah, Kwanza, Ramadan, indeed to *all* holidays year-round.

As an example, take Halloween. For Halloween 2000, Americans spent $2 billion on candy alone, with each household doling out an average of $84 on candy and other Halloween "stuff"—decorations, costumes, pumpkins, candy dishes, doormats that play eerie tunes, and the like. I focus on Christmas because it is the most blatant example of the commercialization of holidays and because it's the holiday most folks would like to change.

For an insightful look at Christmas, past and "present," read Bill McKibben's book *Hundred Dollar Holiday: The Case for a More Joyful Christmas.* McKibben summarizes the reasons for simplifying Christmas, and once again they mirror those for simplifying generally: "The reason to change Christmas is not because it damages the earth around us, though surely it does. . . . The reason to change Christmas is not because it represents shameful excess in a world of poverty, though perhaps it does. The reason to change Christmas . . . is because it might help us to get at some of the underlying discontent in our lives."

Obstacles to Holiday Happiness

From my talks with simplified families, it seems that the biggest obstacles to enjoying a simple Christmas fall into two categories, both of which represent issues to deal with when simplifying generally:

The Big One, of course, is the commercialization of Christmas. According to the National Retail Federation, American families spent, on average, almost $800 on holiday gifts in 1997. And that's just for items under the tree, not the food and drink, gift wrap, "lights in motion," Department 56 villages, "collectible" ornaments, and Cabin in the Woods dinnerware. That year, Americans collectively spent over $163 billion on holiday purchases. On average, it took six months for each family to pay off those holiday excess bills. Even an agnostic/lapsed Catholic like myself can see the irony in the materialistic extravaganza that this season has become. Our present-day holiday celebrations resemble Jesus' birth and simple life very little.

The second big obstacle to truly enjoying Christmas is the "busyness" of the season—the additional family and work obligations, shopping, school programs, travel, and efforts to decorate and entertain. Coupled with the absence of truly meaningful rituals and traditions, the result is often a sadly paradoxical amount of stress during this time of Peace on Earth. (One Internet poster called the season the "Hollerdays," due to all of the yelling.)

What might seem to be a third problem, at first blush, are our expectations about the season. Most of us really love this time of year, or at least we *used* to. But unless those expectations involve picture perfect, "magazine cover" holidays, I don't really think they're the problem. As noted above, these aren't part of most folks' Christmas fantasies.

I believe the commercialization and "busyness" of the season are the true culprits. By dealing with those, I feel that most of us can meet our holiday expectations—those of a peaceful, satisfying time with our family and friends. Most of the other aspects of the holidays that end up frustrating or disappointing us are, it seems, related to these two issues. I'm not sure what to do about the overdrinking uncle or the cousins who fight each year. But simplifying the entire month can't hurt!

ONE FAMILY'S HOLIDAY "EPIPHANY"

Rusty and Kate Rhoad's Chistmas celebrations used to be typical American free-for-alls. "It was a major event," says Kate, of the family of five's presimplifying holidays. "There were huge amounts of presents under the tree, stuff the kids didn't really need or even want."

The excess didn't stop with Kate's nuclear family; gifts to parents and in-laws were also copious. Kate recalls one year when they purchased an Ansel Adams print for Rusty's sister and husband, a microwave for Rusty's parents, and camping equipment for his brother and his girlfriend. "We were trying to make a good impression," admits Kate. "We figured everyone's going to do this and we have to keep up." Kate says they'd spend up to $1,000 on gifts alone each year, even when they had only one child to buy for (they now have three kids).

Trying to find the "right" gift for everyone was "very stressful and tension-filled," she says. They also realized that they were doing too many things, accepting every invitation, without considering the impact on the family.

The result? "It was hectic, we were too busy. The kids felt it too. We just didn't have fun at Christmas," she recalls.

But things changed in 1993. That year, Kate and Rusty decided to simplify their holidays. The family sat down at the end of November with the December calendar. "We made a list of things we *really* wanted to do over Christmas, and put them on the calendar." Some of the things they've done over the years include "adopting" a needy family (buying holiday foods and gifts for them), going caroling with friends, reading Christmas stories and drinking hot chocolate, and celebrating the winter solstice on December 21.

Instead of shopping for impressive gifts all month, Kate, Rusty, and their three kids—Travis, Dakota, and Saxon—make gifts for others. Each year, the entire family cooks up a batch of barbecue sauce and delivers it to neighbors. They make homemade picture frames for in-laws, with photos of the kids in them. They've also made colorful envelopes out of old calendars. The family's annual holiday price tag now reaches about $200 *for everything*—from gifts to decor.

"Our intention is renewal, and all that buying has nothing to do with renewal," says Kate. "Now I have time to be mindful. That's my goal, to be mindful of the season and of my family and have less stress on things. I love the fact that we've made these changes."

A Six-Step Plan for Simplifying Christmas

You can bring renewal and joy back into your holiday season too. The following six-step plan will guide you to a simpler, more meaningful Christmas.

Note: These six steps can also assist you in simplifying

other winter religious holidays your family may celebrate and holidays year-round. Substitute the holiday in question for Christmas where appropriate. Consider some of the down-scaled gift-giving ideas in this chapter, and research other simple rituals for your simplified holiday.

1. SOUL SEARCHING

Does this sound familiar? Chapter 2 asks you to perform some general soul searching. Take a few more minutes now and analyze your feelings about the holidays.

In *Unplug the Christmas Machine,* Robinson and Staeheli note that "being unsure of their values is the source of many people's unhappiness at Christmas." Again, much like life generally . . .

So fish out a pen and paper and answer the following questions. Mom and Dad should answer them with kid input where appropriate.

- What did you love most about Christmas as a child? Try to remember the sights, the smells, the sounds, and the feelings.
- What do you enjoy about Christmas now? It's important to get kid input on this question. They'll undoubtedly mention gifts; take that in stride and ask what *else* they love about Christmas.
- What do you want your focus to be during the holidays? What is it about the holidays that you feel is important?
- Describe your "perfect" Christmas—perfect as in fulfilling your true wishes, not perfect as in Madison Avenue flawlessness.
- What aspects of Christmas do you truly dislike? Possibilities here might include the in-law gift exchange, the entire Christmas card ordeal, traveling to three relatives' homes on Christmas Eve. Then again, these items

might be on your fantasy list. Remember, it's an individual thing.

With the answers to these questions, summarize your feelings about Christmas into (1) those activities or elements of the holiday that are important to you and your family and that you wish to keep or to add, and (2) those aspects of Christmas that you wish to do away with or to change.

2. RESEARCH NEW TRADITIONS

Traditions are a *huge* part of the holiday season. Family traditions are important, say Robinson and Staeheli, because they give kids something to look forward to and because they provide a sense of order and security.

Your family's new traditions will fall into two general categories: the scaling back of spending, if that has been an issue for you; and transforming the unsatisfying "busyness" of the season into meaningful rituals.

The Gift-Giving Tradition

Gift-giving is the most common of all traditions of the season—and the one that folks would most like to change, or even abolish altogether.

Some of the methods for scaling back on gift-giving turn into treasured family traditions. This is true for my extended family. Many years ago we decided to quit exchanging gifts between the adults and substituted a "White Elephant" exchange. (My own family started doing this, and soon afterward my husband's two family gatherings joined in.)

Here's how it works: Everyone—or just the adults—wraps a gift. Some families say the gifts must be something you find gathering dust in your own home; others say it can be either secondhand or very inexpensive. All wrapped gifts are placed before the group. Numbers are drawn. Number one selects a gift. Number two can either take number one's gift or open another. No gift can change hands more than two times—in other words, the third "owner" keeps it.

Like many families who have adopted this tradition, we have some items that circulate year after year: the bottle of "Hog's Breath" beer (which started out as a six-pack many holidays ago), the "lovely" porcelain bird figurine, the fake tie-on "fanny." For me, and I suspect everyone else involved, this raucous exchange is much more enjoyable than receiving a bunch of stuff you don't need that you have to pretend you're excited about getting. My kids have watched us have so much fun with this tradition that now they participate too.

Some families have a rule of no gifts for adults, only children. Other families draw names. Tara Strand-Brown's father and sisters all draw two names and give gifts only to those two. "This works great! Everyone loves it," says Tara. The idea is to come up with a plan that puts a limit on the excess, one that everyone can agree to.

New Family Traditions

Look at your list of traditions/activities you enjoy and those you dislike. If your family already has several traditions that you all look forward to each Christmas and none you find distasteful, consider yourself lucky.

If you're like most of us, your list will be a mix of loves and hates. The key is to have traditions that are *meaningful* to you. Most simple living folks find that the rituals that have most significance are those involving either other people— friends, family, or those in need—nature, or their faith.

Friends and family: Christmas gatherings are for many of us part of the magic of community during the holidays. If they are for you and yet you find them exhausting and stressful, then simplify them! Probably the best simplifying advice for these affairs can be summed up in one word: potluck.

Potluck, fortunately, implies another simplification strategy: casual. Even if you enjoy dressing up, others may loathe it. The important thing is to get together.

One family passes around a "job jar" at holiday get-togethers. Everyone pulls a slip of paper from the jar to find out what their Christmas chore is. This way everyone knows how they can help out before and after the meal, and the host/hostess isn't so overwhelmed. The kids have their own job jar with age-appropriate tasks for them.

The community-enhancing aspects of the holidays can take other forms. Linda McDonough's family stages a "cookie sneak" on St. Nicholas' Eve—the night of December 5. Linda and her two daughters make gingerbread cookies and then "sneak" them around to neighbors, leaving the treats anonymously on doorsteps. It's a great way, says Linda, for her girls to understand the joy of giving while having fun—and cookies!—in the process.

Charity: The holidays are traditionally a time of charity, and many families try to incorporate a "giving" tradition into their family's repertoire of seasonal activities. Giving traditions that focus on children or seniors are particularly appropriate for families. Collecting art supplies and other needed items for a local women's shelter can teach your children many valuable lessons. "Adopt a Family" is popular, as are "giving trees," which feature names of needy kids instead of ornaments and are found in malls (*if* you can stomach going to one). Call your local volunteer bureau for more information.

The charitable tradition can blend with the gift-giving one too. For example, Gerald Iversen's family gives sizable contributions to the needy and limits gifts to one each. Other simple families ask that adult gifts be to the "giftee's" favorite charity. The Alternative Gifts website—www.altgifts.org—allows you to choose from thirty-three national and international relief organizations, make a donation "in honor of" someone, and then have a card sent to the honored individual.

Nature: Many simple living families make a point of getting out into nature during the holidays. For example, Shelby

Pawlina's family decorates an outdoor tree with edible "ornaments" like cranberries and popcorn, for their bird friends.

A common practice for families who aren't practicing Christians—and some who are—is to celebrate the winter solstice on December 21. Some families simply take a walk and then light a candle and enjoy a moment of silence. Others have somewhat elaborate ceremonies, with poetry readings and singing.

Karen Schneider-Chen's family walks down to the dock of a nearby lake and lights a candle. They tell a Native American story about how the sun came into existence and then they sing the winter solstice song, "Light Is Returning." "It's an uplifting ceremony," says Karen.

Faith-based traditions: There are many established, religiously oriented Advent and Christmas traditions worthy of your family's consideration. Linda McDonough's family has adopted a number of these.

One is the Jesse Tree tradition, a reference to King David's father, Jesse, and his descendants. The "tree" is often just a bare branch, says Linda. Each day from the first of December to the twenty-fourth, Linda's daughters add a special ornament that signifies some aspect of biblical history and Linda tells the story associated with the ornament. For example, an ornament of stone tablets represents the story of Moses; a slingshot depicts David. "It helps us to focus on what the season is really about—and the kids love the stories," says Linda.

Some families improvise and create their own faith-based rituals. Kathleen Murphy's daughter Alison thought that a birthday cake for Jesus would make perfect sense. "So now we have a family ritual of baking a birthday cake, candles and all, for Christmas dinner, and singing 'Happy Birthday' to Jesus," says Kathleen.

Often, other cultures can provide inspiration for wonderful faith-based traditions. See the "Resources" section for more ideas.

SIMPLIFYING HANUKKAH

Hanukkah, in reality a minor Jewish holiday, has become a major gift-giving occasion due to its December observation date. Jewish families who'd like to scale back Hanukkah's gift-giving "tradition" might consider some of the suggestions in this chapter for downscaling the exchange of presents.

The key for Jewish families—and for Christmas-celebrating households too—is to focus on meaningful and fun family rituals rather than on the gifts. Playing dreidel, making homemade decorations for the house, eating latkes, and baking Hanukkah cookies are all activities that kids enjoy and look forward to. After lighting the menorah each night during the eight days of Hanukkah, many families read Jewish stories to the kids, another treasured ritual. *Tsedakah,* the Hanukkah tradition of charity, inspires many Jewish families to make volunteering and charitable donations a part of their holiday—and both of these fit with the simplicity theme too. (See "Resources" for some ideas on family-friendly resources to use during Hannukah.)

Focusing on a few special family activities like these can keep Hanukkah simple—and memorable for your kids.

Other traditions: Grandparents and other elderly relatives—particularly those who might be first-generation Americans—are often good sources for ideas on ethnic traditions. A friend with a German heritage introduced us to the "pickle ornament" tradition, a common practice in the old country. After the family decorates the Christmas tree, my husband and I hide a pickle-shaped ornament in the branches while the kids are in the other room. The first child to find it opens a small family gift we've picked out, often a new game or book. The gift isn't the focus, though; the kids ask us to hide the ornament over and over.

In the original pickle ornament tradition, the finder of the pickle received a gift. We modified that aspect of the tradition so that no one would feel left out. It's okay to do this—in fact, amending traditions to fit your family's style and needs is important.

You can find many other ideas for meaningful activities and celebrations at these websites: www.simpleliving.org, www.simplifytheholidays.org, www.adbusters.org, and in numerous books about Christmas. See "Resources" at the end of this chapter.

If nothing else, at the very least *unplug* your television during family holiday get-togethers! Whether it's two dozen assorted relatives or just your nuclear group, ban the boob tube!

3. THE IMMEDIATE FAMILY TALK

Once you've done your soul searching and gathered information on new traditions, it's time for the family to make some decisions. You should have this family talk as early as possible, preferably a couple of months before the holidays.

The family will be answering these questions: Which traditions and activities do we want to keep, change, or get rid of? Which would we like to add? Present a list of simple but meaningful traditions for your family to consider. Get everyone's input. You may need to veto a child's wish to abandon Christmas morning church service. Then again, you may be able to compromise, attending church services on Christmas Eve or later on Christmas Day.

You may also need to keep bringing the family back to the simplicity theme. Too many activities—especially those with a commercial theme—will inevitably contradict the objectives of "simple" and "meaningful." Days of just hanging out together are completely okay! (Working parents may want to schedule extra time off during December, if possible.)

Kids and Christmas

Will simplifying—scaling back on Christmas excess—deprive our kids during the holidays? Authors Robinson and

Staeheli think not. They point to four things that kids *really* want for Christmas, and an orgy of materialism on Christmas morning isn't on the list. The four things are: a relaxed and loving time with the family, realistic expectations about gifts, an evenly paced holiday season, and reliable family traditions. It's clear that simplifying at Christmas, instead of depriving our children, actually benefits them, just as simplifying generally does.

We can also look at how we celebrate our winter holidays—and others throughout the year—as an important part of our parenting mission, and certainly as a lesson to our kids on our true beliefs. "If we [make buying gifts for the kids] the center of the holiday," says Bill McKibben, "we help school them in the notion that transcendent joy comes from things . . . If instead you emphasize others—making presents with your kids, spreading seed to the birds and beasts, visiting the nursing home—it exposes them to the other truth, gives them some chance to see where real joy lives."

Robinson and Staeheli recommend a balance of family activities, community events, and "just plain 'hanging out' time." If you're cutting back on gift-giving for the kids, talk about it with them well before Christmas morning. And consider substituting something else to look forward to, like a special family activity.

One way to alleviate the letdown that many kids (and adults!) experience on December 26 is to schedule a couple of those activities *after* Christmas day. My family always spends a day sledding in the mountains during the postholiday week. The kids have a favorite ritual to anticipate and we all get a taste of a "White Christmas," an otherwise rare event at the lower elevations in our area.

Many of the simple families I interviewed have found that focusing on fun rituals helps the kids to *not* focus on presents. Linda McDonough says that her family's many treasured traditions are the core of the season. "We have so many great Advent and Christmas rituals," she explains, "that they overshadow the gifts."

4. THE EXTENDED FAMILY TALK

After your soul searching and your decisions on new traditions, you'll need to communicate with those outside your immediate family who might be affected by your changes. If you've concluded that gift-giving between extended family members has gotten out of hand, have a family talk with your parents, siblings, and whoever else is involved. The best time to do this is several months before Christmas. Thanksgiving Day, although it seems like a logical time, is too late for many extended families.

The family talk is a great time to hand out "Gift Exemption Vouchers" from Alternatives for Simple Living. Go to their website—www.simpleliving.org—and print them out. (The Simple Living Network site, www.simpleliving.net, also provides a printable exemption voucher.) They'll add a little levity to the meeting.

And remember this: With a solid majority of folks hungering for a simpler holiday, your relatives will likely be glad you brought the subject up.

5. THE CHRISTMAS BUDGET

Perhaps because we simplified years ago, we don't put together a Christmas budget; we know we're not spending anywhere near the national norm during the holidays.

But if budgets work for you, it makes a lot of sense to set some goals for yourself. McKibben's $100 limit seems a lofty target. He's quick to point out that the $100 amount has no magical quality. The point is to focus on the good stuff—which isn't the stuff under the tree.

Some folks may need to take extra precautions. If you're especially weak around the holidays, record purchases in a notebook or keep a running list of expenditures and "rubber-band" it to your credit card.

SIMPLE GIFT IDEAS

Homemade Gifts

One way to keep within a limited Christmas budget is to give simple gifts. According to the Center for a New American Dream, 82 percent of Americans would rather receive a photo album of times shared growing up than a store-bought present. But far fewer than 82 percent of them are receiving those homemade gifts.

Most simple living advocates recommend a return to handcrafted items, from food to soap to bird feeders. Consider a cookbook of treasured family recipes, calendars with family photos, or kids' photos in kid-fashioned frames, made from cardboard or Popsicle sticks and decorated with stickers, beads, shells, or whatever the kids deem festive. Some simple families work together to create a family gift. Possibilities include tapes or videos of the kids performing music or singing. Others have put together "family trees" or assembled family histories, by recording interviews with older relatives.

Gifts of Yourself

Gifts of your time are the essence of simple giving. Offer to babysit for new parents or to take an elderly relative on an outing. Many simple living families use the "coupon" approach. Jan Anderson's family does. "We try to encourage gifts of coupons, like washing the car, doing another's chores for a week, that sort of thing," she says.

Experiential Gifts

Gifts of experiences, customized for the child, also make sense. A car-crazy kid like my eleven-year-old would love the promise of attending the Classic Car Convention a nearby town hosts each year. My younger son would more likely enjoy an Audubon Society book (or another good field guide) and a

(continues)

(continued)

promise to go bird-watching with him. Another child would jump at a chance to go kayaking or to visit the local historical society. Chapter 8 contains more information on selecting toys for kids.

Earth-Friendly Gifts

If you're keeping score, another good reason to down-shift on gifts is the benefit to the environment. Christmas may be a dream for retailers but it's a nightmare for Planet Earth. First, there are the resources wasted by the excessive gift-giving, decorations, and lighting. And then there are all of the leftovers: Americans produce an additional 5 million tons of trash each year between Thanksgiving and New Year's Day.

So, if you're still going to buy some gifts, consider an earth-friendly company like Real Goods or Harmony Seventh Generation (see "Resources"). Alternatively, try to buy locally, benefiting small, hometown retailers while building community. There also might be a Ten Thousand Villages store in your area, where beautiful imports are sold and fair trade principles are practiced.

Gifts to Charities

Finally you can give to a favorite charity in honor of the "giftee." These are truly the most meaningful presents. See www.altgifts.org for ideas.

6. SUPPORT

As with simplifying generally, it can be difficult to make these changes during the holidays when all around you are examples of excess.

Luckily, there are many resources for support. If you belong to a simplicity circle or support group, you'll find plenty of like-minded folks to bounce ideas off or to bemoan the relative who insists on the formal, sit-down dinner. The Internet discussion boards are also good spots to find both sympathy and inspiration. (These are mentioned in Chapter 10.)

Consider joining in with others for "Buy Nothing Day," the day after Thanksgiving, which has become the biggest shopping day of the year. More information is available at www.adbusters.org.

Another wonderful resource for support in making meaningful holiday changes is Alternatives for Simple Living (www.simpleliving.org). This group was formed in 1973 to protest the commercialization of Christmas (yes, it was bad even back then). Alternatives offers a number of publications, among which the pamphlet "Whose Birthday Is It, Anyway?" is probably best known.

What I like about Alternatives is that instead of just talking about the real reason for the season—the birth of Christ—this organization helps folks to focus on, as they put it, "what Jesus wants from us." Not self-righteous rhetoric, but purposeful action in fighting injustice and poverty. "By helping to provide a goat for a farmer in Honduras, a decent home for a family in rural Mississippi, or food for those who are victims of war, you can give Jesus a birthday gift he really wants," their pamphlet points out.

You'll also find much comfort in reading *The Hundred Dollar Holiday* by Bill McKibben. If you belong to a church, show it to your pastor or priest—again, well in advance of Christmas—and ask if they think the parish or congregation would want to adopt a similar project.

A Magical Christmas

What can you expect once you've done these things?

A simpler, more profound observance. Waking up on December 26 with no regrets but with lifelong memories like those of my mother.

If there is a silver lining to the commercialization of Christmas it is the fact that it's become so extreme that nearly everyone recognizes it for the crass attempt it is to buy happiness. If the vast majority of Americans are hungering for meaning during December, it hopefully can't be long before they question the need for excess year-round. Perhaps our willingness to look at the overindulgence of this season and say "Enough!" during the holidays will evolve into our ability to do the same for our overconsumption the rest of the year. That's *my* Christmas wish.

Resources

CHRISTMAS TRADITIONS

Doris C. Baines. *Christmas: Traditions and Legends* (Lake Oswego, Oregon: Kendor, 1997).

Meg Cox. *The Heart of a Family: Searching America for New Traditions That Fulfill Us* (New York: Random House, 1998).

SIMPLIFYING CHRISTMAS IN GENERAL

Bill McKibben. *Hundred Dollar Holiday: The Case for a More Joyful Christmas* (New York: Simon & Schuster, 1998).

"Noel Pax" with Mary Thompson. *Simply Christmas: Great Ideas for a Noncommercial Holiday* (New York: Walker, 1992).

Jo Robinson and Jean Coppock Staeheli. *Unplug the Christmas Machine: A Complete Guide to Putting Love and Joy Back into the Season* (New York: Quill/William Morrow, 1991).

Elaine St. James. *Simplify Your Christmas* (Kansas City, Missouri: Andrews McMeel, 1998).

"Whose Birthday Is It, Anyway?" pamphlet published by Alternatives for Simple Living; www.simpleliving.org

GIFT-GIVING IDEAS

Alternative Gifts: www.altgifts.org; (800) 842–2243.

Harmony Seventh Generation: www.seventhgen.com; (800) 869–3446.

Real Goods: www.realgoods.com; (800) 762–7235.

SERRV International; a catalog of fair trade goods; www.serrv.org; (800) 422-5915.

Ten Thousand Villages stores: check www.tenthousand villages.com for a store near you.

HANUKKAH

The Al Galgalim project: www.hadassah.org/algalgalim/ main.html. Al Galgalim is a Jewish education program that helps families with kids ages two through eight enjoy meaningful celebrations of Jewish holidays.

Marilyn Burns. *The Hanukkah Book* (New York: Four Winds Press, 1981).

Barbara Diamond Goldin. *While the Candles Burn: Eight Stories for Hanukkah* (New York: Puffin Books, 1996).

ORGANIZATIONS/WEBSITES

Adbusters: www.adbusters.org. Sponsors "Buy Nothing Day" and other campaigns.

Alternatives for Simple Living: www.simpleliving.org; P.O. Box 429, Ellenwood, GA 30049; (404) 961–0102.

The Center for a New American Dream's "Simplify the Holidays" website, www.simplifytheholidays.org

Index

ABOUT THE AUTHOR

MARIE SHERLOCK writes for a variety of magazines, including *Family Circle, Your Money,* and United Parenting Publications. She has been living the simple, good life in Oregon with her husband and two children for more than ten years.